Praise for *The Al*

"*The Aleppo Codex* could be read as a thriller. It could also be read as a history of the Jewish people, or as a meditation on history and myth. This great book comes closer to containing everything than any book I've read in a long, long time." —Jonathan Safran Foer

"A superb work of investigative journalism that reads like a detective thriller." —*The Wall Street Journal*

"An incredible story that involves greed, subterfuge, state cover-ups, and the fascinating role of the ancient Hebrew Bible manuscript, the Aleppo Codex, in creating a national identity." —*Utne Reader*

"The story of what happened next—how the codex came to Israel and where the missing pages might have gone—is a murky and often contradictory one, told by many self-serving or unreliable narrators. In his book, the Canadian-Israeli journalist Matti Friedman presents a compelling and thoroughly researched account of the story." —*The New York Times Magazine*

"A thrilling, step-by-step quest to discover what really happened to Judaism's most important book . . . Many of [*The Aleppo Codex*'s] most astute and well-earned revelations are also its biggest surprises." —*The Boston Globe*

"*The Aleppo Codex* builds to a moral crescendo more impressive than the climactic fight scene in any thriller." —Salon.com

"[Friedman] opened a treasure box of history, mystery, conspiracy, and convolutions that would do any biblical thriller proud . . . Friedman has done a remarkable job—finding sources and digging through archives—of getting the Crown's fascinating story out of the shadows and into the light. In the process, he's become the latest in the long line of the Crown's protectors." —*Booklist,* starred review

"Three cheers for Matti Friedman . . . who in his first book got his teeth into a terrific story and investigated and reported it as thoroughly as possible . . . Friedman does an exemplary job of hacking his way through the various thickets that surround the Aleppo Codex."
—*The Jerusalem Report*

"Friedman's account of how the Codex was taken from Syria in the 1940s, later to resurface in Jerusalem, although no longer complete, is full of betrayals, controversy and surprises—and raises larger questions about the ownership and preservation of historical treasures."
—*The Jewish Week*

"Friedman gives a masterful account of a major religious document . . . [He] delivers an atmospheric, tense story about the destruction of a sacred relic, raising inevitable questions about who owns a people's historical treasures."
—*Publishers Weekly*, starred review

"The story of the Aleppo Codex's survival, which Friedman recounts in almost cinematic detail, is as unlikely as it is astonishing . . . Friedman's writing shines most when he resurrects a time and a place now vanished . . . We read *The Aleppo Codex* expecting to be educated about a book lost, but we are captivated by a world lost instead."
—*Haaretz*

"Stirring . . . Friedman rightly sees the Codex as a valuable document and does diligent research to learn what happened to it, especially to the missing pages. What and how he discovers reads like an intriguing mystery story that rivets the attention of readers who become eager to learn the outcome . . . He has ably brought to our attention a little-known episode in Jewish history that is eminently worthy of our high regard."
—*The Jewish Post and Opinion*

"Friedman creates a riveting story, one that the reader will have a hard time putting down."
—*The Advocate*

"Friedman's painstaking investigation of just what happened to the Aleppo codex—and when—is a fascinating account of the role of sacred relics in creating a national identity, and also of the lure of old and treasured objects." —*Maclean's*

"Friedman's clear writing and dogged pursuit of some otherwise overlooked assumptions read more like a detective novel than history . . . Friedman has written an important account in accessible, gripping prose." —*The Christian Science Monitor*

"Thrilling . . . A real-life *National Treasure* that reads like fantastical fiction." —*CultureMob*

"A cracking good yarn . . . Matti Friedman does a masterful job of untangling the puzzle." —*Jewish Tribune*

"Sharply etched . . . A carefully paced narrative of purloined Judaica." —*Kirkus Reviews*

"[A] brilliant nonfiction thriller about an ancient copy of the Torah. Highly recommended." —Paulo Coelho, author of *The Alchemist*

"Matti Friedman is a stunningly talented writer, a once-in-a-generation discovery. *The Aleppo Codex* has enough betrayals, conspiracies, surprise plot twists, sacred flimflam men, and well-dressed contraband dealers for the best of thrillers—but every bit of it is meticulously researched fact. Cancel your appointments, bury your cell phone—you won't want to be interrupted—and read this book."
—Gershom Gorenberg, senior correspondent for
The American Prospect and author of *The Accidental Empire*

"A beautifully woven tale of epic proportions about a sacred book and its all-too-human custodians. I did not put it down until I had finished it at the crack of dawn. Absolutely riveting!"
—Oren Harman, author of *The Price of Altruism*

"Weaving a millennium of Arab Jewish history with several versions of how the codex came to Israel, Friedman details a mystery story full of ambiguity and obfuscation, particularly by certain individuals connected to the Ben-Zvi Institute in Jerusalem. Think of this book as a real-life version of Umberto Eco's *The Name of the Rose*."

—*Jewish Herald-Voice*

"With a journalist's nose for truth and a writer's passion for eloquence, Friedman sifts through the past and unearths a thrilling tale of deceit, lawsuits and the precious book at the center of it all."

—*Jspace*

"Part historical exposé, part international thriller, and part meditation on the passions awakened by religion and religious artifacts . . . Friedman painstakingly guides readers through the labyrinth of misconception and propaganda surrounding the Crown, leading them to a conclusion worthy of the most shocking of spy thrillers. *The Aleppo Codex* is superbly written."   —*ForeWord Reviews*

"From the very first page to the last Friedman has the reader's attention by means of artistic turns-of-phrase and meticulously researched logical precision . . . Anyone, moreover, who loves a detective tale; or anyone who loves mystery; and again, anyone who loves to read a finely crafted story will put this book down, having completed it, with one simple word on their lips: wow."

—Jim West, Quartz Hill School of Theology, in the blog *Zwinglius Redivivus*

THE ALEPPO CODEX

THE
ALEPPO
CODEX

In Pursuit of One of the World's Most
Coveted, Sacred, and Mysterious Books

BY

Matti Friedman

ALGONQUIN BOOKS OF CHAPEL HILL   2013

Published by
Algonquin Books of Chapel Hill
Post Office Box 2225
Chapel Hill, North Carolina 27515-2225

a division of
Workman Publishing
225 Varick Street
New York, New York 10014

The Library of Congress has cataloged
the hardcover edition of this book as follows:
Friedman, Matti.
    The Aleppo Codex : a true story of obsession, faith, and the
pursuit of an ancient Bible / Matti Friedman — 1st ed.
        p. cm.
    Includes bibliographical references.
    ISBN 978-1-61620-040-4 (HC)
    1. Aleppo Codex — History. I. Title.
    BS715.5.A43F75 2012
    221.4'4 — dc23   2012002327

    ISBN 978-1-61620-278-1 (PB)

10 9 8 7 6 5 4 3 2 1

For my parents,
Imogene and Raphael Zev,
and my wife, Naama

Until then I had thought each book spoke of the things, human or divine, that lie outside books. Now I realized that not infrequently books speak of books: it is as if they spoke among themselves. In the light of this reflection, the library seemed all the more disturbing to me. It was then the place of a long, centuries-old murmuring, an imperceptible dialogue between one parchment and another, a living thing, a receptacle of powers not to be ruled by a human mind, a treasure of secrets emanated by many minds, surviving the death of those who had produced them or had been their conveyors.

—UMBERTO ECO, *The Name of the Rose*

This is a work of nonfiction. Quotations from documents, recorded materials, and my own interviews appear inside quotation marks. In acknowledgment of the inexact nature of memory, quotations recalled by those interviewed do not. Notes on sources appear at the end.

CONTENTS

DRAMATIS PERSONAE

ASHER BAGHDADI: Sexton of the great synagogue of Aleppo.

BAHIYEH BAGHDADI: The sexton's daughter.

SHAHOUD BAGHDADI: The sexton's son.

DAVID BARTOV: President Ben-Zvi's chief of staff.

ITZHAK BEN-ZVI: Israel's second president (1952–63), a scholar, and the founder of the Ben-Zvi Institute.

MEIR BENAYAHU: An aide to Ben-Zvi and the institute's first director.

UMBERTO CASSUTO: A Bible professor sent to Aleppo in 1943 to study the codex.

ITZJAK CHEHEBAR: A prominent rabbi who fled Aleppo in 1952 and went on to lead the exile community in Buenos Aires until his death in 1990.

EDMOND COHEN: An Aleppo accountant responsible for concealing the codex in the 1950s.

IBRAHIM EFFENDI COHEN: An Aleppo textile merchant responsible for concealing the codex. Edmond Cohen's uncle.

MOSHE COHEN: Edmond Cohen's son. Escaped Syria in 1972.

MURAD FAHAM: The Aleppo cheese merchant who smuggled the codex to Israel.

EZRA KASSIN: A former Israeli military investigator and amateur codex sleuth.

SHLOMO MOUSSAIEFF: A jewelry tycoon and renowned collector of ancient artifacts and manuscripts.

YITZHAK PESSEL: An Israeli agent in Istanbul responsible for the Syria-Turkey-Israel immigration route in the 1950s.

AMNON SHAMOSH: An Israeli novelist, Aleppo born, who wrote the first history of the codex.

ISAAC SHAMOSH: A scholar sent to Aleppo in 1943 to try to bring the codex to Jerusalem. Amnon Shamosh's brother.

ISAAC SILO (pseudonym): A resident of Alexandretta, Turkey, and an Israeli immigration agent from the 1940s until his death in the 1970s.

SHLOMO ZALMAN SHRAGAI: The director of Israel's worldwide immigration network in the 1950s.

RAFI SUTTON: A former Mossad agent, born in Aleppo, who carried out his own codex investigation.

MOSHE (MUSSA) TAWIL: The chief rabbi of Aleppo who decided to send the codex to Israel.

SALIM (SHLOMO) ZAAFRANI: An Aleppo rabbi who, along with Tawil, sent the codex to Israel.

INTRODUCTION

IN THE SUMMER of 2008, in a dark underground room at Israel's national museum in Jerusalem, I encountered one of the most important books on earth. I had never heard of it. Up a winding flight of stairs from where I stood, in a hushed sanctuary dedicated to the Dead Sea Scrolls, a busload or two of tourists filed reverently past the glass cases containing the parchment celebrities of Qumran, but in the gallery below I was alone.

Off to one side, a bulky volume was open under a dim light. I was struck first by a certain air of dignity about it, a refusal to beg for attention: This book boasted no gold leaf, no elaborate binding, no intricate illuminations in lapis lazuli or scarlet, nothing at all but row after row of meticulous, handwritten Hebrew in dark brown ink on lighter brown parchment, twenty-eight lines to a column, three columns to a page. The margins contained tiny notes added by a different hand. It was open to the book of Isaiah. From the labels I learned that the volume was no less than the most perfect copy of the Hebrew Bible, the singular and authoritative version, for believing Jews, of God's word as it was sent into the world of men in their language. This lonely treasure and millennium-old traveler was the Aleppo Codex, and it would come to occupy much of my life for the next four years.

I was intrigued by the little I knew of the manuscript's story and by the strange juxtaposition of its significance and its anonymity, and a few months after that first visit, amid my other journalistic tasks as a staff reporter at the Jerusalem bureau of the Associated Press—at the time, these tended to involve maintaining a stream of staccato wire copy from the Middle East describing incessant and fruitless political maneuvering and occasional carnage—I found time to make my first attempt to write about it. As I understood it then, the manuscript's story was this: It was hidden for centuries in the great synagogue of Aleppo, Syria, where it became known as the Crown of Aleppo, or simply as the Crown. It was damaged in a fire set by Arab rioters in 1947, concealed, smuggled to the new state of Israel by the Jews of Aleppo as their community disappeared, and entrusted in 1958 to the country's president, coming, in the words of one of the official versions of the story, "full circle." This bound volume of parchment folios—a codex—had been kept intact for many hundreds of years, but a large number of leaves had mysteriously gone missing at the time of the synagogue fire. This hindered a quest by scholars to re-create the perfect text of the Bible, as the Crown had never been photographed and there were no known copies. A few vague theories existed about the fate of those pages, which I duly reported, along with a new attempt to find them by the codex's custodians, scholars of the prestigious Ben-Zvi Institute in Jerusalem. I read some of the available material about the manuscript, interviewed several academics, and filed thirteen hundred words to an AP editor in New York City.

At the time of that article's publication, I did not yet recognize the disappearance of the Crown's pages for what it was—a real-life mystery with clues still hiding in forgotten crates of documents and in aging minds. And I did not see that there was another mystery hidden inside the story, one that turned out to be at least as interesting as the first: how, precisely, had the codex moved from a dark grotto in Aleppo to Jerusalem? I did not imagine, at the time, that there could be much new to say about something so old, and it certainly did not occur to me that the true story of the manuscript had never been told at all.

I would like to say I discerned that something was off about the codex's story and that this is why I found myself thinking even months later about the volume I had seen in the museum. But I discerned nothing, and when eventually I began work on this book, I still imagined an uplifting and uncomplicated account of the rescue of a cultural artifact that was shot like a brightly colored thread through centuries of history, and of its return home. My reporter's sense, a certain mental hum alerting me to the presence of a story concealed, began tingling only after I had spent a few bewildering months walking into locked doors.

I met the head of the Ben-Zvi Institute, a government-funded academic body named for the man who was given the manuscript upon its arrival in Israel: Itzhak Ben-Zvi, ethnographer, historian, and Israel's president between 1952 and 1963. Though the manuscript is safeguarded at the national museum, the late president's institute, set among trees in a quiet Jerusalem neighborhood and dedicated to studying the Jewish communities of the East, remains its official keeper. The professor, a polite and careful man, spoke to me at length and then, when I moved beyond generalities and requested access to documents pertaining to the Crown in the institute's archive, stopped returning my e-mails.

Searching for details about what had happened to the manuscript since the 1947 synagogue fire in Aleppo, I found a Hebrew book published in the 1980s by the institute. Though it offered much detail about the Crown's history before 1947, it was oddly blurred and contradictory about everything that had happened since. I got the impression, the amplitude of which inched upward with the page numbers, that the author was going to great lengths not to reveal something, or many things, and I closed the book with the unsettling feeling that I knew less than I had when I opened it.

I called another official at the institute and told him I was hoping to write a book about the Crown of Aleppo. "There already is a book," he said.

I learned of a trial that had taken place in Jerusalem more than fifty years before and that seemed to have been linked somehow to the manuscript, and then found that no one appeared to have any official record of it.

I called one of the world's foremost experts on Hebrew manuscripts, a former director of Israel's national library and, in introducing myself, made a casual reference to a "page" of the Crown. "Not *page*," said the librarian, his voice brittle with contempt. "*Leaf.*" If I did not know the difference, he said, perhaps I should write about something else—a layman, he seemed to mean, had no business poking around this story. (In the technical language of the library, a page is one side of a leaf. Outside the halls of academia the words mean the same thing, and I have used them interchangeably throughout.) He then suggested several articles I should read, all of them written by him, and hung up.

Gradually I discovered a subculture of people fascinated by the Crown and its story, scholars, collectors, and Jewish exiles from Aleppo who became immediately attentive at the mention of its name. I began to think of them as a kind of Aleppo Codex Underground.

I went to a small store crowded with Hebrew books near the open vegetable market in west Jerusalem, whose owner, I had been told, was an Aleppo Jew who might have information about the manuscript. The bookseller, a bearded man with a black skullcap, apologized: he could not help me. He had also asked questions, he said, in vain. "In the Aleppo community there is a conspiracy of silence about the Crown," he said.

Hearing rumors that agents of the Mossad, Israel's covert intelligence service, had somehow been involved, I contacted an old spy I had befriended while working on an earlier piece for the AP, a former Mossad station chief in Beirut and Tehran who now spent his days padding around a Tel Aviv apartment in slippers. "You want to speak to Rafi Sutton," he said. Sutton, Aleppo born and approaching eighty, was a veteran of the Mossad and several of Israel's other intelligence arms. Twenty years earlier, after retiring from professional spy work, Sutton had conducted his own investigation into the Crown's recent history.

At one of our first meetings, he placed a thick file folder on his coffee table, leaned back, and gave me an interrogator's stare so finely honed that I could almost feel his thick fingers rummaging through my brain. "What do you know?" he asked, and then he scoffed when I told him. I knew nothing. "The whole story is in here," he said, nodding at his file folder, his imposing nose pointing down past the disconcerting glint of his grin to a tuft of white hair sprouting from his tracksuit. But spies do not just give information away. The folder was a prop, a come-on, and for now he had no intention of letting me see what was inside.

Through my new contacts in the Aleppo Codex Underground, I met Ezra Kassin, a man in his forties who could describe in minute detail the great synagogue of Aleppo and the grotto where the Crown had been concealed. But he had never been there; he was born to an Aleppo Jewish family in Israel, where he served in the army as a military police detective and later ran a center for the study of Jewish mysticism. Kassin was preoccupied to the point of obsession with the missing pages of the Crown, as if by reconstituting the book something much more important could be put back together. Like Rafi Sutton, the old Mossad agent, Kassin had run his own amateur Crown investigation, documenting it in binders and computer files that he kept in the home he shared with his wife and two-year-old son.

"Listen," he told me when we met in a café, "you're entering a minefield." I nodded, pretending I knew what he meant. He shook his head. I had no idea.

"There are traps and pitfalls and mirages and cats guarding the cream," he said. "Say the wrong thing to the wrong person, and ten other doors will slam shut." He raised his cappuccino to his lips, enjoying himself.

My first visit to the gallery at Israel's national museum should have prepared me for what came afterward. The volume I saw open to the book of Isaiah, the one that launched me on this enterprise, was not the Crown of Aleppo at all. Only the two pages on top were real, resting upon a dummy tome cleverly arranged to look like the original. For reasons of conservation and security, I later learned, the rest of the manuscript was kept in a vault elsewhere in the building. Access required three different keys, a magnetic card, and a secret code. In the display case was a curator's trick meant to give visitors a sense of the real thing; like so much else in this story, it was a useful deceit.

With persistence, the doors did crack open. The story begins at the moment when something new was being born and something very old was ending, and unfolds between two cities not all that far away from each other—Aleppo and Jerusalem—branching out to other cities on other continents. I first thought the story was about the power of a great book, and it still is, though in a manner far darker than I had originally intended. Considering the devastating insight into the nature of human beings contained in the Crown's pages, one might be forgiven, whether one believes the Bible's words to be prophetic or merely wise, for seeing this tale as that of a book that foresaw its own fate.

The Crown's twin mysteries, I came to believe, were connected to each other, and both were connected to the unwillingness I encountered to tell the truth or speak at all about the manuscript's journeys in the twentieth century. This is a true story, not a neat whodunit, and the tools necessary for a definitive solution to the first mystery, that of the missing pages, would include power of subpoena and a time machine. I understood that certainty would necessarily be elusive. Yet I progressed further than I first thought possible and discovered a considerable amount of surprising information, known to few and never made public, that allowed me to sketch the contours of an answer. The solution to the second mystery—how, precisely, the book ended up where it did—is recounted here in full for the first time.

In discussing the pursuit of the true knowledge hidden in the Bible, the great physician and philosopher Moses Maimonides, whom the reader will shortly encounter in twelfth-century Cairo, wrote,

> You should not think that these great secrets are fully and completely known to anyone among us. They are not. But sometimes truth flashes out to us so that we think that it is day, and then matter and habit in their various forms conceal it so that we find ourselves again in an obscure night, almost as we were at first. We are like someone in a very dark night over whom lightning flashes time and time again.

Maimonides—who used this very codex in preparing his most enduring masterpiece of Jewish law—was referring to matters grander than journalistic inquiry, but I found myself returning to his words as I struggled to piece together what had befallen this book. At first the few fragments of information I was able to assemble did not seem to suggest an intelligible explanation, but slowly my investigation began to bear fruit and the fate of the book was illuminated. While it is beyond my power to restore the missing pieces of the Crown of Aleppo, I found that many of the missing pieces of its story were waiting to be rescued.

This book began as a project driven by my curiosity. But as the facts became more garbled and disappointing, as I became adept at panning for secrets in file folders and began spending much of my time with old men, grasping at memories crumbling like burnt parchment, I discovered another motivation. If the Crown of Aleppo could not be whole, everything had to be done so that its history would be; this was owed to the people who wrote it, read it, swore by it, and guarded it with their lives for a thousand years.

PART ONE

I

Flushing Meadow

THE FIRST LIMOUSINES pulled up beside bare trees and a grove of flagpoles at Flushing Meadow, on the outskirts of New York City, discharging their passengers into a gray building that had once housed a skating rink. Crowds gathered in the chill outside. An auditorium inside was full of spectators and delegates. It was November 29, 1947, a Saturday afternoon.

Grainy footage filmed that day shows men in suits seated in rows before a raised podium where three officials had their backs to a giant painting of the globe. Aides arrived and departed from the podium with sheaves of paper and expressions befitting the gravity of the occasion: the delegates to this new world organization, the United Nations, were about to alter the course of history simply by holding a vote.

"We will start now," said the man in the middle—this was the assembly's presiding diplomat, a Brazilian—and a silver microphone on the podium picked up those words in accented English and relayed them to Jewish garment workers clustered around radio sets on the Lower East Side of Manhattan, then across the Atlantic to camps for the refugees of the Second World War, which had ended barely two years before, and farther east to Arab students in Damascus, merchants in Jaffa and Cairo, store owners in sandy Tel Aviv, a city not yet thirty years old. Some had pencils ready to tally the votes. A two-thirds majority meant Palestine, ruled by the British since 1917, would be partitioned into two states, one for Jews and one for Arabs. The vote followed months of desperate diplomacy and strong-arm politics influenced by the horror of recent events in Europe. For supporters of the Jewish national movement, Zionism, passage of the resolution would mean justice for a persecuted people and the realization of a two-thousand-year-old dream of national rebirth. For the Arabs of Palestine and of surrounding countries, it would mean the imposition of a foreign entity in the heart of the Middle East, an unbearable humiliation, and certain war.

In the north of Syria, six thousand miles away from New York, it was evening. An aviator arriving from the west across the flat screen of the Mediterranean might first have seen that night's full moon reflected on the water and then a dark expanse of tribal grazing lands and farming plots stretching inland toward the Euphrates and the deserts of the interior. Aleppo would have appeared below as a cluster of lights at the meeting point of the rail lines and roads that converged from all directions, the city spreading around a nucleus of bazaar streets by the crumbling mass of the Citadel. Down in those streets, the stores now shuttered, the women of the *manzul* were receiving clients, and men were submerged in café smoke like deep-sea divers, tubes between their lips, inhaling the rose-scented oxygen of water pipes. From the outskirts of the Old City, labyrinthine passages led into the quarter where the Jews had always lived, and in the heart of this quarter, behind high walls, was their great synagogue. Inside the synagogue, at the end of a corridor and down a few steps, was a dark grotto. In the grotto sat an iron safe with two locks, and in this safe was the book.

In Aleppo, the sexton of the great synagogue—Asher Baghdadi

was his name—a thin man in a robe that fell to his ankles, would have been making his rounds at this time, after the Sabbath had ended and the last of the worshippers had left, walking through the rooms as he always did, through the courtyard where prayers were held in summertime, past the grotto known as the Cave of the Prophet Elijah, with the safe inside. The double lock served as an additional precaution, this one against the treasure's own guardians, requiring the two elders entrusted with keys to be present and to watch over each other when the safe was opened. It rarely was. The sexton was not important enough to have one of those keys, though he did have an iron key to the synagogue's gate that was as long as the forearm of a small child. The sexton crossed a narrow alleyway and climbed the three flights of stairs to his home, where the windows looked down into the deserted courtyard of the building he had just left. Kerosene streetlamps flickered in the alleys.

Most of Aleppo's Jews appear to have been only vaguely aware of the events at Flushing Meadow, if at all; many believed Palestine had little to do with them, and only a lucky few owned a radio. Among those who did understand the gravity of the events afoot was fifteen-year-old Rafi Sutton, the retired spy I would encounter six decades later. Rafi was in his living room, in a modern neighborhood that was home to middle-class Jews, Muslims, and Christians who had fled the crowding and poverty of the Old City. He sat with his parents and sisters next to a Zenith radio housed in a wooden cabinet.

In the broadcast from Flushing Meadow, a flat American voice replaced that of the Brazilian. The new voice began reading from a list.

"Afghanistan?" he asked, and then repeated the inaudible answer from the assembly floor: "No.

"Argentina," he said. "Argentina? Abstention.

"Australia?" he said. "Yes."

In the days and weeks leading up to the vote, Arab leaders and diplomats had moved beyond threatening to eradicate the Jewish enclave in Palestine by force to threatening the Jews of the vulnerable Diaspora archipelago strung throughout the lands of Islam—Baghdad, Aleppo, Alexandria, Tunis, Casablanca. There were eight hundred thousand Jews in Arab countries, and another two hundred thousand in non-Arab Islamic states like Iran and Turkey. These people were not Zionists, for the most part, but that didn't matter: they were hostages now. "The lives of a million Jews in Muslim countries would be jeopardized by the establishment of a Jewish state," an Egyptian representative warned. If the resolution passed, Iraq's prime minister said, "severe measures should be taken against all Jews in Arab countries." The fate of the Jews in Arab lands could become "very precarious," a Palestinian Arab delegate had reminded everyone. Though Arab governments might do their best to protect them, he said, "governments, in general, have always been unable to prevent mob excitement and violence."

"El Salvador?" the American voice continued. "Abstention.

"Ethiopia? Abstains.

"France?"

In the hall at Flushing Meadow, many held their breath; the French had been wavering and were expected to abstain.

"Yes," said the American voice, and raucous cheers swept the auditorium.

"Excitement," remembered one Zionist delegate who was in the hall, "became a physical pain."

Rafi's radio emitted a knocking sound—this was the Brazilian rapping for order with his gavel on the other side of the

Atlantic. Rafi and his parents were worried about his three older brothers, who had left home to join the Zionist project in Palestine years before and whom Rafi knew mostly from their letters. His mother, who was illiterate, had him read the letters aloud before she wedged the enclosed photographs of suntanned young men into the wooden frame around her wardrobe mirror. The Suttons were not yet worried about themselves.

"Ukraine?" the American voice was saying. "Yes.

"South Africa? Yes.

"Soviet Union? Yes.

"United Kingdom? Abstains.

"United States? Yes," said the American voice.

When the voting ended, the Brazilian banged again with his gavel. Those present in the hall saw him put on his spectacles. "As he spoke," one of the Jewish delegates later recalled, "a feeling that grips a man but once in his lifetime came over us. High above us we seemed to hear the beating of the wings of history."

The Brazilian diplomat read from a paper. "The resolution of the Ad Hoc Committee for Palestine was adopted," he said, "by thirty-three votes, thirteen against, and ten abstentions." Shouting erupted in the hall.

In British-ruled Jerusalem, crowds poured into the streets. Trucks with loudspeakers drove through the Jewish section of the city, waking people up to celebrate, and the staff of a winery rolled a barrel into the middle of downtown and began handing out free drinks. Golda Meir, a future Israeli prime minister, addressed revelers from the balcony of the low headquarters building of the Jewish Agency, the Zionist leadership in Palestine. "For two thousand years we have waited for our deliverance. Now that it is here it is so great and wonderful that it surpasses human words. Jews," she said, "*mazel tov!*"

Arab leaders and diplomats responded with stunned fury. "My country will never recognize such a decision," the Syrian delegate to the United Nations warned before he and the other Arab representatives walked out of the assembly in protest. "It will never agree to be responsible for it. Let the consequences be on the heads of others, not on ours." Soon the clerics at the Islamic seminary of Al-Azhar in Cairo would release a call for a "worldwide jihad in defense of Arab Palestine." The Syrian chapter of the Muslim Brotherhood would echo the call for holy war, saying the battle was one of "life or death" for Arabs, "whom the vilest, the most corrupt, tricky and destructive people wish to conquer and displace."

In Aleppo, Rafi Sutton's parents switched off the radio. There was no sound from the streets outside. Nothing had changed. Not yet.

In the ancient synagogue where the Crown had been kept for two hundred thousand nights, this night, which would be the last, seemed no different.

The Crown had arrived in the synagogue from a world in which wars were fought with swords and arrows and which extended no farther west than the Atlantic coastline. Whatever had changed outside the Crown's grotto since then, its keepers still came from generation after generation of Jews from the same Diaspora outpost, one that had been in place before the birth of Islam or Christianity. The Jews of Aleppo swore oaths on the Crown, lit candles in its grotto, and prayed there for the welfare of the sick. Each generation added to the protective web of stories that surrounded the treasure, though almost none of those who venerated it had ever set eyes on it. The moral of these stories was always the same. Once, long ago, one tale went, the elders took the Crown out of the synagogue, and plague swiftly struck the Jews, abating only when the Crown was returned. In another, the Crown was similarly moved, only to reappear, miraculously, in its place. If ill befell the treasure, according to traditions of great age and import, or even if it ever left the synagogue, the community was doomed. This might have been fanciful, many admit now, long after the events in question, but then they invariably point out that in the end it did turn out to be true.

An inscription in the book read as follows:

Blessed be he who preserves it
and cursed be he who steals it
and cursed be he who sells it
and cursed be he who pawns it.
It may not be sold and it may not be defiled forever.

The delegates at Flushing Meadow had set in motion the events that would lead to a war in Palestine, a Jewish victory, and the birth of the state of Israel. That is well known. But they also began a very different chain of events known to few: the story of the Crown of Aleppo, one that must be rescued from decades of neglect, myth, and deliberate deception.

2

Aleppo

ALEPPO CAME WARILY to life the day after the vote.

On an ordinary morning, the sexton, Asher Baghdadi, might leave his small apartment next to the synagogue and walk to the market for pita bread with sesame seeds, or a pot of *sahlab*, a sweet concoction of milk, orchid powder, cinnamon, and chopped walnuts. His daughter Bahiyeh, who recounted this to me years later, appears in a family photograph from the 1940s as a child with round cheeks and untrusting eyes. By the time I sat in her living room, she was a chain-smoking grandmother in slacks and rubber clogs. She lived in another country, spoke another language, and was known by another name. As she looked up at the ordinary light fixture bolted to her ceiling in a town south of Tel Aviv, she described the crystal chandeliers she saw as a child when she followed her father on his rounds through the great synagogue. She remembered strange noises, and secret rooms, and one spot where she would stand to feel a mysterious gust of cold air. Though Bahiyeh's role in this story is small, I came to see her—her child's memories, her half-forgotten Arabic, and her freezer stocked with Syrian spices—as an untarnished vestige of Jewish Aleppo, a world that ended, for her, when she was eleven.

Bahiyeh and a shifting assortment of her dozen brothers and

sisters woke up each morning on mattresses laid out on the floor and ate bread with date honey or the jam their mother made by leaving apricots under a plate of glass on the roof. Then they would all tear down the stairs and out into the streets of their city. But not this morning.

In one of the streets of the Old City not far away, Murad Faham was making his way from his home to the bazaar when he met an acquaintance bearing a warning. Faham was a cheese merchant approaching forty. Like most of the city's Jews, he had yet to hear the news from Flushing Meadow or from Palestine, where fighting had already erupted that morning. Faham's account of these events is found in oral recollections that were taped and transcribed thirty years later.

Where are you going? asked the man.

To the market, Faham replied.

Tell the Jewish store owners to close their stores at once, the man said. Then he put his head close to Faham's and whispered in his ear: Today the Jews took the land, he said, and these people want to do something to us that the Creator of the World does not wish upon us. Tell them it would be better to close their stores.

Faham did so and was hurrying back home when this time he met a Muslim businessman he knew.

Murad, why are you walking around outside? Go home, the businessman said. He was escorting him when they encountered a crowd of schoolchildren shouting slogans against the partition vote. They were just children, but for the first time that morning Faham was afraid.

For my sake, go home and don't come out, the businessman pleaded. We know that something not at all good is about to happen.

Outside the Old City, in the modern neighborhood of Jamiliyeh, Rafi Sutton was awake and alert, even though he had stayed
up late listening to the radio the night before.

At the time of these events at the end of 1947, Rafi was the
teenage king of a little world that required an hour to cross on
foot: from his home across from the Mazreb delicatessen, whose
French-style baguette sandwiches were popular with older Jewish boys trying to impress their girlfriends, down shady boule-
vards where more and more automobiles mixed with fewer and
fewer horse-drawn carriages, past the Cinéma Roxy, past the
brothel, and into the medieval tangle of the Old City and the
souks, seething and heaving with life, the air heavy with centuries of spice, to the great synagogue that housed the hidden
book. If he took *le tramway*—a remnant of the French colonial
rule that had ended only the previous year—the trip was even
faster, and for Rafi the tram was free: He would jump on one of
the yellow cars with their smart blue stripe, boarding through
the front door and then moving to the back ahead of the conductor collecting fares. By the time the conductor reached him
he was gripping the two handles on either side of the rear door,
bending his knees, and then he was airborne, a boy in shorts,
the streetcar still in motion, landing on his feet and vanishing
among trucks and snorting horses.

During the years of the Second World War, before things began to change for the worse, Rafi's life was a blur of torch-lit Boy
Scout ceremonies—*l'éclaireur toujours prêt!*—capture the flag,
lessons in Torah and French. Food was rationed, and Rafi was
sent to stand in line for raw brown sugar that left an unpleasant froth on the surface of tea. He and his friends entertained
themselves with rumors of the Nazi spies who were said to be

The great synagogue of Aleppo in the early twentieth century.

erecting antennas on Aleppo rooftops and relaying secret messages back to Hitler in Morse code. Recounting this to me, Rafi seemed to think these preoccupations foreshadowed the career he eventually chose, after this world expelled him and he looked back on it with the eyes of an enemy, as an agent for the Mossad.

In these years his world orbited the majestic Zenith, which had a place of honor in his family's apartment, up a curved staircase in the neighborhood of Jamiliyeh, where most families had more money than his did. A half oval of burnished wood and circuitry, the radio had returned with his mother after one of her visits to her wealthy brothers, who were jewelers in Beirut. They had purchased a newer model and let her take the old one back to Aleppo on the train. That was how Rafi's family, despite his elderly father's years of sickness and financial hardship, came to have a radio, a luxury that drew relatives and friends to their living room in the evenings to keep up with the war. The Zenith informed the adults of the German victories as it told them of the astonishing collapse of France, the land of the soldiers and policemen Sutton had always seen on the streets, of the deli's baguette sandwiches, and of the language that many of the Jews here claimed, as a point of pride, to speak better than their native Arabic.

With the fall of Syria's French rulers to the German blitzkrieg in Europe in 1940, Aleppo came under the control of the Nazi puppet government of Vichy. Rafi did not need the radio to tell him about this or about the attendant threat of persecution of a kind the Jews here had never known, or about the merciful invasion the following year of a bewildering array of new soldiers: Canadians, Nigerians, New Zealanders, Indians, an infinite number of foreigners of different shades and uniforms. Rafi's parents sometimes sent him to look for Jewish soldiers—there were even some of these in the British Commonwealth horde that descended on the city—and bring them home for Sabbath meals. And he did not need the Zenith to inform him of the troubles that began in earnest in Aleppo at war's end, with France back in control and many Syrians agitating for an end to colonial rule. At first the anger on the street targeted only the French. The Jews, who benefited from French influence, relied on their protection, and were terrified by the thought of an independent Syria, made sure to join the mass protests with as much enthusiasm as they could feign. Even Rafi demonstrated. A protest leader riding on someone else's shoulders would shout to the crowd, *Ana de Gaulle, hibouni!* I am de Gaulle, love me! And the crowd would answer, *Hara aleik!* Shit on you! Then they would shatter a few storefronts or turn over a tram.

On one occasion, Rafi saw a crowd of men stop a French army jeep, order the soldiers out, tie their hands, and force them to lie down on the street with their heads on the curb. Then they crushed their skulls with stones. In 1946, the French gave up and left the people of Syria to govern themselves, and with the French gone, the Jews were at the mercy of their countrymen. Rafi's French-language Jewish high school, the Alliance Israélite, was promptly shut down.

At the time of its demise, Rafi's world consisted of perhaps ten thousand people with a small number of recurring family names and roots deeper than those of nearly any other Jewish outpost on earth, a mix of people who had always been there or who had washed up over the centuries, fleeing persecution or pursuing trade. The Jews of Aleppo were an old community by the time Roman legions destroyed the Jewish temple in Jerusalem in AD 70, and an ancient community by the time Muslim conquerors arrived in the seventh century. They had been here for two and a half millennia, though time-honored local estimates would not admit to a year under three millennia. Tradition linked the community's roots to the capture of the city by Yoav, the general of King David's army, in an episode given brief mention in the Bible. According to one story—of the type that seeks to aggrandize something very old and impressive by claiming it is even older and more impressive—it was the general himself who laid the foundations of the great synagogue, and of the Aleppo Citadel as well.

The Arab residents called the city Halab. The Jews still occasionally called it by the name the Bible gave it, Aram-Tzova; this made the point that they were no one's guests. Among the Jews were families like the Dayans and Tawils, who traced their lineage in the city back thousands of years, and families like the Suttons or the Kassins, who had run from the Spanish Inquisition. There were the di Picciotos, one branch of a Tuscan merchant family, and the Baghdadis, like the sexton's family, who were from Iraq, and even families with names like Hornstein and Goldman, who had come from eastern Europe. Conservative, traditional, and paternalistic, they nonetheless included a small number of freethinkers, a smattering of Zionists, and at least one communist, who named his sons Lenin, Stalin, and Karl.

Since the rise of Islam, Jews had lived as a tolerated minority, or *dhimmi*, a status granted to Jews and Christians because they were monotheists. Despite a growing tendency in our own times to paint the premodern Islamic world as an Eden of religious tolerance in which Jews flourished, they always lived by the whims of fickle rulers and the mood of a hostile majority. In the eyes of that majority they were effete, lacking in honor, and powerless by definition, but as long as they accepted the supremacy of Muslims they were usually allowed to live and observe their faith and occasionally to prosper. Rafi's father, like everyone's father, did business with Muslims, and most Jews in Aleppo bought pastries from Muslim bakers and kosher meat from Muslim butchers who employed Jewish ritual slaughterers. But the old contract was already eroding by the time Rafi was born.

With the appearance of the French and other European powers in the lands of Islam, Jews had begun to forget their place, learning foreign languages, improving the education of their children, succeeding in business, and often leaving Muslims behind. In Algeria, they assumed French citizenship, which was not granted to Muslims. In downtown Cairo, under British rule, Jews built a grand synagogue modeled on the architecture of the pharaohs. Arab Muslims, who increasingly saw themselves as a national group—one that might admit Arab Christians but not Arab Jews—resented the growing incursion of Western countries, while the Jews were emboldened by foreign protection and patronage. When other Jews, Europeans, began arriving in Palestine in large numbers, the antagonism grew worse, forcing the Jews of the Islamic world to plead their loyalty to their neighbors. "The Jews of Syria have no connection with the Zionist question," read one plaintive advertisement that a Jewish youth club in Damascus, Syria's capital, published in local papers in 1929. "On the contrary, they share with their fellow Arab citizens all their feelings of joy and sadness." Muslims, it read, must "differentiate between the European Zionists and the Jews who have been living for centuries in these lands."

During the Second World War, Syria's citizens came to overwhelmingly support Hitler, and the leader of Palestine's Arabs spent part of the war in Berlin engaged in Nazi propaganda work and raising units for the SS. The *Protocols of the Elders of Zion,* a Tsarist forgery purporting to reveal a Jewish conspiracy

to control world events, was translated into Arabic and circulated widely. Iraqis in Baghdad, where one-third of the population was Jewish, massacred 180 Jews in their homes and shops in
1941. Four years later, mobs in Libya killed 130 more, and there
were less noteworthy incidents in between.

The number of insults Rafi suffered on the street began to
rise with the number of lurid newspaper headlines trumpeting
the atrocities inflicted by the Jews on the Arabs of Palestine. He
became used to hearing the word *yahudi*—Jew—spat at him.
The teenage son of one of the city's chief rabbis, who used to
wear a black beret like a Frenchman, gave up and went bare-
headed after Muslim toughs took to knocking it off. One man
I interviewed, who was a small child at the time, remembered
that getting home from school in those days meant a mad sprint
through the streets and then shouting, as soon as he saw his
building, for his mother to open the door.

As the day of the vote at Flushing Meadow approached, the
rabbis and notables of Jewish Aleppo, like their brethren across
the Islamic world, tried to distance themselves publicly from
Zionism. One of the community's leaders, Rabbi Moshe Tawil,
stood at Rafi's synagogue one Sabbath and delivered a sermon
condemning the Jewish national movement in Palestine. Young
Aleppo Jews in Palestine, living among secular socialists from
Europe, were eating food that was unclean and abandoning the
faith of their fathers, the rabbi warned the congregation, not
untruthfully. The Jews of Aleppo belonged in Aleppo and had
nothing to do with the foolhardy ambitions of other Jews in
the land to the south. The rabbi raised his hands to heaven and
surprised Rafi by bursting into tears.

3

The Fire

RABBI MOSHE TAWIL'S teenage son, Isaac, learned of the United Nations vote after he woke up that morning in his home near Rafi's, outside the Old City, and heard shouting from the street: *Sayouni, sayouni*. That meant "Zionist." Now an elderly man, a rabbi like his father, he punctuated his recollections by periodically slapping his hand on the table and causing my digital recorder to hop in the air. He went downstairs, he said, and eventually found himself in a crowd that had swelled to thousands of men.

Filastin biladna, wal-yahud kilabna, they were shouting: Palestine is our land, and the Jews are our dogs. Isaac quickly did what the Jews had been doing throughout the years of nationalist ferment in Syria: he joined the mob, raised his fist, chanted along with everyone else, and prayed he would not be noticed.

Standing inconspicuously opposite the neighborhood's grand modern synagogue down the street, Isaac saw policemen hoisting rioters through the windows and into the sanctuary. Some had cans of kerosene. The community's most venerated sage, Moises Mizrahi, a bent man in a red fez whom everyone believed to be a century old, was inside. Isaac saw the same policemen escort him out. On the street outside the synagogue, the rioters constructed an enormous pile of prayer books, Torah scrolls, and tractates of the Talmud and then set it on fire.

By this time, most of Aleppo's Jews had locked themselves in their homes. Roving mobs burned the neighborhood's other synagogues and a Jewish youth club where young people who had stayed up listening to the proceedings at the United Nations the night before had smashed wineglasses in jubilation and foolishly sung the Zionist anthem loud enough for the neighbors to hear. Rioters shattered the window of the Mazreb delicatessen, leapt inside, and ransacked it. They set fire to smaller prayer halls, the religious seminary run by Isaac's father, dozens of Jewish stores, and heaps of prayer shawls and phylacteries.

The fires spread down the city thoroughfares toward old Aleppo and the Jewish Quarter, where, in an apartment not far from the great synagogue, one nine-year-old boy—a tailor in his seventies when I interviewed him in a Tel Aviv apartment—heard rioters battering at the gate leading into the courtyard of his family's building. The banging stopped only when the rioters gave up and began scaling the wall instead. Howls of rage came from outside. The Jews in Palestine, someone screamed, were cutting Muslim babies from their mothers' wombs. His parents barricaded the family in the main room of the house, under wheels of cheese hung from the high ceilings to keep them from the cats. Then the rioters were at the door, and the boy escaped barefoot through a window into a side alley as they broke in. When they had taken his family's valuables, they used the kerosene and coal his parents had been storing for winter to set the building alight.

Bahiyeh Baghdadi, the sexton's daughter, was huddling not far away from the boy's burning house, in the basement of her

The Baghdadis of Aleppo, around 1940. Asher Baghdadi, the sexton, is in a striped robe. Bahiyeh is seated on a stool to his left.

family's building. Dull animal roars followed each crash of glass outside. She knew the mob was already across the alley inside her father's ancient synagogue.

Indna jabas, indna tin, wa-indna yahud a-sakin, came the chanting from the street above. This was meant to be a joke: We have watermelon, we have figs, and we have Jews on the knife. An apostate woman, a Jew who had become a Muslim, was at the entrance, pleading with the rioters in the name of their prophet to spare the building: *Dahilkom, dahilkom,* she was crying—Please, please. As the sexton's daughter, now an elderly woman, recounted this to me, she stared through me wide eyed.

The sexton, Asher, rose and wrapped his head in his cloak like an Arab. He was going to save the Crown. Bahiyeh's twelve-year-old sister, Carmela, grabbed him and begged him not to go, then followed him out when he went anyway. Carmela made it a few steps into the alley before a rock thudded into her head and drove her to the ground, unconscious. The sexton lifted her up and retreated inside under a barrage of stones.

Arab neighbors came and told the sexton's family to run or they would burn with the building, but the Baghdadis were too afraid to venture out. Asher, Asher, come see your synagogue, the rioters taunted him from outside. The sexton stayed in the basement. By this time, people looking from their roofs in Rafi's neighborhood outside the Old City could see black smoke rising from the Jewish Quarter. From belowground, though, Bahiyeh and her family could see nothing.

Inside the great synagogue, the rioters found a metal box hidden in a grotto and carried it into the courtyard. They must have assumed it contained something worth stealing. It had two locks but was not much of a safe; they simply pried off the back and flipped it over. Out fell a few old books.

One of them was bigger than the others. It had five hundred parchment pages, each with three columns of neat Hebrew script, twenty-eight lines to a column. What was left of the volume's ancient binding disintegrated, and leaves scattered on the smooth stones of the courtyard. And just like that, the cobwebs of belief that had preserved the Crown perfectly for centuries were brushed away.

Someone lit a match and touched it to spilled kerosene.

A MONTH LATER, the January 2, 1948, edition of the Hebrew daily *Haaretz* went on sale in Tel Aviv with the following headlines on the front page:

OVER FIVE HUNDRED IMMIGRANTS LAND ON THE BEACH AT NAHARIYA

A ship carrying Hungarians, Lithuanians, and Poles, survivors of the war in Europe, had braved the British sea blockade imposed to quell Arab anger by keeping Jewish refugees out of Palestine. The immigrants had landed safely on a beach near a Jewish town on the Mediterranean coast.

DOZENS OF ARABS KILLED IN 2 HAGANA REPRISALS IN HAIFA AND SALAMA

3 HAGANA MEN KILLED NEAR HAIFA, ONE JEW STABBED TO DEATH IN JERUSALEM

The Hagana was the Jewish military organization in Palestine. The war between Jews and Arabs was growing in violence as the British prepared to pull out. There were daily ambushes on the roads, bombings, reprisals, and reprisals for reprisals. The declaration of the state of Israel, and the invasion of regular Arab armies, was four months away.

And, among the day's stories, this:

THE BIBLE OF ALEPPO

If the news published in the newspapers matches the truth, the famous Bible that was the glory of the Jewish community of Aleppo, the Bible that according to tradition was used by Maimonides himself, was devoured by fire in the riots that erupted against the Jews of Aleppo several weeks ago. The "Crown of *Aram-Tzova*," as it was commonly known . . . is lost and gone, according to what we have heard.

With the Jewish enclave in Palestine at war, its very existence in doubt, the writer—a Bible professor—was in mourning for a book. "We might still hope," he wrote,

that perhaps this information is no more than false bragging on the part of the rioters and that in fact this wonderful book has survived yet again. But this is nothing but a slim hope, and in the torching of the ancient synagogue of Aleppo this beloved relic of the wisdom of the Middle Ages is likely to have gone up in flames.

Perhaps it is difficult to grasp, in our times, how a book could elicit such passion. The codex had outlived the age of its creation, when a book was an object of vast worth, a product of great craftsmanship and scholarship, and a repository of irreplaceable knowledge. It had survived into the time of the printing press and the photograph but had retained its singular value because of the zealousness of its keepers: there were no known copies.

A closer examination of the parchment leaves scattered in the courtyard of the Aleppo synagogue will enable a grasp of what this book was. On its pages were inscriptions that served as passport stamps, revealing much about why the Crown was created and where—for the Aleppo Codex was not from Aleppo at all and was ancient by the time it arrived there—and where it had been since, and what its loss meant to the people who revered it.

4

The Swift Scribe of Tiberias

Tiberias, circa AD 930

THE MEN WHO created the Crown would have looked out every day over the same landscape I saw when I traveled to their town more than a millennium later: across the level face of the Sea of Galilee to the barren rise of the Golan plateau on the other side, the specks of fishing boats the only blemishes on the water's surface. Tiberias was a cluster of markets and stone buildings on the western shore.

"This is the full codex of the twenty-four books," read an inscription on the Crown, "written by our master and rabbi Shlomo, known as Ben-Buya'a, the swift scribe, may the spirit of God guide him."

Shlomo Ben-Buya'a, the swift scribe, sat on the floor or on a mattress. He would have placed a wooden plank on his knees, then spread out a parchment folio.

The scribe worked under the direction of another man, a master who knew every consonant and vowel of the holy text and whose fame exceeded his own. This scholar, Aaron Ben-Asher, the same inscription tells us, was the "lord of scribes and father of sages." Perhaps he was in the room as the scribe looked at the first empty page, already scored with a sharp instrument to delineate a grid of columns and lines, and then touched his quill to the parchment. *In the beginning,* he wrote, *God created the heavens and the earth.*

I imagine Ben-Buya'a pronouncing each word out loud, following the tradition of Hebrew scribes, before applying ink to the rectangles of animal skin, hanging his angular letters from the horizontal lines.

In those years, nine of every ten Jews in the world, including the scribe and the scholar, lived in the lands of Islam. Tiberias, ruled by a Muslim dynasty from Baghdad, was renowned among Jews as a center for the study of Hebrew. The city attracted Jewish scholars from afar, like a certain Eli, son of Judah, the Nazir, the latter title indicating that he had taken monk-like vows to refrain from drinking wine and cutting his hair. Eli seems to have arrived here at about this time to study the holy tongue; one of his interests was the pronunciation of the letter *r.* "I would spend a long time sitting in the squares of Tiberias and its streets," this scholar wrote—in Arabic, for though he was studying Hebrew, Arabic was the language of Jewish scholarship— "listening to the speech of the simple men and the crowd and studying the language and its basic principles."

Reading this, I pictured Eli, the linguistic pilgrim, trolling open-air markets where merchants hawked olives, dates, and fish from the Sea of Galilee, listening for interesting Hebrew words and turns of phrase, as the scribe Ben-Buya'a sat in a room nearby transcribing the divine book in that same language, line by line.

It had been nine hundred years since Jesus of Nazareth walked this shoreline. Only slightly less time had elapsed since Roman legions razed the temple in Jerusalem and crushed what Jewish sovereignty existed in the province of Judaea. While some

Jews remained in the land of Israel, many of them in Tiberias, most had dispersed, drifting farther into distant countries until the gravitational pull of their homeland could scarcely be felt. They would acknowledge the authority of kings other than their own and be exposed to gods other than the one who, as they understood it, created the heavens and the earth. Their lifeline to Judaea and Jerusalem was long, and getting longer, and with the years it would become more tenuous.

And the earth was unformed and void,
with darkness over the surface of the deep,
and the wind of God sweeping over the waters

And so the scribe continued, printing twenty-eight lines before beginning a new column, filling three columns before moving to a new page.

The book the scribe was copying was woven from interlocking stories of complicated characters interacting with a single transcendent deity to whom the Jews believed their fate was linked. These were stories their ancestors had told each other long before to explain their connection to this God, their land, and each other and to raise themselves from anarchy into order and law. It was their guide to the world. The book began to take shape before the first temple in Jerusalem was destroyed by a Babylonian army in 586 BC. During the reign of King Josiah a few decades earlier, the Bible recounts in the book of Kings, one of the priests found a "scroll of the law" in the temple, a hint in the text itself that the stories were already being written down. Later, in exile in Babylon, scribes continued to write and redact, and by the fifth century BC the work that we know as the Torah, the Five Books of Moses, or the Pentateuch had come into being.

These five books, the Torah, are the heart of the Jewish religion. It is the Torah that is read out loud from a scroll every week in synagogue in a yearly cycle of portions that begins with the creation of the universe and ends with the death of Moses. Other books were added later: the moral and social prophecies of the humble Amos; Ezekiel's vision of God, experienced along the river Chebar during the Babylonian exile; the sexually evocative language of the Song of Songs. Other books were left out. By the first century of the Common Era, after the Jews had returned to their land and had then been exiled yet again, this time by Rome, the Bible's books had been selected, edited, and refined into the text we know.

At first these stories were one of many threads making up the national life of the Jews. They also had a land, and a language, and a temple that was the center of their religion. But that changed with the destruction of the temple by Rome in AD 70 and the exile of the Jews. There was no precedent for a scattered people's remaining a people; dispersion meant disappearance. If the Jews were to be an exception, instead of being bound by a king, a temple, or geography, they needed to be bound by something else, something portable. What emerged was the idea that a people could be held together by words.

On Mondays, Thursdays, and the Sabbath, in synagogues anywhere on earth, a member of the congregation opens an ark and removes a book. It is a double scroll because this is the way books were once written. Written inside is the Torah, the first five books of the Hebrew Bible. On top of the scroll there is often a silver crown: the Jews dress their book up like a king and stand up in respect when it is taken from the ark, just as they would if a dignitary entered the room. The Jews, in exile, would no longer have their own king to protect them or rule over them. They would have no political power themselves. Instead they would have a book that would connect them, wherever they were, to each other and to the power and protection of the King of Kings.

A member of the congregation places the scroll on a table and rolls the two sides of the scroll away from each other, revealing long columns of black Hebrew letters, preparing to read it aloud. But the book cannot simply be read. Hebrew, like Arabic, is written without most of its vowels, and a reader is supposed to recognize the word and fill in the vowel sounds from memory. To demonstrate the problem this creates, imagine encountering the word *mt*. Is it *mat? Meet? Mate? Moat?* Now imagine more than three hundred thousand words written without vowels: this is the Hebrew Bible. There is also no punctuation, and some words are written one way but read another. And yet despite this absence of adequate information, reading the scroll with the utmost precision is imperative: When the reader chants the text, there are people standing on either side of him listening for errors. Congregants sometimes call out corrections, upon which the reader has to go back and repeat the words. On rare occasions, a reader will find a mistake in the scroll itself—a scribal error, or a letter worn away by age or by the constant rolling of the parchment—and the reading comes to a halt. The most learned worshippers gather around and peer at the scroll, and then, if it is deemed flawed, it is returned to the ark; even the tiniest defect renders the entire scroll unusable. Later it will be taken to be corrected by a scribe. Another scroll is brought out, and only then does the reading continue.

Behind these stringencies lies the contention that there is only one text and that anarchy in these matters is an abomination. Catholics have Rome, a single religious institution holding all of the church's constituent parts together, but after the Jewish exile, Jerusalem was just an idea, not an organization. Judaism had no central institution, only thousands of self-contained communities linked by the content of their religious belief and practice. The Jews could not be held together by a book if they were not reading precisely the same one, because minor differences in the text could lead to diverging interpretations and a splintering of the faith. And yet much of the information crucial to reading the book properly could not be found in the book itself.

There needed to be another book, then, that would tell people how to read the first. It had to be written down before this key supplementary knowledge, which had been transmitted orally for centuries, was lost in the Diaspora. This is why the Crown was created.

The language of the Bible had to be clear and not in dispute. Spelling and pronunciation had to be standardized, and punctuation inserted. But there is more to it than that, because the biblical text means more than might be conveyed by the simple meaning of the words. The text tells many truths—those on the surface, and those hidden beneath it. The text must be perfect because an imperfect text loses information vital to the book's divine message. It is not just that we must know exactly what the words mean, Jewish tradition tells us, because we do not and cannot know exactly what they mean; perhaps we did once, and perhaps we will again one day, but for now the information must be preserved even if it is beyond our understanding. A tiny vowel sign, one that makes only a minute difference in how a word is pronounced—prolonging the syllable *ah*, for example, into *aah*—might be sheltering precious and secret information. So might the mysterious fifteen dots that are written above certain words in the text, or the baffling rules instructing scribes to make certain letters big and others small. If we lose these, we lose knowledge that God wanted us to have, even if we don't know why.

One tradition recounts that the sage Akiva, who lived in Roman times, used to expound not only on individual letters but on their tiny calligraphic flourishes, the "crowns of letters." Even these were important. Another tradition tells us that the Five Books of Moses are actually one very long version of the name of God, which is another way of saying that you must not get anything wrong. Yet another tradition reminds us that when God created light, he did not just create light. He *said,* "Let there be light." He created the world with words, which are therefore a kind of blueprint for creation and for the nature of the universe. Any tiny aspect of the text, no matter how useless we may foolishly believe it to be, is part of the code.

Hundreds of years had gone by after the destruction of the temple when a group of scholars in Tiberias began the work of compiling the authoritative text of the Bible, inventing a system of tiny lines, hooks, and dots that served as symbols for vowels and cantillation—the tune to which the text is chanted, which also serves, crucially, to add punctuation and emphasis. The project, which took centuries, became known as the Masora, from the Hebrew word meaning "to pass on." Their goal was to collect and record oral traditions, to reach consensus where there was disagreement, and ultimately to create the text of the Bible on which all others would be based.

Of the rabbis engaged in the project, the greatest were those of the Ben-Asher dynasty, which produced five or six generations of scholars. The family's greatest scion was Aaron, and his greatest work—the one that marked the end of the process of attaining perfection in the text—was this one. There were many biblical codices produced in later centuries, and certain examples of particularly high quality came to be called crowns of the

Torah, or just crowns. This codex, the final achievement of hundreds of years of scholarship and the most accurate and famous
of them all, became known as *the* Crown. While there are many
tens of thousands of Torah scrolls, there is only one Crown.

The rabbi Aaron Ben-Asher and the swift scribe Shlomo
Ben-Buya'a worked together for several years. Because the book
was meant to be a reference guide, not a ritual object read in
synagogue, it did not need to be a scroll; scrolls, by this time,
were already obsolete for recording practical documents. Instead
it would be a bound codex, or what today we would refer to
simply as a book. The invention of the codex allowed scholars
to easily flip through text without rolling yards of parchment
back and forth.

Tanners soaked, stretched, and scrubbed the animal skins, removing traces of hair from one side and innards from the other.
Ben-Buya'a wrote the letters in indelible ink made from powdered
tree galls mixed with iron sulfate and black soot. Above, beneath,
and beside those letters, on just under five hundred parchment
leaves, Ben-Asher added the marks indicating vowels and cantillation. He added thousands of tiny notes in the margins. Some
were merely one letter: A Hebrew letter *lamed*, for example, indicated a word that appears nowhere else in the biblical text. A *bet*,
the second letter of the Hebrew alphabet, indicated a word that
appears twice. Longer notes warn of words that are not to be read
as they are written or point to other passages where a certain rare
word can be found. Ben-Asher could do this because he knew
the entire text by heart. When the scribe and the scholar were
finished, the new codex was ready to be sent into the world. More
than a thousand years later, scholars of the Hebrew Bible would
still have no more important book than theirs.

PART TWO

PART TWO

5

The Treasure in the Synagogue

THE CANTOR IN the synagogue sang the Hebrew words — *For the beloved of my heart, Elijah the prophet* — to an old Aleppo tune, and two young women in short dresses tottered around the sanctuary in high heels, holding a silver tray with a few dozen lit candles and a loose pile of dollar bills for charity. The men were clean shaven and wore dark suits or leather jackets and black velvet skullcaps. Some had both phylacteries and BlackBerries. They shook hands and kissed one another on both cheeks. One had his prayer shawl in a cloth bag embroidered with the family name Sha'alo, one of the Aleppo clans. The women, in their own section, tended toward dark haired and gorgeous. From one of the back rows, I took all of this in.

A new mother, dressed in white, her belly still swollen, entered the sanctuary from the back, her own mother carrying the newborn boy on a pillow. The young father took him from the women and carried him toward a huddle of men near the front. They chanted the traditional blessings of the circumcision rite as one of the men readied his sharp instruments, and then the baby wailed and the ceremony was over. People kissed the mother and said, "Mabruk," Arabic for congratulations. "Many more, *inshallah*," one grinning man her age added: if Allah wills it.

I slipped out of the synagogue onto a wide boulevard lined

with trees and red brick American homes, and a yellow taxi zoomed by just then as if to confirm that I was, in fact, in Brooklyn, New York.

Jewish Aleppo is gone. Today the Syrian city's great synagogue sits empty in the middle of a Jewish Quarter with no Jews. The Crown's grotto, the secret nerve center of the community's spiritual life, contains nothing but dead air, and the volume that was kept there is as absent as its guardians. Using the portable survival mechanism built into their religion—the book— the exiles have regrouped in small, tightly knit colonies across the globe, in Buenos Aires, Panama City, Tokyo, and Milan. The largest is in this New York borough, the petri dish where fragments from lost Jewish worlds are cultured and regrown, where today the Jews of Aleppo exist among other communities, synagogues, and rabbinical seminaries bearing the names of lost towns in Poland and Ukraine. They and their descendants have survived and prospered, but in the city of their origin a world thousands of years in the making simply vanished. Few besides the Aleppo Jews themselves seem to have noticed.

On the day of the riots in 1947, eighteen Jewish houses of prayer had been gutted by the time the Syrian government finally sent troops in to disperse the mobs at nightfall. The Crown, as far as almost anyone knew, had gone up in flames along with countless other texts in the inferno at the great synagogue.

The rioters had also torched fifty shops, five schools, and an unknown number of homes belonging to their Jewish neighbors. Stories circulated among the Jews about rioters who had fashioned gloves and bags from the parchment of looted holy books. Aleppo's wealthy Jewish families, the ones whose money maintained the synagogues and schools and provided dowries for needy brides and who had the clout to intervene with the government, had already fled down to the Mediterranean coast and the cosmopolitan quarters of Beirut. They would soon be on ships bound for Europe and America and would not be back. Within days of the riot the community was rudderless and destitute.

Only one house of prayer was left unharmed: a modest building overlooked by the rioters because of its location off a particularly narrow alley. It was here, on the first Sabbath after the riots, that many of the Jewish men who remained in the city went to pray.

Some of the people who gathered at the synagogue that Sabbath morning still believed life would return to normal. Some understood that it would not. But they were all wounded and furious, and so an extra prayer was added to the regular service: chapter 83 of the book of Psalms. Isaac Tawil, the rabbi's son, shouted the lines with everyone else, pouring his anger into Hebrew verses that the "cursed ones," as he called them, could not understand if they heard them, as they surely did, from windows nearby. Not far away was the gutted great synagogue, its courtyard littered with parchment, the broken safe in one corner. *Lord, do not keep silent, be not quiet, Lord, be not still,* they intoned with emotion, just as the rabbi's son did when he sat opposite me in Tel Aviv more than sixty years later, his eyes closed.

> See how your enemies are astir, how your foes rear their
> heads . . .
> Make them like tumbleweed, Lord, like chaff before the wind
> As fire consumes the forest, or a flame sets the mountains
> ablaze
> So pursue them with your tempest and terrify them with your
> storm.

Accounts of the Aleppo riot usually repeat the claim that the mob killed dozens of Jews, as if without death the violence would not register on the scale of Jewish tragedy. That claim is false. No one was killed, raped, or even seriously hurt, and if the immense destruction was a telling indication of the extent of local Muslim tolerance for Jews, we must acknowledge that this fact was, too. In the middle-class quarter where Rafi Sutton lived, there were Muslims who stood outside the doors of Jewish homes and faced down the marauders, and Rafi himself took refuge with his family in the apartment of Muslim neighbors. Some of the Jews in Aleppo saw the fact that the rioters killed no one as a reason for hope that all was not lost; it was the 1940s, and this was a people with no good options and little expectation of kindness. Others saw it as proof that the authorities were in control, encouraging the devastation of property, and thus of the community's livelihood and future, but halting the disturbances before blood was shed.

Though it would take time, the destruction of the community was under way; it was the Jews, not their enemies, who would now be driven like chaff before the wind, until none remained. But the loss of the community's most sacred possession was a clever falsehood.

The Syrian authorities knew of the codex and knew its value, and they might have considered the manuscript a cultural artifact that was part of the history of their new country. Agents of the regime had already questioned one of the rabbis about it. A wealthy Armenian doctor from the city, perhaps a collector of manuscripts, had also contacted the same rabbi and had inquired about purchasing the book. The Crown was in danger, and to mislead those seeking it, the Jewish elders spread the lie that it had been destroyed.

Later, what had actually happened to it became a matter of almost comic disagreement. If all the stories told over the years by Aleppo Jews about people spiriting the Crown from the synagogue are true, then no fewer than a dozen different men were there at the same time, individually removing the same book.

In one story, a rabbi who later emigrated to Mexico City went into the great synagogue after quiet had returned to Aleppo, or so he would tell a writer in his adopted home many years later. Inside he discovered the Crown, charred. He picked it up and hid it in the ruins of the synagogue, where it was later recovered.

Another version was recounted in a book written by an Aleppo Jew in Brooklyn: During the riot the Crown was stolen by no less a personage than a minister of the Syrian government, who fled with it to Lebanon. Upon his return he was caught by Syrian authorities and sent to the gallows, and the book was returned to the Jews.

Yet another account came from Murad Faham, the cheese merchant who heard about the United Nations vote as he walked to the bazaar and who will soon reappear as one of the key players in this story.

After the riots, Faham recounted much later in his taped oral testimony, he dressed like an Arab, in a woolen cloak, and went out onto the street. It was almost dawn. He walked to the great synagogue, passing the shells of Jewish stores, and went through the gate, seeing that the fire had blackened the walls and melted the metal supports under the pews. He found the safe that had been in the Cave of the Prophet Elijah. Inside was the Crown, which was still on fire but somehow had not been consumed; here is a magical element inspired, perhaps, by the Exodus story of the burning bush. "I took it in my hands, a ball of fire, and wrapped it in my outer coat," Faham recounted. His cloak "was like that of a Bedouin, thick and made entirely of wool, and I did not feel the fire." A few Arabs came by, but they took him for an Arab himself, greeted him without much interest, and continued looting the synagogue, taking pieces of silver from the pomegranate-shaped decorations placed on top of Torah scrolls.

Faham went to the house of the sexton, Asher Baghdadi, who was too frightened to open the door.

Don't be afraid, Faham called to him.

I can't come down to the synagogue, Baghdadi said.

Don't go down to the synagogue, just open up, I want to talk to you, Faham said. When the sexton finally opened the door, Faham handed him the package and told him what it was.

I don't want to take it home, he said. Take it and give it to-morrow to one of the elders of the community.

This account, the most dramatic and detailed of them all, is the one I quoted credulously in my first article about the Crown. It remains my favorite. Like the others, however, it is fiction.*

I heard another version from a rabbi I met six decades after these events. He was hunched and weak, drinking tea over a book of Talmud in a synagogue outside Tel Aviv. I was with Ezra Kassin, the former military investigator and amateur Crown sleuth, who warned me that the rabbi had suffered several strokes and might not be lucid. Ezra introduced himself as the grandson of a man from Aleppo whose name was also Ezra Kassin. The rabbi mumbled something, and I motioned to Ezra that we should leave; the man was clearly infirm. Ezra ignored me. The rabbi spoke another sentence that I could not make out,

---

* In 1958, Faham testified that in the fall of 1957, ten years after the riot, he had not even known the Crown had survived the synagogue fire, contradicting his claim much later to have saved it himself.

and then said, "Your grandfather was a tailor in Aleppo." Ezra nodded. "He was a simple, pure man," the rabbi said. "There are no people like that anymore." Then he started talking as if he had been waiting for us to come. His good eye looked at me sharply, and I imagined that his other eye, milky and blind, was peering back in time.

"They attacked synagogues," he said, pausing to cough violently, "study halls, the Jewish school. They burned Torah scrolls, and they came closer and closer. We stayed at home for three days." But on the third day, he wanted to go to the great synagogue. "We felt so much sorrow that we cried and read songs of lamentation," he said, referring to poems Jews read to commemorate the destruction of the temples in Jerusalem. "We saw Torah scrolls torn into pieces, pieces, pieces in the synagogue . . . I—I myself—saw the Crown, on the floor . . . I drew close and picked up the Crown. I put it in a bag," he said. Then he gave it to one of the men in charge of the synagogue. "Afterward, the goyim thought it was burned."

Some of the stories—and there are others—overlap in places, and some contain grains of truth. Some might be explained by the simple fact that there were many holy books in the great synagogue and almost no one had ever seen the Crown or knew what it looked like: what they thought was the great book might have been another manuscript. But the proliferation of stories, it seems clear, is rooted in the role of the Crown as the talisman and symbol of the Aleppo Jews. If the book was safe, so were they, and if it was not, they were not either. Now it had come to symbolize the moment of their community's destruction, and everyone wanted to be part of the story.

The most trustworthy account, the only one corroborated by numerous other sources—and the one that simply makes the most sense—credits a man who never bragged about it or thought to write it down. This was the sexton himself.

Asher Baghdadi was not just the man in charge of the synagogue's upkeep but also the person who lived in closest proximity to it, and could thus reach it with relative ease. Early in the morning after the riot, the sexton took one of his adult sons, crossed the alleyway between his house and the synagogue, and entered the courtyard, finding it full of charred books and pieces of parchment. He got down on the ground and began looking through the pages to find pieces of the Crown.

"I saw my father crying like a baby," his son Shahoud recalled in a TV documentary forty years later. "I said, '*Abba*, what happened? Get up, why are you sitting there?'" Shahoud bent over and began to help his father sort through the piles. What he found will be a matter of interest to us later on.

At the sexton's home, which had been looted but not burned, his daughter Carmela—the one who had been hit on the head with a stone during the riot—woke up that morning and saw that her father was gone. She remembered him returning with a burlap sack. Shaking with emotion, he said, *Hear, O Israel*, repeating the prayer Jews say in times of great danger or in the moments before death.

Look what they did, he told his children, and he opened the sack. Inside were parchment leaves.

I saved what I could, he said.

After a period that might have been several days or several weeks, Baghdadi gave the book to one of the community's remaining leaders, who gave him a modest sum of money for his trouble. The elders secretly passed it on to a Christian merchant whom they trusted and thought no one would suspect. At the same time they spread the story of its loss. When the city re-gained a semblance of normalcy, four or five months later, the leaders moved it to a storeroom owned by a Jewish textile mer-chant, Ibrahim Effendi Cohen, in one of the Old City bazaars. The Crown would remain there, undetected, for a decade.

6

The Jerusalem Circle

BY THE TIME two months had passed since the United Nations vote, the Jewish sector of Jerusalem was strangled by Arab ambushes of the supply convoys coming up the highway from the coastal plain. Communication links with the outside world were spotty, and food supplies scant and shrinking. Jewish and Arab terror squads waged bombing campaigns against civilians of the other side. "Jerusalem is becoming virtually isolated behind a curtain of fear," wrote a *New York Times* reporter.

"Every time we go to sleep, we are not sure we are going to wake up," an Arab mother confided in a letter to her son. "It is not the bullets we mind so much, but the dynamiting when you're asleep. People wake up in the middle of the night under the debris of their houses."

On January 17, men from the Jewish Irgun militia rolled an oil drum packed with dynamite into a crowd of Arab commuters waiting at a bus stop, killing seventeen. At dawn on February 22, six British army deserters and former policemen working for the Palestinian Arab command left four stolen army vehicles parked on Ben-Yehuda Street, in the center of the Jewish part of the city. The explosives inside, prepared by an Arab bomb maker trained by the SS, went off at 6:30 a.m., destroying four buildings and killing fifty-eight people.

Less than three weeks after that, and less than a week before another deadly bombing in the Jewish sector, three scholars at Hebrew University held an urgent meeting. The subject was the Crown of Aleppo and, specifically, dramatic news that had just arrived from Syria with a woman who had fled. "The entire community there has been destroyed and only the remains are left, the poor people, without a leader or a steward," read the minutes of the March 5 meeting. The woman, whom the scholars clearly considered a trustworthy witness, "happened to visit the synagogue, and the sexton revealed to her that he managed to save remains of the Crown, and they are now in his hands." The book had survived.

The Aleppo Jews and the Syrian government were not the only ones with their eyes on the codex. Jerusalem, too, was home to a circle of men who were preoccupied with the same book and had already tried, unsuccessfully, to obtain it.

The leader of the Jerusalem circle was Itzhak Ben-Zvi. Born Isaac Shimshelevich in Ukraine, Ben-Zvi was a Zionist leader and would later become the second president of the state of Israel—an influential, if largely ceremonial, position. He was also an ethnographer and anthropologist. He is remembered today as one of the giants of Israel's history. Nearly every town in the country has a street named for him, and his image appears on the 100 shekel note. In 1935, on a visit to Aleppo, the future president had been allowed a brief glimpse of the codex by the community elders and had never forgotten it.

By the early 1940s, scholars at Hebrew University in Jerusalem—then still firmly under British rule—had decided to produce a new edition of the Hebrew Bible, the most accurate ever, ending the enduring disgrace that other modern editions had been published by Christians. For this, they decided, they needed the Crown, the most accurate version of the text. As there were no copies, they needed the original. Because they were not just scholars but also Zionists, Ben-Zvi and his colleagues believed Judaism's greatest book belonged in Jerusalem, the spiritual center of the Jews' national renaissance. They also feared that Syrian authorities or collectors might get their hands on the book—in those years before the riot, it was common knowledge in Aleppo that would-be buyers had offered the community a fortune for it—or that it could be lost in the upheaval of the Second World War, which was then at its height. Not understanding the intensity of the Aleppo Jews' connection to the book or their belief that it could never be moved, the scholars hoped it would be enough to send someone to Aleppo and simply to ask for it.

In early 1943, Isaac Shamosh, a young lecturer on Arabic literature from Hebrew University, stepped off a train in Aleppo. Shamosh must have been aware that he had little chance of success. He had been born and raised in the city, which is why he had been chosen for the mission. He had once been, simultaneously, an avid Zionist and a Syrian nationalist (there was a brief time when this actually made sense) and had moved to Jerusalem to assume his teaching position after an Arab gunman killed the previous lecturer with a bullet shot through the window of his home during an earlier period of unrest.

When he approached the Aleppo elders, he received the blunt answer he no doubt expected: the book would never leave the great synagogue. As he prepared to return via Beirut to Palestine, however, several of the lecturer's old friends from Aleppo, young men in modern suits and with modern ideas who saw the community's traditional leadership as hopelessly backward, came to see him. Shamosh later recounted their conversation repeatedly, his younger brother told me many years after Isaac's death, because he came to see it as one of the pivotal moments in his life.

We know the Crown is in danger here, the men said, and we know the identities of the two men who have the keys. Tell us the number of your carriage on the Beirut train and the time of your departure and bring along an empty suitcase.

Perhaps Shamosh thought of the inscription on the Crown— "cursed be he who steals it"—or of the tradition that promised the community's doom if the book were moved. Perhaps he was simply afraid. He returned to Palestine empty handed, and when he told the other scholars in Jerusalem what had happened, Ben-Zvi replied with a wry sentence that the scholar always remembered: Too bad we sent an honest man. Those words haunted the envoy afterward, when news of the book's destruction arrived, because by stealing the book he could have saved it.

A few months after arriving back in Jerusalem, Shamosh returned to Syria, this time accompanied by the secretary of Hebrew University. The Jerusalem scholars had adjusted their expectations and now hoped only to get the Aleppo elders to agree to allow them to photograph the codex. In the previous century the predecessors of these same rabbis had allowed two men, an Oxford scholar and a Christian missionary, to photograph individual pages of the book, but now even this was out of the question. Allowing a copy to be made, they believed, would render their treasure worthless. "I had a very hard week, which is not what I had hoped," the secretary complained on hotel stationery to the university's president. "Why? Our Jews in Aleppo have not decided to allow us to copy and compare, and only after many efforts did they call a meeting of the community council and agree to say yes, but—but they are not satisfied

with the matter of security to prevent theft." He suggested in a
memo marked "Top Secret" that even if permission to take photographs was denied they might try to do it anyway, in a covert
fashion. During the exchange the Aleppo Jews told the scholars they were unwilling to receive any letters postmarked from
Palestine, concerned they could be singled out as Zionist sym-
pathizers; this, sniffed the secretary, was the "fear of Diaspora
Jews." In the end the Aleppo elders agreed only to allow one of
the scholars access to the manuscript without photographing it
or removing it from the synagogue.

The two envoys returned to Jerusalem, and another member
of the Jerusalem circle, Professor Umberto Cassuto, an Italian-
born Bible expert who had once been chief rabbi of Florence,
traveled to Aleppo that December. An old photograph of Cassuto
shows a man with a pointed white beard and a mustache curled
extravagantly at the ends, peering at a book through round
spectacles.

Cassuto's reception was of a type that will be familiar to many
who have tried to do business or report a story in the Middle East. "When I arrived there," Cassuto wrote later, "they
did receive me graciously, but with regards to the Crown they
told me right at the beginning: If Your Honor wants to see
the Crown—certainly, we will gladly display it for a quarter of
an hour." More wrangling and pleading followed. He set up a
meeting with one of the elders; the elder did not show up, then
apologized and promised to come the next morning but did
not, and so forth, until Cassuto threatened, rather unconvinc-
ingly, according to his diary, to "look for another community
that wants to help with this sacred work." Of course, no other
community had the Crown. He said he would have to tell his
colleagues at the university that the Jews of Aleppo "refused to

offer us any help." He was finally led through the Old City to the great synagogue, where he was met by the two elders with the keys. Each opened one lock, and then one took out the Crown. The visiting scholar was accompanied by several guardians, he wrote later, men who were there "in order to guard the Crown, and maybe, who knows, also to guard me so I would not take photographs, God forbid."

The guards, young rabbis, had themselves never seen the Crown before, and remembered the stranger's visit long afterward. One of them was the ancient rabbi with one blind eye whom I met in the synagogue near Tel Aviv almost seventy years later and who had recounted his own version of the codex's rescue. "We guarded him," the rabbi said of Cassuto. "What did we do? Opened the Crown, the fabric covering, I remember that." He saw the Crown was special, he said, because of the unflagging precision of the scribe's work. "The beauty of the Crown was not that it was a splendid manuscript—there are more beautiful ones—but its beauty was that from beginning to end, from Genesis to Chronicles, it was the same writing. The same shape. That was the beauty."

The professor sat in the synagogue taking detailed notes, noting words in the text whose spelling was a point of argument. The Crown, he wrote in his diary, was in a wooden box covered in red leather, the covers of the codex attached to the two halves of the box. "The sewing of the folios has come apart in several places and the book is separated into different pieces," he wrote. On some of the pages, he saw, the words had faded and had been reinforced with new ink by nameless scribes over the centuries.

The elders had eventually agreed to allow Cassuto several hours with the manuscript, instead of fifteen minutes. When his time was up, the men with the keys came back and returned the

Professor Umberto Cassuto.

codex to the safe. This routine was repeated over the better part
of a week before the scholar returned to Jerusalem, having gone
over only a small portion of the text. Other matters weighed on
him. In November 1943, weeks before his arrival in Aleppo, the
SS had begun the liquidation of the Jews of Florence, where Cassuto's son, Nathan, served as a rabbi. Nathan and his wife, Chana,
were sent to Poland and interned in the concentration camp at
Auschwitz. Nathan died there. Cassuto's daughter, Hulda, eluded
the Germans, but her husband, Saul, also died at Auschwitz. As
the professor studied the Crown in Aleppo, his six small grandchildren were hidden to evade capture, the boys by Catholic families and the girls by the nuns of the convent of La Calza.

After the Aleppo riots, when news of the book's destruction
reached Jerusalem, it was Professor Cassuto who penned the
newspaper obituary. His distress over the book's loss can only
seem more poignant when one understands that Cassuto was a
man who knew real grief. The Jews of Aleppo, he wrote, had
lit candles in front of the Crown's safe and had prayed there for
the healing of the sick, and believed it protected them and their

community from harm. He described the safety measures—the two locks, the men who guarded him at all times. "The cloak of legend was unfurled over this book, as if it were surrounded by clouds of honor and the fog of purity," the article read. "But secret wisdom and hidden treasure are of no use, and all the care and zealousness of the local people made it impossible to learn from the book or enjoy the wisdom inside." The stringent security measures, he wrote, his pique apparent in the old newsprint, were "more than enough to distance those who wanted to learn, or to make their work harder, but unfortunately were apparently no good whatsoever against the gangs of rioters."

When the Hebrew University scholars met in March 1948, two months after that article was published in *Haaretz*, to discuss the news of the book's survival, Cassuto was present; it was now apparent that his sorrow over the Crown's loss was premature. Ben-Zvi, who as a political leader was preoccupied with the growing ferocity of the war against the Arabs, was not there but was informed. The scholars held a second meeting a few days later to discuss the same news, all of this as the university was engulfed, quite literally, in violence. Students and professors from the physics and chemistry departments were manufacturing gunpowder and explosives. Two months before the meeting, in mid-January, thirty-five Jewish fighters, most of them students from the university, had been ambushed and killed as they tried to reinforce a group of besieged settlements south of Jerusalem. Ben-Zvi's son, Eli, who was defending a kibbutz in the north, fell in combat that month. Five weeks after the meeting, on April 13, Chana Cassuto, the professor's widowed daughter-in-law, who had survived Auschwitz and reached Israel, would be in a Jewish convoy ambushed as it tried to get through an Arab neighborhood to the hospital on Mount Scopus, next to the university campus. She would be among the seventy-eight dead.

The scholars weighed the possibility of making another attempt to bring the Crown to Jerusalem. The border between Palestine and Syria was still open, most of the stubborn Aleppo elders who had foiled the 1943 attempt were now gone, and the scholars thought the sexton Asher Baghdadi still had the manuscript and might be persuaded to turn it over. The scholars had old information; by this time the sexton had already given the codex to the remaining community leaders. In any case, Professor Cassuto was opposed. "It must not appear as if the university is interested in exploiting the Aleppo community's disaster and is trying to obtain what it failed to obtain in a time of peace," he said. Furthermore, "The sexton is only a temporary guardian of these remains and is not authorized to turn them over to other hands, and we have no permission to receive them from him."

Nothing was done. Two months later, with the termination of the British Mandate for Palestine, the declaration of Israel's independence, and the invasion of five Arab armies, the frontier with Syria was sealed for good, with the Crown out of reach on the other side.

Jerusalem had housed the codex once, long before, only to have it seized by foreign marauders. It would have to wait awhile longer for the Crown's return.

7

The Sack of Jerusalem

Jerusalem, AD 1099

THE CHRISTIAN KNIGHTS and foot soldiers serving under Duke Godfrey de Bouillon were encamped opposite one corner of the city wall, by the Jewish Quarter. Behind them to the northeast was Mount Scopus, where Hebrew University would sit many centuries later.

The doomed souls trapped inside Jerusalem could certainly hear the soldiers shouting in unfamiliar tongues, the sound of their carpenters finishing the great siege machines. On Sunday, Monday, and Tuesday of that week in July 1099—170 years or so after the creation of the Crown in Tiberias, several days' journey to the north—Godfrey's men carted in timber from afar and prepared their assault tower. They suffered so badly from a shortage of water that "for one penny a man could not buy sufficient to quench his thirst," according to one knight who left us a detailed account of those events, the *Gesta Francorum*, but not his own name. Another crusader force, this one under Raymond of Saint-Gilles, Count of Toulouse, was preparing to attack the fortress guarding Jerusalem's western flank. The privations of the thirsty crusaders paled in comparison with the suffering of the people trapped in the city that week, and that suffering, in turn, would be rendered insignificant by what was coming.

Three and a half years had passed since Pope Urban II preached the Crusade at Clermont, in France, and five weeks had passed since the Christian fighters reached the hilltop tomb of the prophet Samuel and gained their first glimpse of the object of their quest. Jerusalem, home to the sepulchre of Jesus and yet ruled by the followers of Muhammad, must have seemed to them a modest enclosure, dwarfed in grandeur by Constantinople and other cities they had passed or sacked on the way. There were perhaps twenty-five thousand people within its walls. The dome of an Islamic shrine dominated the city from the Temple Mount. As the siege reached its climax on Wednesday and Thursday of that week, the anonymous knight tells us, bishops and priests preached to the Christian soldiers and instructed them to pray, give alms, and fast. Then, as the sky lightened on Friday, the crusader forces surrounding Jerusalem assaulted the city walls. They met savage resistance.

"On Friday at dawn we attacked the city from all sides but could achieve nothing, so that we were all astounded and very much afraid," wrote the knight serving under Godfrey. The attacking force found, according to another chronicler of the battle, that part of the Muslim garrison was actually made up of Jews.

> Mox gentilis adest, Judaeus, Turcus, Arabsque,
> Missilibus, jaculis obsistitur, igne, veneno.
> At nostri jaculis opponunt pectora nuda.

This was the French monk Gilo of Paris, who wrote his poem some years after the events in question.

Suddenly the heathen were there, Jews, Turks and Arabs:
they were assailed with missiles and spears, fire and poison,
yet our men presented their chests all exposed to the missiles
    and spears,
bearing this hard scourging as a penance.

According to custom, the residents of a city would be called up
to defend the part of the wall closest to their homes. Godfrey's
assault came in Jerusalem's northeast corner, opposite the Jews'
quarter, so Jews were among the defenders.* Today this area
inside the walls is the Muslim Quarter, and Godfrey's staging
ground outside is a busy urban thoroughfare, an archaeological
museum, and an Arab school.

At sunrise on Friday, July 15, after the night had "left respite
for the Jewish people," wrote the monk Gilo, the Christians finally moved up their assault towers.

Rocks coming down on the woven wicker coverings smashed
    through them
and timbers, shields and men were tumbled from the top of
    the siege castle.
Even on the point of death the enemy were not lacking in
    courage.

The patchwork force defending the city fought off wave after
wave of attackers, including the anonymous knight. "Yet, when

* Gilo of Paris, the French Cluniac monk who wrote this poetic account of Jews resisting the crusaders, was not an eyewitness, but other
crusader chroniclers give similar accounts. One was Albert of Aachen,
who tells in his *History of the Journey to Jerusalem* of "a very stubborn
defense" of the port of Haifa by "citizens of the Jewish race."

that hour came when our lord Jesus Christ deigned to suffer for us upon the cross," he recounted, "our knights were fighting bravely on the siege tower, led by Duke Godfrey and Count Eustace his brother." The first crusader to leap from the tower onto Jerusalem's wall was a knight named Lethold. The defenses finally collapsed, and the Christians surged into the Jewish Quarter and then the rest of the city. Many residents fled for safety toward the Al-Aqsa mosque, which the crusaders called the Temple of Solomon.

"Our men went after them, killing them and cutting them down as far as Solomon's Temple," wrote the anonymous knight, "where there was such a massacre that our men were wading up to their ankles in enemy blood." Here all of the Christian chroniclers compete to provide the goriest depiction: the accounts differ on whether the blood reached the fighters' ankles, shoe tops, calves, or knees or the bridles of the horses. The crusaders butchered several thousand people on the Temple Mount. A group of men and women were cowering on the roof of Al-Aqsa, and in a singular act of mercy, two crusader commanders gave them their banners to protect them from harm. But later other Christian fighters made their way up onto the roof and killed them all anyway, throwing their bodies below. Elsewhere in the city, the crusaders decapitated soldiers and noncombatants and forced others, wounded by arrows, to leap from towers. Still others were tortured and then burned to death. Provençal soldiers who had missed the plunder on the Temple Mount took corpses that had already been stripped of valuables and clothes and disemboweled them, finding in the viscera money swallowed for safekeeping. Then they burned the bodies and sifted through the ashes looking for gold. The Christians seized horses and mules, commandeered homes, and ransacked houses of prayer. Many of the city's Jews fled to one of the synagogues, according to one Muslim chronicler, upon which "the Franks set fire to it with them inside."

The Jewish people, at this time, were split by the most dangerous schism in their history, and there were two sects of Jews in the city. The first were Rabbanites, who followed the oral traditions and laws of the rabbis; these are the predecessors of today's Jews. The second were their rivals, adherents of the Karaite heresy, who obeyed only the laws written in the Torah and dismissed the rabbis, their strictures, and their loopholes. The Karaites thrived in the lands of Islam, and Jerusalem was one of their centers. They are all but extinct in our times, but their strength, for a while, challenged the Judaism of the rabbis. For the Karaites, only the words of the Bible were sacred, and nothing was to distract them from the book. Their name meant "people of the text"; it was fitting, then, that they owned its most perfect copy.

Sometime in the eleventh century, a wealthy Karaite benefactor had purchased the codex created by Ben-Asher, who was, many scholars now believe, a Karaite himself. A dedication recorded in the Crown tells us that this donor's name was Israel, son of Simha, that he was from the city of Basra, in modern-day Iraq, and that he was "wise, clever, righteous, honest, and generous." Israel gave the manuscript to the Karaite synagogue in Jerusalem, where it was to be kept by the "great leaders" of the Jerusalem Karaites, Josiah and Hezekiah. It was not to leave their hands. Three times a year, on festival days, according to the inscription, the leaders were to take out the treasure and show it publicly to the "communities of the holy city." This appears, surprisingly, to have included even the rival Rabbanites; the importance of this codex was such that it transcended the Jews' sectarian feud. On those days, the people were to "read it and look at it and teach from it as much as they want and choose," and if at any other time during the year a scholar wanted to use the codex, the leaders were to "take it out to him so that he may see and become wise and understand."

Even before the arrival of the Christian armies from the West in 1099, the Jews had experienced several bewildering and violent decades of turmoil. The power of the Abbasid caliphate of Baghdad, with its black banners, had shifted to the Fatimid dynasty in Cairo, and then marauding forces of the Seljuk Turks had arrived in Jerusalem with armies of mounted archers, controlling the city before being expelled by the Fatimids not long before the Christians arrived. Based in part on a calculation that one thousand years had now passed since the destruction of the temple by Rome, many Jews in the Middle East and Europe, looking in their prophetic books, concluded that the dark events of the last decades of the eleventh century meant the End of Days was near.

"Stem of the son of Jesse, until when will you remain buried?" wrote the Andalusian Jewish poet Solomon Ibn Gabirol. This was a reference to King David, son of Jesse, from whose lineage the Messiah was to come. "Why should a slave rule the son of the nobles? It is a thousand years that I am enslaved," he wrote. Another story from those years before the Crusades told of a man in France or Spain who climbed to the treetops at night and flew from one to the other, thus fulfilling a prophecy in the book of Daniel: *One like the son of man came with the clouds of heaven.* The local Gentile authorities had the imposter executed.

"I saw the troops of the Westerners moving in their masses, and I do not know where they will turn," a certain Menachem, son of Elijah, wrote from somewhere inside the Byzantine

Empire as the crusaders advanced. A pretender claiming to be the prophet Elijah, harbinger of the Messiah, had revealed himself on the Dardanelles, he reported, and news had come from the Jewish kingdom of the Khazars that seventeen communities were traveling into the desert to meet the ten lost tribes of Israel. The Messiah was close. "When the Westerners, all of them, go to the Land of Israel, the threshing floor will fill up and then God will command, *Arise and thresh, O daughter of Zion*," he wrote, quoting the prophet Micah.

If some saw portents of redemption, others saw catastrophe. When peasant crusaders hacking a bloody path toward Jerusalem in 1096 put to the sword entire Jewish communities in the Rhineland, one Jew wrote, "We hoped for peace but there is grief; we looked for redemption but there is terror." Word of that slaughter reached Jerusalem perhaps two years before the crusader army arrived, and one can imagine the effect on those trapped inside the walls.

The forces assaulting the city came driven by their own interpretation of the same divine books. According to one chronicler, the crusaders remembered God's wrath at King Saul when he spared an enemy king instead of following orders to slaughter every living soul he found. "With drawn swords our people moved quickly through the town," one crusader historian wrote, "nor did they spare anyone, even if he begged for mercy." The anonymous knight saw bodies stacked "in mounds as big as houses" outside the walls. "No-one has ever seen or heard of such a slaughter of pagans, for they were burned on pyres like pyramids, and no-one save God alone knows how many there were," he wrote. When the cleric Fulcher of Chartres arrived at Jerusalem in December of that year, five months after the fighting, to celebrate Christmas, he reported that the stench of the dead was still so strong that he and his comrades were forced to cover their noses and mouths. The crusaders destroyed the Jews' quarter, including synagogues and, with them, we may assume, hundreds or thousands of holy scrolls and codices. They took some of the surviving books as loot, knowing the Jews would pay to redeem them. One of the surviving volumes was a Hebrew codex with three columns to a page, twenty-eight lines in each column.

News of Jerusalem's fate quickly reached the prosperous Jewish community in Fustat, on the Nile, beside the Islamic metropolis of Cairo. The community's leader performed mourning rituals when he heard, rending his garments "and weeping for the dead and the desecrated scrolls of the law," according to one witness. "The Franks arrived and killed everyone in the city, whether of Ishmael or Israel, and the few who survived the slaughter were made prisoners," wrote another Jew in Egypt. Yet another described a "great disaster" that had befallen the Jews of Jerusalem: their synagogue was burned, he wrote, and many were killed or captured along with their Torah scrolls.

The Jews of Fustat seemed nearly as preoccupied with the books as with the people, and the correspondence of the time regularly mentioned both. Responding to the pleas coming from the Holy Land, these Jews gathered in their synagogue, sent out letters, and raised money and within a month had dispatched 123 dinars with an emissary and instructions to "redeem the Scrolls of the Torah and to [attend to] the ransoming of the people of God, who are in the captivity of the Kingdom of Evil, may God destroy it." The books, in that sentence, came first. One wealthy man from the coastal city of Ascalon took a loan and redeemed one hundred copies of the books of the Prophets, eight Torah scrolls, and 230 Bible codices. The captives purchased from the

Franks were brought to Fustat overland through the desert because crusader warships now prowled the coast. Many Jews perished along the way.

The codex from Tiberias, intact, left the sacked city and went into exile in Egypt. One of the Crown's inscriptions ordered that it never be redeemed, a preemptive attempt to prevent it from being stolen in the first place. But this command was ignored, and of course ransom was paid anyway. Along with other flotsam of Jerusalem's destruction, the book crossed the desert and reached safety in Fustat, where it was handed to a scribe. "Transferred by right of redemption from the spoils of Jerusalem, the holy city, may it be rebuilt, by the community of Egypt," he wrote.

8

The Jump

THE SEXTON'S DAUGHTER, Bahiyeh, repeated the question to me as she heard it all those years ago—in a whisper. Informers were everywhere, she knew, though she was only twelve.

"Fi tafeh?" Is there a jump?

It was the fall of 1948. The new state of Israel, declared that May, was locked in battle with the combined armed forces of the Arab world, including the Syrian army. Bahiyeh knew that a "jump" meant a group leaving illegally for Israel. Escapees risked imprisonment or worse. Jews were not allowed to leave Syria or even to move between its cities; the regime did not want local Jews strengthening the Zionists' numbers, and it appears to have seen them as bargaining chips and a useful outlet for public anger. Soon the government would be stamping their passports in red with the term *mousawi*—"Mosaic," from "Moses," meaning "Jew"—so they might be more readily identified. There were already stories about what happened to those caught fleeing, and there would be more and worse in the months and years ahead: Escapees were thrown into the regime's prisons, where they were tortured and starved. Others simply disappeared en route. But there were good reasons to try anyway. In August 1948, a month or two before Bahiyeh began hearing in earnest about the secret "jumps," a mob in Damascus killed thirteen Jews, including eight children. There were Israeli agents working secretly in Syria, and there were Syrian Arabs willing to help for money. There were ways out for those willing to take the risk.

The sexton would not leave his home and his ruined synagogue. But Bahiyeh's mother, Gratzia, wanted to get her three teenage girls—Frieda, Carmela, and Rachel—out of Syria because she feared they could be raped or kidnapped by Muslims. This would have been impossible not long before, when the old social order and the Jews' place in it were secure, but the old order no longer applied. One of Bahiyeh's adult brothers made the arrangements, and a smuggler transported the three older girls across the border into Christian-dominated Lebanon, which was still relatively safe. From there, they walked across Israel's mountainous northern border to a frontier kibbutz. That left Bahiyeh and six of her siblings.

Bahiyeh's jump came at ten o'clock one night at the end of 1948. Packing nothing but a small purse and her jewelry, Gratzia Baghdadi loaded the children into the backseat of a taxi. Bahiyeh had nothing but the dress and shoes she was wearing. Her mother bribed a soldier to get through a checkpoint on the road south to Damascus, where the taxi dropped them off at the house of a Christian family that had somehow become a way station on the underground route to Israel.

Bahiyeh remembered a woman coming out of the house, her finger to her lips: If they find you here, they'll send you back, she told the children.

Another taxi picked them up, ferried them across the Lebanese border, and dropped them off at a synagogue in Beirut.

The floor was covered in mattresses and crowded with other refugees. Someone gave each of the newcomers a chunk of halvah and a slice of bread.

Remember, I don't know you and you don't know me, an Arab man told the family the following evening as he took them and a few dozen others to a rendezvous point somewhere outside Beirut.

Walk with your children as if you're going for a stroll, he told Bahiyeh's mother, as if it were normal for a Jewish family to be out strolling in the Lebanese countryside at night. He warned them not to say a word. It was winter, when the citrus fruits ripen, and low-hanging fruit bumped Bahiyeh's head as she followed her mother through a grapefruit orchard. Bump, bump, bump: this is what the sexton's daughter remembered best decades later.

Soon they reached the shoreline. Fishing boats were waiting for them, and a man threw her into one as if he were heaving a sack of flour. The boat was so overloaded that Bahiyeh could reach over the side with her little girl's hand and touch the waves. It began to rain, and one of the fishermen suggested that whoever had a God should start praying. A woman was crying because she could not find her child, who must have been put on a different boat.

After a few hours at sea, Bahiyeh was lifted out of the boat, and she waded onto a beach that looked much like the one they had just left. Men in blue work shirts were waiting to greet them. They gave the newcomers blankets and hot tea. They also gave them pickled herring, an eastern European delicacy, and must have thought they were being kind. Bahiyeh, raised on the cheese and spices of her city, thought it was vile. She would never see Aleppo again.

Twelve-year-old Bahiyeh Baghdadi was one of the one hundred thousand people from Europe, North Africa, and the Middle East who entered the new state of Israel that year as the war
with the Arabs raged. Eventually, nearly all the Jews living in
Arab countries would be pushed out, two-thirds of them arriving in Israel: French-speaking, middle-class professionals from
cities on the Mediterranean coast and clansmen from squalid
villages in the interior, streams of the displaced from Morocco
to Iran. Most were poor; the better-off preferred Europe and
the Americas. Israeli immigration agents were bringing them to
chartered propeller planes idling on desert tarmacs or to boats
floating surreptitiously in dark coves along the North African
coast and then to the sunlit bedlam of the new state.

These new arrivals had little in common with the European
Jews who had previously made up the majority. Some of Israel's leaders, as they struggled to house, clothe, and employ the
newcomers, saw them as inferior specimens necessary for the
new state largely because its intended manpower pool in Europe
had been annihilated. They were inclined to discuss all the new
immigrants, including Europeans, in the cavalier ethnic gener-
alizations of the time. One government report declared immigrants from Europe to be lazy and above manual labor; Syrians,
Iraqis, Iranians, and Libyans to be "generally healthy"; and
North Africans "mostly destitute, hot-tempered, unorganized
and nationalistic," and "of low cultural and social level." Turks
were "good human material," and Yemenis were "quick wit-
ted." One member of Israel's parliament, the Knesset, described
the Jews from Arab countries as generally "medieval." At the
peak of the immigration wave that followed Israel's founding,
the Foreign Ministry sent a memorandum to its representatives
noting that most of the newcomers were from the Middle East:

"This will affect all aspects of life in the country," it read, warning that the "preservation of the country's cultural level demands a flow of immigration from the West, and not only from the backward Levantine countries." A senior official in the Jewish Agency, which was in charge of immigration, said, "Perhaps these are not the Jews we would like to see coming here, but we can hardly tell them not to come." Despite these reservations and prejudices, however, immigration was never restricted to any significant degree, and Israel went to great lengths to bring as many Jews as possible as fast as possible, regardless of their origins, and to absorb them to the best of its ability.

At about the time of Bahiyeh's escape, a poster went up on a wall next to the Shika Café in Aleppo with a list of boys slated to be drafted into the Syrian army. Several of them were Jews, who were officially considered Syrians like everyone else and were not exempted from service. One was Rafi Sutton, the retired spy I met as an old man. He was seventeen.

By this time, Rafi had spent months watching young Muslim men march and ride in open trucks through the streets before leaving in high spirits for the battlefield in Palestine. Many of them were kids he knew from the neighborhood. They had rifles that they sometimes fired into the air, and wore checkered headdresses, and performed calisthenics and weapons training on a soccer field near his home. As the fighting wore on and went increasingly badly for the Syrians, he saw soldiers, some bandaged and supporting themselves with crutches, coming home in jeeps and trucks pocked with bullet holes.

Rafi reported to the draft office in May 1949 as directed. Rafi had heard stories about what awaited Jewish soldiers in the army, and when he exited with a new military identity card and an official draft date in a few weeks' time, he stood on the building's wide steps and swore he would find a way out.

Rafi's family had arrived in Aleppo four and a half centuries before, after Spain's Christians expelled the Jews. The story of how they arrived was contained in the family's name—not the Anglicized version, Sutton, but the original, Setehon. One of the exiles from Spain, the story goes, was a rabbi whose family name was Seton. Reaching a port, he was forced to decide where to go. The known world did not extend much to the west; not far away was Gibraltar and what Gentile scholars called the *finis terrae,* with unknown seas beyond. So the rabbi would travel east. He had heard about a city past the eastern edge of the Mediterranean where Jews had lived, somehow, for thousands of years without interruption: Aleppo, a lighthouse for a man reduced to bundles of belongings and books, a wife, and a huddle of homeless children. To win divine providence for the perilous sea journey, he took the Hebrew letter that represents the name of God—*heh,* pronounced like the letter *h*—and inserted it into his family name. God had done this to the idolater's son Abram in the book of Genesis, making him Abraham. Seton became Setehon, and this, the rabbi hoped, would see his family delivered safely to their new home. He must have been proud of his foresight when they were.

The rabbi's descendants were now on the move again. For Rafi, the way out led through the taxi stand outside the Baron Hotel, a grand Aleppo landmark where T. E. Lawrence had stayed in his days as Lawrence of Arabia and where Agatha Christie was a guest while writing *Murder on the Orient Express.* Jews, as a rule, were not taxi drivers, but there was one exception: a man universally known by the nickname Ufo, who worked the Aleppo-Beirut line for the Al-Karnak Taxi Company. Rafi found him in the hubbub of drivers and hustlers outside the Baron.

The border crossings from southern Syria leading directly to Beirut were all heavily guarded, the driver said. Instead they would try to get into Lebanon from the north, driving on the coastal highway toward the city of Tripoli, where the crossing was less traveled and the guard would be lighter. Rafi was to dress like an Arab, in a white skullcap and robe, and was to bring nothing else with him. They would set out at a time when no one would suspect Jews to be on the road: the Sabbath, when driving is forbidden. Rafi had never desecrated the Sabbath, and the thought made him ill.

Still, on the last Sabbath in May, at five o'clock in the morning, Ufo parked outside a mosque near Rafi's house, switched off the headlights, and knocked on the door. Rafi's father pressed his hand against his son's forehead in blessing. His mother wept, and his sister said a hurried good-bye from the doorway as he rushed out. Inside the cab were two other Jewish boys. They took off their European clothes and donned Arab garb. The first soldier they encountered at the checkpoint on the outskirts of the city asked a few questions and waved them through. They stopped in a town along the way to kill time, because the driver wanted to reach the border crossing after dark, and then they continued toward the frontier, passing through little villages along the Mediterranean coast. It was close to midnight when the taxi finally approached the Lebanese border. A military guard post was a few hundred yards away, downhill. The lights were off.

The driver cut the engine, flicked off the headlights, and let the car roll. Fifty yards away from the checkpoint, he braked.

They all listened: silence. The driver got out of the car and walked over to the border post, where he saw two soldiers asleep inside. He gingerly pulled the rope raising the barrier, then returned to the car, left the door open to avoid unnecessary noise, and continued rolling down toward the checkpoint. Rafi thought his frantic heartbeat might wake up the guards; the fear was so intense he could feel it eating away at his leg muscles. But then they were through, and then they were past Tripoli and the gardens and churches of Jounieh in the suburbs of Beirut, and then his uncles, the jewelers who had given Rafi's family their Zenith radio, were lifting their heads from their desks as the shop door opened and in walked their sister's son from Aleppo.

Rafi wanted to cross into Israel overland, but that plan was scuttled by news that the usually laissez-faire Lebanese authorities had decided to show they were taking action against Israel and had cracked down on Jewish refugees sneaking across the border. Not long before he arrived, the Lebanese had arrested a group of Syrian Jews on the frontier at night and sent them to prison. At loose ends in Beirut, Rafi took to hanging around at the Café Bahrain, near the port, where one day a fisherman who looked about thirty asked him for a light. Rafi did not smoke. The fisherman was wearing a necklace with a cross and said his name was Michel. After a few casual meetings with Michel over a period of weeks, Rafi gathered his nerve and undertook a trial run. He told the fisherman he knew a man who needed to deliver a box to the island of Cyprus. Would Michel be willing to do the job?

It would depend on the price, Michel said, in Rafi's recollection. A fair sum would be five hundred pounds. Rafi nodded. A few days later, he went back to Michel and mentioned that he

Rafi Sutton in Beirut, 1949.

knew two people without papers who needed to get to Cyprus. Would he take them? Yes, Michel said.

A few days after that, Rafi informed Michel that the two had changed their minds and now wanted to go in another direction.

What other direction? asked Michel. Where could you go from here except to Palestine?

Let's say to Palestine, Rafi said, and he thought, There, I said it.

Michel was perhaps not as surprised as Rafi had hoped. Why start with the bullshit about Cyprus and the box? he said. Tell me you want to escape to Israel and I'll take you.

This was getting too complicated for a teenager, and soon figures in the Jewish community of Beirut had taken over the planning. Before long, the group had grown from the three Aleppo boys into a group of several dozen, mostly Syrians, along with a few Iraqi Jews who had also washed up in Lebanon. By the end it had swelled to more than 150 people. Instead of one fishing boat, they would take two large boats manned by Michel's relatives. The date was set for the Rosh Hashana festival for the same reason that the boys had set out from Aleppo on the Sabbath: no one would suspect a smuggling attempt on the Jewish new year.

Taxis brought the escapees in small groups in daylight to the busy fishing port in Beirut, and launches ferried them out to the waiting boats. They brought no luggage and dressed for a sightseeing excursion. Rafi sat by the prow, crushed among other bodies, the shoes he had bought the day before submerged in ankle-deep water. He was wearing all the clothes he owned, including five pairs of socks, four pairs of underwear, and multiple undershirts and pants.

One of the boats was soon blown off course, and then its engine broke down, and the passengers lost sight of the shoreline. One boat towed the other. In Rafi's boat was a man he recognized as a prominent lawyer from Aleppo, and when the man took off his sunglasses a few hours later, Rafi was amused to see their shape imprinted in pale white on the sunburnt skin of the lawyer's face. The weather changed, darkness fell, chilly winds followed periodic downpours of rain, and a trip that was supposed to take only hours stretched overnight and into the next day. The escapees were shivering with cold and exhaustion when they finally heard the crunch of hull on stone.

Rafi splashed through the tidal pools in his ruined shoes, avoiding the jagged rocks of the Galilee coastline, and collapsed on the sand. Before long he saw the lights of a jeep, and then something that almost could not be real: two policemen running toward the beach, shouting in a language he knew from synagogue. The refugees mobbed them, grasping at their hands, weeping. It was the fall of 1949, the second day of the Jewish new year.

9

The President

WHEN ITZHAK BEN-ZVI became president of Israel, he did not
forget the Crown of Aleppo. Instead he used the weight of his
new station to aid his pursuit. His young chief of staff, David
Bartov, heard about the Crown shortly after his boss took office
in 1952, and then regularly after that. Bartov believed the country had more pressing problems and joked with the other staffers
about the president's "hallucinations," he told me when I met
him much later, a dignified, slow-moving man in a Jerusalem
home for the aged.

Jerusalem, where the president's office was located, was a divided city. Gunfire crackled regularly along the urban frontier
line between the western, Jewish side and the Jordanian-held
Arab sector in the east. Israel was a chaotic, heroic, and desperate refugee camp, a four-year-old country that had more than
doubled its population since independence, its cities and absorption camps overflowing with the remnants of European Jewry in
jackets and caps, women with numbered tattoos, herders from
the Atlas Mountains with robes and hennaed hands, Yemenis,
Russians, Romanians, Greeks, a confused, impoverished mass of
humanity that was somehow at once homeless and home. "The
'ingathering of the exiles,' as the Zionists call this heartbreaking
irruption, is the principal point of pride—and also the principal

burden and growing despair—of the State of Israel," a writer for the *New Yorker* reported in a dispatch at about this time. Absorbing these immigrants, and especially the ones from the East, into a viable state will require miracles, he wrote, but he added thoughtfully, "Everywhere a visitor goes in that country, he sees symbols of the imminence of these miracles."

After assuming the presidency, a figurehead position that bequeathed to its holder little political power but considerable public stature and authority, Ben-Zvi met with a prominent American Jewish leader and tried to persuade him to fund an attempt to obtain the Crown. The American, exiting the president's office, met the young chief of staff and twisted his finger against his temple: Ben-Zvi was crazy. The president tried the country's prime minister, David Ben-Gurion, but found him preoccupied with other matters. On a different occasion, the president told his chief of staff to summon the head of the Mossad. The new intelligence service had agents in Syria who were organizing illegal emigration and collecting information, and perhaps they could help. Bartov was not present at the meeting but remembered an incredulous Ben-Zvi telling him afterward that the country's top spy had no idea what the Crown of Aleppo *was*. For several days afterward, the president asked Bartov if the Mossad had returned an answer, and each day the chief of staff was forced to say no. Eventually he had to inform Ben-Zvi that Israel's spies were otherwise engaged and would not be able to take on the president's mission.

Itzhak Ben-Zvi was one of the state's most important leaders and symbols. Like Ben-Gurion, his friend and colleague, he was a member of the small group of utopian revolutionaries who had fled persecution and grinding poverty in the Pale of Settlement in the early twentieth century for a life of relentless labor, repeated bouts of malaria, furious ideological arguments, and pursuit of an unlikely dream in Turkish Palestine. In the end, Ben-Zvi and his comrades had willed a Jewish state into being against impossible odds, almost against the very logic of human events; they had glared at history and watched it bend to their will. "With the tenacity which Latins devote to love and Frenchmen to food, they pursued and served the idea of Zion Revived," the Israeli historian Amos Elon wrote of this generation. "Their main relaxation consisted of composing argumentative, quarrelsome, ideological diatribes against one another upholding the superiority of one notion of socialism, or Zionism, or an amalgam of both, over all others."

Ben-Zvi, like the country's other leaders, had his eyes fixed firmly, ruthlessly forward, but he differed from most of them in allowing himself a fascination with the past. He was an avid traveler and was said to be proficient in eight languages. Observing the various costumes and tongues of the world's Jews, Ben-Zvi saw traces of a shared nationhood "not extinguished by the snowstorms in the farthest corners of the north nor by the storms of Yemen." He was an archaeology enthusiast, seeing the pursuit of physical remnants of the past as a way to establish a physical link between the people of Israel and their land. The new pioneers, though, marching as they were into a glorious socialist future, had little use for the past and often carelessly destroyed artifacts they turned up; Ben-Zvi held symposiums on how to educate the New Jew he had helped create to respect what was old.

The president was also different from many of his peers in Israel's leadership in his approach to the new immigrants from the East. He shared the casual paternalism of his colleagues, but not their disdain. He saw a culture "overflowing with rich tradition and carrying powers," albeit one "hidden beneath a shroud of primitivism and Levantinism." He was fascinated by these Jews and set up an academic center to study them, the Institute for the Study of Jewish Communities in the Middle East. His new institute had chosen "the most backward Jewish tribes," he said in 1952, people "whose cultural possessions have no responsible curator."

The exile of the Jews was over, as far as Ben-Zvi was concerned; it was now to be studied and memorialized in museums. The mystique of the Crown, which had been written in the land of Israel and then preserved by one of Judaism's most venerable outposts in the East and which was now tantalizingly unavailable, played simultaneously on several of his interests. Such a potent Jewish symbol needed to be in Jerusalem, the capital of the new state that had superseded the Diaspora. More specifically, it had to be in Ben-Zvi's institute, where, he dreamed, it would be studied by scholars and not hoarded in secrecy by rabbis.

The state archive contains a letter written in 1953 by Israel's chief Sephardic rabbi, Ben-Zion Ouziel, in flowery Hebrew peppered with quotes from scripture and addressed to the heads of the Aleppo community in exile, pleading with them to send the Crown to Jerusalem. Like the president, the rabbi had been granted one glimpse of the book in the Aleppo synagogue and had never forgotten it. He believed the Crown was still in the hands of the Christian merchant, reflecting the difficulty of obtaining accurate information about the location of the manuscript, which had been moved to Jewish hands years before. "Since I learned of the destruction of the ancient synagogue in Aram-Tzova," wrote the rabbi, "and the removal of the Crown from its place and from the faithful hands that guarded it—as I saw with my own eyes at the time, when it was kept in an iron box as a precious treasure, and so indeed it is, as it is said: *She is*

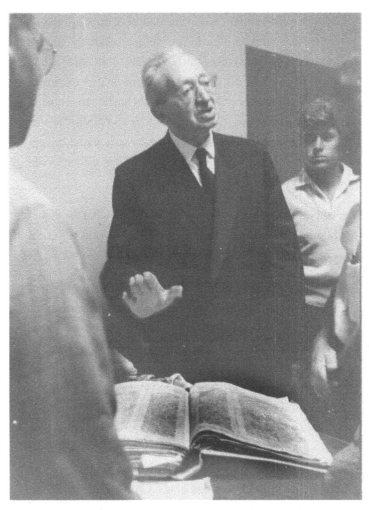

President Ben-Zvi and a Hebrew manuscript.

more dear than pearls, and all of your possessions cannot compare—
I have been filled with fear about the fate of this precious manuscript." He continued,

I have heard that it is now held by a Gentile and kept in a
secret place. I would like to assume that this Gentile keeping

it is a trustworthy man, but in the end he is no more than a transient person who even in his lifetime could change his mind in the circumstances of these times. I am thus afraid that the Crown will fall, during his lifetime or after his death, into foreign hands from whom we will be unable to rescue it. If this precious Crown, which our fathers and rabbis labored to pass on to the sons of their community so it would be kept and guarded in the hands of Israel, is lost, our silence would be considered a sin.

After this introduction, the rabbi moved to what he believed was the heart of the problem: the curse on anyone who moved the book.

I have heard it said that the sons of Aram-Tzova are afraid of touching this holy book because of what is written about anyone who moves the book from its place. But now, because the Crown has been torn from its place and taken from the hands that guarded it, this is a vain fear, and it is forbidden to leave it in foreign hands. There is no doubt that this was not the intention of those who wrote the book and that on the contrary their opinion and desire is for the Crown to be kept under zealous and careful guard by Israel. And if we do not do this, we are all responsible before God, the giver of the Torah, and before the writers of the Crown, for we did not do all that we might have done in order to save it.

The letter did not help, and the rabbi died not long afterward.

Ben-Zvi kept trying. He met with Isaac Dayan, the rabbi who headed the small community of Aleppo Jews in Israel, and pressed him unsuccessfully to get the book out. "We had the impression that Rabbi Dayan has the desire but does not see the urgency," the president's secretary wrote after the 1955 meeting. The president met with Isaac Shalom, a wealthy Aleppo Jew who lived in New York and owned a refrigerator company in Israel, hoping the businessman would pull strings in Aleppo, then followed up with a letter several months later. Since their meeting, Ben-Zvi wrote in July 1955, "I have not heard anything from you about the 'Crown.' I don't know if you have already been in touch with Aleppo about this matter." New information was trickling into the president's office, and Ben-Zvi had now been told that the Crown was in the charge of four members of the Aleppo community. "In light of this information," Ben-Zvi wrote, "I believe the time has come for the matter to be put into action. The responsibility for the Crown is in the hands of these four people, and there is a chance to influence them and demand it from them." Israel would cover any expenses incurred, he wrote, and its ambassador in Paris would help get the Crown out through diplomatic channels.

The president was prepared to go further. The Aleppo community depended heavily on funds sent by American Jews through an organization known as the Joint Distribution Committee. The president thought threatening this money—which meant threatening the community's survival—might help pry the book away. "I am therefore asking you to use all your influence in this matter and renew the financial pressure on the Aleppo community," the president wrote to Isaac Shalom in New York. "As I mentioned to you, the directorate of the Joint, which sends the Aleppo community's budget, demanded this of the community. I ask you to be in touch with them as well." Covert Israeli representatives in Syria were standing by, he hinted:

"The people holding the Crown must know that after we receive their agreement, a person charged with receiving it will contact them."

Bartov, the president's chief of staff, remembered thinking—but not daring to say out loud around the president—that the Aleppo rabbis would never agree to part with their book, and that even if they did, getting it out of an enemy country would involve more difficulty and danger than it could possibly be worth. He was underestimating Ben-Zvi.

10

The Merchant's Mission

THROUGHOUT THESE YEARS, as millennia of Jewish life in Aleppo came to an end—the Crown's guardians growing fewer and fewer, the remaining Jews subject to official discrimination and popular hatred and dependent on charity from abroad—the manuscript was hidden in the Old City, in the care of the wealthy merchant Ibrahim Effendi Cohen and his adult nephew, Edmond Cohen. Nobody knew this outside a tiny group that included a few of the community's remaining leaders and the keepers themselves.

Ibrahim Effendi was an Aleppo Jewish archetype. He had once had an important job at city hall and a trading office up a flight of stairs in the corner of the Aleppo souk known as Khan al-Jumruk, the Customs Caravanserai. His title of respect, *effendi*, was left over from the time of the Turks. He wore a vest with a pocket watch on a chain, and he had a great wooden desk and a gold letter opener. In one corner of his office was the telephone he used to capitalize on the Aleppo diaspora, one that had begun decades before the riot as the community's sons began leaving the economically depressed Middle East for better lives in the West. Ibrahim Effendi traded with relatives and Aleppo emigrants in the cotton and textile exchanges of Manchester and in offices in New York, São Paulo, Buenos Aires, and

Tokyo. In an Aleppo business, a relative in Milan might keep an eye on what fashionable Italian ladies were wearing and send the specifications to Aleppo, where a different relative still in the mother city—Ibrahim Effendi, in this case—would arrange the purchase of cotton and have it shipped east to a relative in Calcutta for processing, then back west to another relative in Manchester for sale. Ibrahim Effendi, who never touched a piece of fabric, took a percentage; he was known as a *commisionji*. Now the merchant's office was empty most of the time, as Jews were prohibited from moving freely through the country or doing business with the outside world. The great traders of an earlier age, like Ibrahim Effendi, with his pocket watch and obsolete Ottoman honorific, were gone or unemployed.

In Aleppo the Jews were vanishing one by one, in pairs and in small groups, fading across the border, bribing and bluffing their way out. By the mid-1950s, some two thousand remained, a third of them destitute. They lived in the shadow of malicious government propaganda and in fear of the mob, forced into increasingly uncomfortable accommodations with the secret police, the *mukhabarat*, who set up their headquarters in the spacious house of a Jewish family that had fled. The Jews lived, "if not in terror, certainly in constant fear, bedeviled by the Syrian security forces," wrote one visitor in 1957. With the benefit of hindsight we know that these were the community's last years, but this was not immediately clear. It was never inevitable that if the state of Israel existed, the Jewish communities in the lands of Islam would not, and it took several years for this to become apparent. In the fall of 1957, when the Jews realized the end was close, the remaining rabbis finally did the unthinkable.

Here, once again, the story returns to the cheese merchant

Murad Faham, who had appeared on an Old City street on the morning before the riot and who much later remembered being the one who had saved the Crown from the synagogue. In 1957, Faham was nearing fifty. He had lost his father as a boy and had taken over the family's cheese business while still a teenager. In the years after the Aleppo riot, Faham would later recount, he helped distribute charity funds from America to the Jewish poor and also smuggled Jews to Israel. In the mid-1950s, the cheese merchant's actions on behalf of the Jewish community led to his arrest and torture by the Syrian secret police in the notorious al-Mezze prison. (Al-Mezze retained its notoriety for another half century, until it was shut down by the regime in 2000.) Interrogators "put out cigarettes on my skin, and they lit matches and stuck them in my mouth until my throat burned," Faham said in the oral testimony he recorded in the late 1970s. He protested that he had undergone an operation not long before, and they asked him where; when he pointed at the spot, they beat him there. Other beatings caused him to lose nearly all his sight in one eye. Faham dramatically embellished his recollections, and details of these events are impossible to confirm, but this account appears to contain at least a grain of truth and so is worth citing here nonetheless.

Over the years, some of Aleppo's Jews had managed to obtain foreign passports, which afforded them a measure of protection. Faham held Iranian citizenship, and it may have saved him from worse treatment. The secret police released him—he was a "broken man," his son told me—and then expelled him and his family across the border into Turkey, allowing them to take only mattresses and a few personal belongings. Faham traveled to Iran, where he lobbied to return home, if not permanently, then at least to sell off his possessions and collect money from debtors. The Syrians agreed only to let him back in briefly, in that fall of 1957, to collect his belongings and then leave again for good.

One night just before his departure from Syria, Faham went to the synagogue, where he met the community's two chief rabbis, Moshe Tawil—the rabbi who had spoken against Zionism at Rafi Sutton's synagogue years before—and Tawil's colleague, Salim Zaafrani. As a rule, Jews were not allowed to leave legally, and the rabbis realized that Faham's departure, under government orders and with a foreign passport, presented an opportunity that might not repeat itself.

"Rabbi Tawil said he had secrets to tell me, but that he was afraid of the authorities," Faham said in testimony recorded in writing the following year. "I told him not to be afraid, and that we should trust in God."

"The Crown that survived the fire must be taken to Israel," Tawil told him, acknowledging, in effect, that the Jewish community of Aleppo was dead.

It would be dangerous, the rabbi warned. The authorities wanted the book, and they had been told the lie that it was lost; if the Crown were discovered as it was being smuggled out, the courier and the community's leaders would be imperiled. "This must be done in complete secrecy," Tawil recalled telling the merchant, in the rabbi's own testimony a year or two later. "We were afraid that the government would hear and we would suffer grievous harm."

"He told me that if I did not take it with me, no one else would be able to take it," Faham remembered, and he agreed. The rabbis ordered the codex removed from its hiding place.

Murad Faham.

Faham's wife, Sarina, was overseeing the final arrangements for the family's departure at their home in the Old City when Edmond Cohen, who was something of a surrogate son to the unmarried and childless Ibrahim Effendi, arrived with a cloth bag. Inside were two books. One was the Crown of Aleppo, and the other was a smaller and less significant fourteenth-century Pentateuch manuscript known as the Little Crown, which had also been kept in the synagogue safe and rescued after the fire. Sarina did not look inside the bag, she remembered thirty years later in a videotaped interview, but wrapped it in a square of white fabric of the kind used for cheese and placed it inside their washing machine. She put bags of seeds and onions on top. When all of their belongings were wrapped and tied into large packages and loaded on a truck, the Faham family—the cheese merchant, his wife, and their four youngest children—drove out of their city in the direction of Turkey.

When they reached the customs post at the Turkish border, Faham remembered, an official wanted to open the family's packages. Faham proffered his Iranian passport and tried to talk his way out. The clerk would not budge at first, and the argument became heated, but then a more senior official intervened and waved the family and the concealed treasure through the checkpoint and out of Syria. The book was on the move for the first time in six hundred years.

11

Maimonides

Cairo, circa AD 1170

THE DOCTOR'S NAME, as it was known to the scholars, poets, and courtiers orbiting the royal court in Cairo—al-Ra'is Musa Ibn Maymun al-Andalusi al-Isra'ili—told much of his life story: He was a *ra'is,* a head of his people, and his name was Musa, Moses. He was the son of a man named Maymun. He was from Andalusia, Islamic Spain, born around the year 1138 on the Gua-dalquivir, among the 132 towers and thirteen gates of Córdoba, where, in the perfumed gardens of Muslim kings, courtier-rabbis composed with equal flair legal tractates in Hebrew and poetic Arabic paeans to the physical beauty of young men. He fled the religious terror of the camel-mounted Almohad fanat-ics of the High Atlas Mountains of Morocco and was forced to live, for a time, as a Muslim, reading the Koran and praying in mosques before traveling east and finding a haven in Fustat, Egypt, next to the capital in Cairo. His language was Arabic, and his life was lived, in its entirety, under the rule of Islam. And yet he remained, the last part of his title tells us, a Jew. Western civilization, which remembers him as one of its greatest thinkers, knows him as Maimonides. It is on his desk that the codex next appears, having been ransomed from the crusaders and brought to Fustat four decades before his birth.

When Maimonides was in his thirties, the lands of Islam were being squeezed from both sides by Christianity. In the West, Muslims were slowly losing Spain to the Reconquista, while in the East the Holy Land was controlled by the crusaders and their Kingdom of Jerusalem. The warrior king Saladin took full control of Egypt in 1171, after a series of baffling alliances, intrigues, and double crosses finally ended two centuries of rule by the Fatimid dynasty, whose last scion—a twenty-year-old who had ruled Egypt since he was nine—died of implausibly convenient natural causes precisely when Saladin took over. The Assassins, a fanatic sect loyal to the old regime and based in a mountaintop redoubt in Persia, sent suicide squads to kill Saladin on several occasions as he waged his wars against Muslim rivals and the Franks. One group of killers disguised themselves as Saladin's own soldiers. This was the world Maimonides knew.

Saladin, upon taking control of Egypt, retained many of the previous dynasty's officials, including a powerful and famously wily administrator named Al-Qadi al-Fadil. This master of intrigue, whose name literally proclaimed him the "Excellent Judge," adeptly made the transition to the new regime, bringing along a coterie of talented protégés; the Spanish Jewish doctor was one of them. Maimonides commuted to the palace in Cairo from Fustat, just upriver, where he lived in a prosperous neighborhood south of the markets around one of the great mosques. There were three synagogues in Fustat—one for Karaites, one for Jews who followed the rabbis of Babylon, and the third, known as the synagogue of the Jerusalemites, for Jews who followed the rabbis of the land of Israel. It was in the last, the inscription tells us, that the Crown was kept after it was ransomed from its captors and arrived in Egypt.

Maimonides was deeply involved in life at court, treating Saladin himself and members of his family and entourage. He wrote a treatise on aphrodisiacs, *On Sexual Intercourse,* for an amorous nephew of the king and penned another about a popular political tactic of the time—*On Poisons and Antidotes*—dedicating it to his benefactor, the vizier whose vast library, reading hall, and literary salons were at his disposal. Another man in the circles around the vizier was a poet, Ibn Sana al-Mulk, who once wrote fancifully that if the doctor Ibn Maymun were to use his knowledge to treat the present time,

He would cure it of the disease of ignorance
Were the full moon to ask him for treatment,
It would obtain the perfection it claims.

Maimonides's preoccupation, however, was not politics or medicine but the spiritual and political well-being of his scattered people, threatened everywhere by the lure and fear of the majority, by the pull of voluntary conversion or the threat—one he knew well from his brush with the Almohads in Morocco years before—of conversion by the sword. He corresponded with Jewish communities across the world, his missives carried by travelers leaving on the Nile boats from the piers at Fustat, trying to guide them with a steady, rational hand, to keep them from surrender and apostasy on one hand and from the dangerous illusions of false messiahs on the other. Maimonides saw the decline of Jewish scholarship as a threat to the survival of a people tied together only by their understanding of certain texts and laws, and in writing he bemoaned the fact that there

were nearly no cities producing Jewish study of any quality. One
of the few towns he did mention as exceptional was the Syrian
trading center of Aleppo, where the doctor's star pupil, Joseph,
son of Judah, eventually ended up as a scholar-physician-courtier
like his master.

It was to Joseph in Aleppo that the doctor dedicated his
most famous philosophical work, *The Guide of the Perplexed*.
The *Guide* was an attempt to present—in an oblique and concealed fashion, in riddles and parables designed to confuse the
ignorant—the true knowledge of God that was hidden inside
the text of the Bible, and to help a wise student see that though
laws were important, knowledge was more important. Much of
the book's first section is dedicated to an analysis of the language of the Bible. This was crucial, because by understanding
the Hebrew precisely, it was possible to infer the book's concealed meanings. The Bible was not an ordinary book, it was a
labyrinth, and if you did not fully understand its language you
would not find your way.

The *Guide* was meant for an Arabic-speaking intellectual
elite, but it was to strengthen the flagging minds and souls of
ordinary people that the doctor wrote his greatest work of law
in Hebrew, the *Mishneh Torah*—literally, the "Repetition of the
Torah"—fourteen books that would become one of the central
pillars of Judaism. Jews could no longer be expected to know
about the arguments between rabbis or how they had reached
their decisions on points of law; they needed a simplified version
of their laws and rituals and a book that would tell them, in a
straightforward fashion, how to conduct their lives.

Around 1170, as Maimonides worked on his legal project, his
only brother set out on a business trip. David, who was about
twenty years old, took a boat 350 miles up the Nile, stopping

before the great tombs and temples of the pharaohs at Luxor, then traveled east by caravan across the desert, braving thirst and brigands, to a Red Sea port. Arriving there, he found nothing to buy but indigo, so he decided to press on across the sea to India. He wrote a letter home to his brother, recounting the story of his journey thus far and asking him to reassure his wife, whom he called "the little one." Then he boarded a boat bound for the port of Aden and was never heard from again.

"The worst disaster that struck me of late, worse than anything I had ever experienced from the time I was born until this day, was the demise of that upright man—may the memory of the righteous be a blessing—who drowned in the Indian Ocean," the doctor wrote later. For a year after receiving the news, he wrote, he was "prostrate in bed with a severe inflammation, fever and mental confusion," and was thereafter inconsolable. Here is a description of a scholar's grief: "He had a ready grasp of Talmud and a superb mastery of grammar," the doctor wrote of his brother. "Whenever I see his handwriting or one of his books, my heart is churned inside me and my sorrow is rekindled."

Books also helped him find solace, and he completed his legal compendium. The *Mishneh Torah* included a section on the rules governing the writing of the Torah, the foundation text upon which generations of scholars like him had erected the Jewish religion. Here, from all of the many Bible codices that must have been available to the leader of a rich and long-established community, he chose the one he clearly considered the authoritative version of what he called "the book that has illuminated the darkness of the world." It was one the Jews of Fustat had ransomed from the crusaders decades before. "And the book we relied upon in these matters," he wrote,

is the well-known book in Egypt, which contains twenty-four
books, which was in Jerusalem some years ago, to revise the
books from it, and everyone relied on it, since it was revised
by Ben-Asher, and he worked meticulously on it for many
years and revised it many times.

Maimonides died in 1204, evidently leaving the codex in his
library and in the possession of his descendants. Sometime in
the latter half of the fourteenth century, a rabbi named David,
son of Joshua—the doctor's great-great-great-grandson—left
Cairo at a time of political upheaval and traveled to Aleppo.
He brought along much of his illustrious ancestor's library. The
codex appears to have been among the collection that reached
the Syrian city.

Travelers in the centuries that followed mentioned the city's
great Bible. One account from 1479 says, in a reference to Maimonides, "The book upon which the great sage relied is today in
the city of Tzova, called Aleppo, and it is written on parchment,
with three columns on a page, and at the end it is written, 'I,
Aaron Ben-Asher, edited it.'" Over the years, it came to be venerated less as a source of wisdom than as a precious possession
of great age and worth, like a jewel or an ornament. The value
of the Crown of Aleppo was such that even individual pages
were seen to have great worth. This, much later on, would be
its undoing.

The codex had traveled from Tiberias to Jerusalem, then
to Cairo, and from there to Aleppo. It witnessed the devastating sack of the city by the Mongols in 1401, and then the
arrival of the Ottoman Turks in the following century. It survived an 1822 earthquake that killed more than half the city's
inhabitants.

It would remain there for six hundred years, until the Jews in the lands of Islam—the world of Maimonides—disappeared.

EIGHT CENTURIES AFTER the death of Maimonides, I descended in a passenger jet into the perpetual dome of smog that covers the modern descendant of his city. Even before Aleppo became a battleground in the Syrian civil war, I was barred from going there by the state of war that exists between Syria and my country, Israel. I wanted nonetheless to see the traces of Jewish life in places where today such life is unimaginable. In Cairo, I thought, I might find a remnant that would evoke something of Maimonides, that would allow me to imagine him seated at his desk with the Crown, which I felt tied me to him in some intangible way.

Ibn Maymun is still known to some Egyptians as a philosopher and physician from Saladin's court, a figure from a time when Muslim societies tolerated Jews in their midst. The Jews have left, driven out by the riots of the 1940s, the fatal bombings in Cairo's old Jewish Quarter, the rise of the pan-Arab nationalism of Gamal Abdel Nasser, state-sanctioned persecution, and the theft of property. Two generations ago the Jewish community in Cairo numbered about sixty-five thousand people; today there are a few dozen, all of them elderly. Within a few years there will be none.

The grand synagogue in downtown Cairo is kept open by the government and guarded by squads of lethargic troops in white uniforms. When I visited one Sabbath morning, half hoping to find even a handful of people praying, no one was inside but an Arab maintenance man. He took me by the hand and showed me a scroll on a table in the middle of the sanctuary. "Torah," he said, and he stuck his hand out for a tip.

In Fustat, which has been swallowed by Cairo and was a short subway ride from my hotel, I visited the synagogue where the Crown was once kept, now open as a tourist site. Upstairs, in a hollow space behind a wall in the women's gallery, is the place where Jews secreted centuries' worth of handwritten documents— contracts, letters, holy books, anything that contained the name of God and thus could not be thrown out. When the Cairo *genizah*, as it became known, was discovered in the nineteenth century, in one of the great scholarly finds of our time, the documents included many of Maimonides's writings in his own hand.

In central Cairo is an area of market streets still known as the Jewish Quarter, though there are no Jews there. The quarter was packed with shoppers buying clothes, and toy tanks with cannons that lit up, and stuffed birds in unnatural shades of yellow. Further into the slum alleys, the bustle receded and the streets grew dirtier. There was an abandoned synagogue somewhere here, on a site where some traditions said Maimonides used to teach or treat patients. It was named for him: Musa Ibn Maymun. The regime of Hosni Mubarak, who was deposed not long afterward, was renovating the building and planned to open it for tourists, a peculiar act of concern for the country's Jewish heritage that came just as Egypt was trying to get one of its top cultural officials elected head of the culture arm of the United Nations. This attempt had been complicated by the same official's past statements in favor of burning Hebrew books.

There were no signs for the synagogue, and the people I asked for directions responded with unhelpful shrugs. Within a few minutes I was lost. Walking down one alley, I peeked into an open door and saw an older man and a teenager sitting in a dark workshop.

"Sorry—where is Musa Ibn Maymun?" I asked. They looked surprised. The teenager said, "Would you like some tea?"

It was the middle of the holy month of Ramadan, when Muslims fast from sunrise to sunset, and I was avoiding eating or drinking except in my hotel. I thanked them and shook my head. The young man pointed to a picture on the wall depicting Mary and baby Jesus. They were Coptic Christians, he said. Some Copts were left in the Jewish Quarter, but the Jews were gone, except for one eighty-year-old woman, the older man told me, but the teenager corrected him: she was gone, too. He waved his hand to sum up the whole situation. "Gamal Abdel Nasser," he said. I wasn't sure if he was explaining the cause of the exodus or merely the time frame.

The teenager's name was Emad. After a brief discussion with his father, who looked about sixty and seemed to remember the Musa Ibn Maymun synagogue, he declared that he could take me there. He led me farther into the Jewish Quarter, depositing me at my destination a minute or two later. I had imagined a building that would bring Maimonides to mind, but instead I found a roofless shell—a stone wall around dirt-floored rooms. I snapped a few pictures until a man who wore a pink civilian shirt but spoke with military authority appeared and told me to stop. I put the camera away, and when he went back around a corner, I slipped inside and found myself in what had once been the sanctuary. A young man looked up at me through blue-tinted sunglasses. His name was Muhammad, he said, and he was the engineer in charge of the renovation. He offered to show me around. This is the bima, he said, pointing to a low stone rectangle under a tarpaulin and carefully pronouncing the Hebrew word for the stand on which the Torah is read. And this, he said, pointing to a niche in the northern wall, is the ark in which the scrolls were kept. He took me into an adjacent room where steps led down to a floor flooded knee-deep with foul greenish water. This was Ibn Maymun's hospital, he said.

In this room were a few members of a teenage work crew. One of them, a boy of no more than fourteen in rubber boots and surgical gloves, spotted me and splashed over, much to his comrades' amusement. He grinned an endearing grin of brown teeth, put down the wooden plank he carried, bowed, and shook my hand with exaggerated warmth. "Welcome," he said in English, and then, his vocabulary exhausted, he pointed at his grubby white undershirt and introduced himself.

"Musa Ibn Maymun," he said, and his friends cracked up.

The book was gone. Maimonides was gone. His people were gone. Nothing was left but this: Walls around empty rooms. An absence.

12

Alexandretta

ONCE ACROSS THE border between Syria and Turkey, it took the cheese merchant and his family about half an hour to reach the rough Turkish frontier town of Alexandretta, on the Mediterranean coast.

In the center of town stood a clothing store that doubled as a transit station for Jews fleeing to Israel. It was run by a man we will call Isaac Silo, one agent in a far-flung network directed from Jerusalem by an outfit known as the Aliya Department, a sister agency to the intelligence-gathering Mossad. *Aliya*, which literally means "going up," is the poetic Hebrew term for immigration to Israel. The department, equal parts spy service and travel agency, was in charge of what the nine-year-old state saw as the reason for its existence and guarantee of its continued survival: the ingathering of the Jews.

Behind that lofty end lay the technical minutiae of tens of thousands of people in transit. Agents were chartering boats and airplanes, putting immigrants on buses and trains, paying their fare, arranging hotels, lying to local authorities, forging passports, bribing police, wiring money into the bank accounts of cabinet ministers in dozens of countries, working with smugglers and criminals, and generally doing whatever was necessary

to speed Jews from their homes in the Diaspora to their new
homeland in Israel.

The immigration agents of those first years sometimes received secret instructions from their controllers in a song-
request program aired on Israeli radio. At the time, the Israelis
were often paying cash in return for Jews—the Bulgarians were
given $50 a head, the Hungarians $300. "We opened Swiss bank
accounts for the Moroccan cabinet ministers. The Sultans of
Yemen preferred dollars in cash. The Romanians, too, wanted
cash," Shlomo Zalman Shragai, the official who ran the Aliya
Department at the time, said of these early years. It was, another agent said, "a mad operation at a mad time." By 1957, when
Faham and his family pulled up outside Silo's store, one tiny
corner of the Aliya Department's worldwide operations, the
wave of incoming Jews had ebbed since those first days but was
far from over.

Isaac Silo was a Turkish citizen, a Jew who was born in
Aleppo, a shopkeeper, a trained kosher butcher, and a prominent member of Alexandretta's tiny Jewish community, made
up of a few dozen families. He had first encountered refugees
during the world war, when groups of Jews fleeing the killing
in Europe and trying to get to Palestine found themselves in
this remote corner of Turkey. Silo began independently taking
them in. By the 1950s he was receiving orders and money from
Israeli agents in Istanbul and was the first stop for Jews coming
out of Syria—the ones exiting legally, with foreign passports
or legal permits obtained by bribes, and the ones leaving illegally, brought across the frontier by Silo's network of smugglers. From Silo's store the refugees were usually taken to a
hotel, where they remained until Silo could book them passage
on the *Marmara*, the boat that left once every few weeks from

Alexandretta and sailed southward down the coast to the Israeli port at Haifa. Sometimes he would bus them to Istanbul, where they were put on El Al planes and flown to the airport at Lod, outside Tel Aviv.

The Israelis covered Silo's costs. Some of his Turkish neighbors seem to have been unhappy about Silo's work—the Jewish Agency archive preserves two threatening letters sent to Silo—but although his activities were technically illegal, the Turkish authorities, who had generally good ties with Israel, tended to leave him alone. From Alexandretta, Silo maintained contacts in Aleppo, feeding his Israeli handlers information on that city's Jews. According to one report sent by Silo at about this time, of some two thousand Jews left in Aleppo, more than 90 percent wished to leave for Israel. The Israelis wanted them out quickly. "We are certain that you will do everything you can to achieve the holy and longed-for goal: to save our Jewish brothers rotting in the exile of Ishmael," two of the immigration agents in charge of Silo wrote him during this time.

The correspondence of the agents tasked with getting Jews out of Syria combined that almost biblical tone with an exacting attention to detail. In one letter to Silo, the Israelis sent him a list of Aleppo Jews about whom they wanted information. They included one Avraham Intabi, seventy-five; his wife, Mazal, sixty-five; and their daughter, Betty, twenty-three. They also wanted to know about Rahamim Dishi; his wife, Haviva; and their children, Shaul, Isaac, Moshe, Jacqueline, Linda, and Yvette. The Israelis were spurred on by pleas from Aleppo Jews who had already made it out. The Jews of Aleppo, one rabbi in Buenos Aires wrote the immigration officials in Jerusalem, "are sorely pressed by the cruel enemy, and every day letters of warning arrive here pleading, 'Help, help, before it is too late.'

"We are certain that you will quickly answer our appeal," the rabbi wrote, "and just as you have saved other communities all over the world you will move quickly to save these prisoners, and you will be blessed."

The messages among the Israeli agents took on a tone of desperation. "There is no need to emphasize, of course, that the problem is painful and extremely urgent," the immigration envoys in Turkey wrote to Jerusalem headquarters, asking for more money to get Jews out. They mentioned the hostility of Syria's population toward the Jews and "wild incitement" on the part of the Syrian government. "We must look at these matters with our eyes open, because our brothers' lives depend on it," they wrote.

Amid all this, in the fall of 1957, the Aliya Department and its agents were paying special attention to one immigrant: Murad Faham of Aleppo. Unusually, the cheese merchant and his family were put up not in a hotel but in Silo's home, a close relative of Silo's told me when I met him in the United States. He did not know why Faham received this special treatment at the time, he said, and he heard about the Crown only much later.

The Israeli agent responsible for Silo and the immigration route through Turkey—and, it seems, for other intelligence functions as well—was Yitzhak Pessel, a stout, efficient officer requisitioned from the military and sent to live with his wife and young children in Istanbul. When the cheese merchant arrived, Pessel made sure to inform Jerusalem, sending a letter not to his immediate superiors but directly to the top—to Shlomo Zalman Shragai, the immigration chief.

Shragai, a Polish-born political operator and a former mayor of Jerusalem, was a member of Israel's frugal, unyielding, and humorless elite, the kind of man you want on your side if you

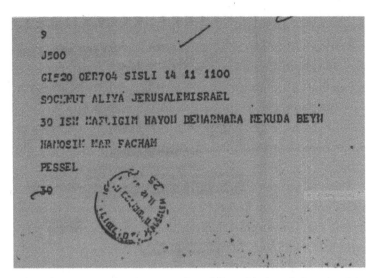

The telegram sent by the agent Pessel from Turkey, informing his
superiors that Faham was en route to Israel with the Crown.

are trying against long odds to will a country into existence. He
was a tireless writer of newspaper articles and letters to the editor, and crucially for this story, he was an Orthodox Jew, a rare
specimen in Israel's ruling class, a leading member of a minority
in Israel that had not replaced Judaism with Zionism but had
instead combined the two. Nearly forgotten today, Shragai was
an influential official at the time, overseeing one of the twentieth century's great movements of people from his office in the
Jewish Agency building in Jerusalem. He was a man involved in-
timately in the mechanics of dismantling Jewish worlds. Among
his concerns at this time were the Jews of Cochin, India, 350 of
whom were left, he told a meeting of the Jewish Agency leadership, their departure to Israel held up by difficulties in selling
their synagogue. Despite his many preoccupations, the head of
the Aliya Department promptly responded to the agent Yitzhak

Pessel's letter in the fall of 1957 informing him that the codex had arrived. Although Silo typically handled direct contact with the refugees, this time Pessel personally met with the merchant in Istanbul. This meeting would become key to the battle that was about to erupt for possession of the manuscript. According to Faham's testimony in court the following year, he spent two or three hours with Pessel. The topic of discussion was the Crown.

A few weeks after Faham's arrival in Alexandretta, Pessel sent his superiors a typed list of the passengers slated to sail to Israel aboard the *Marmara,* including Faham, his wife, Sarina, and four of their children.

On December 11, 1957, Pessel sent a telegram to Jerusalem: 30 ISH MAFLIGIM HAYOM BEMARMARA NEKUDA BEYN HANOSIM MAR FACHAM. This was Hebrew written phonetically in Latin characters. It meant, "Thirty people are sailing today on the *Marmara.* Among the passengers is Mr. Faham."

13

The Brown Suitcase

THREE WEEKS LATER, two messengers walked in from a chilly night in Jerusalem's Jewish sector and climbed the stairs of 8 Jewish National Fund Street, an apartment building just across from the headquarters of the Jewish Agency. One of them carried a brown suitcase.

The men knocked on a door and were shown into an apartment full of books. This was the home of Shlomo Zalman Shragai, the head of the Aliya Department. The immigration chief's grown son Eliyahu was there that Monday night—January 6, 1958—and remembered it well when I met him years later. He was used to strange visitors at strange hours: members of parliament, the director of the Mossad, anonymous men who would appear briefly, whisper something to his father, and disappear. He had been brought up not to ask questions. Eliyahu heard the knock, and when the door opened he saw two men whose appearance was unremarkable but for the brown suitcase. His father appeared to be expecting them. They crossed the living room to his father's study, and the door closed behind them. They emerged a few minutes later and left without their suitcase. This, in itself, was not an entirely unusual occurrence, but what happened next was.

Shlomo Zalman Shragai (left) with Israel's first prime minister,
David Ben-Gurion, in 1951.

The immigration chief beckoned Eliyahu into the study,
where he saw the open suitcase. Inside was a package wrapped
in a white fabric of rough weave, which he recognized as the
kind used to wrap cheese. His father peeled it away, revealing a
stack of yellowing parchment folios.

"This," Shragai told his son, emotion evident in his voice,
"is the Crown of Aleppo." He quickly replaced the shroud and
closed the suitcase.

Shragai had been notified immediately when Faham arrived
with the treasure at Haifa. Once Faham's goods had cleared customs, a process that took several weeks, the immigration chief
ordered his Jewish Agency subordinates in charge of new arrivals at the port to drive to Jerusalem and bring the Crown

directly to him. On January 8, with the book now in his hands, he penned a brief note to the courier Faham, who was staying with one of his sons in Kfar Saba, a town among citrus orchards on the coastal plain. "Two days ago Mr. Zvi Grosbach brought me the suitcase with the Crown of the Torah," Shragai wrote. He asked that Faham come to meet him and provide more details about the Crown.

Faham replied a few days later with a letter that would soon be used against him in court. "I am the immigrant Mordechai, son of Ezra Faham Hacohen," the courier wrote, introducing himself with his Hebrew name,

> who was exiled from the city of Aleppo, in Syria, and who arrived in Israel with my family on December 16, 1957. We brought with us the Bible of Ben-Asher, who lived in Tiberias at the beginning of the tenth century and who was one of the last masters of the Masora and who marked the beginning of the time of the grammarians.
>
> This Bible is a guide for the eyes of the scribes and copyists, and it was upon it that Maimonides based his book, and he used it in clarifying the matter of when to leave full or empty lines, as is discussed in the Laws of Torah Scrolls, section eight, chapter four.
>
> The tradition kept by the residents of Aram-Tzova (Aleppo) is that this Bible, the one called the "Crown of the Torah," is from the days of the second temple and the plunder taken from Jerusalem, and that it was only edited by Ben-Asher, and that is why it was named for him—the Crown of Ben-Asher.
>
> At the time of my departure from Syria, the rabbis and the heads of the rabbinic court in our city, Rabbi Moshe Tawil, descended from Elia the Priest, may he be deserving of a

good and long life, and Rabbi Shlomo Zaafrani, may God
protect him, gave me this Bible to bring up to the land of Israel and to give to a man who seems to me to be honest in his
worship of God and in his fear of sin. That is why I decided
to give it to your honor, Mr. Shragai, may God protect you.

In the accepted version of the Crown's story, the one upon
which I relied in my original article about the manuscript, the
envoy from Aleppo brought the book to Israel and gave it to
the country's president. Here was the first deviation I found
from the official narrative. Slight as it was, it alerted me that
something in the story was not right. Presenting a book of the
Crown's importance to Israel's head of state had a certain logic
to it; the fact that the Crown had actually been presented to a
lower-ranking functionary was peculiar, as was the fact that the
immigration chief was mentioned nowhere in the material I had
read. Yet Faham's instructions from the two rabbis, as he had
written, did not mention the president at all: Faham was only to
spirit the book to safety in Israel and entrust it to a man of his
own choosing, providing he was religious. He chose Shragai, a
rare Orthodox Jew in a position of power, and had thus fulfilled
his mission.

In Eliyahu Shragai's recollection, his father, awed by the
Crown's age and sanctity, told him the book was too holy to
remain in his hands and had to be given promptly to President
Ben-Zvi. His father went the very next morning to the president's residence, a five-minute walk away, Eliyahu told me, and
gave him the Crown. When it was placed on Ben-Zvi's desk,
remembered the president's chief of staff, David Bartov, "the
happiness was beyond anything I had seen before."

By this time, the official narrative's small but curious inconsistencies with what my own research was turning up, and the resistance I was encountering to my inquiries, had convinced me that there was more to this story than was immediately apparent. I redoubled my efforts to penetrate the Aleppo Codex Underground, making more phone calls to scholars, a small number of whom became my allies; laboriously expanding my circle of contacts in the insular Aleppo Jewish community, a nearly impossible task for an outsider that began to succeed only after the amateur Crown sleuth Ezra Kassin volunteered to make introductions and to serve as my guide; spending more time in the Israeli government's archive in Jerusalem, where I found an old file bulging with papers and marked "Crown of Aleppo"; and sifting through documents at the Ben-Zvi Institute, where, after several months of hesitation and delay, the current head of the institute and its academic secretary—neither of whom had been there in the years around the Crown's arrival—eventually decided to grant me access to their archive.

As I dug deeper, I noticed enigmatic references to a trial that had taken place in Israel after the manuscript arrived. The official history of the Crown, published by the Ben-Zvi Institute in 1987, gave this trial only the briefest mention, making it seem little more than a communal spat of scant consequence. When I met the author of that history, he told me he was not interested in "legal fights over ownership" and had barely read what information he had found. The story seemed to be becoming more opaque the more I learned, and I grasped at the trial as a possible key to understanding the lacunae and contradictions of the existing narrative. I met no one who had seen a transcript of this trial, but I was told on several occasions that such a transcript did exist; it was, however, classified and off limits. This made it seem all the more alluring. I spent months looking.

The trial, I learned, took place not in a civil court but in a rabbinic court, part of a parallel religious legal system the government of Israel instituted after the state was founded. The rabbinic courts dealt mainly with matters like marriage and divorce, but sides in a dispute could also choose to have their case adjudicated in a religious court by rabbis instead of civil judges. When I contacted the Jerusalem Rabbinic Court—housed in a cluttered, hectic building whose main elements of interior design are piles of yellowing file folders and hurried clerks in black skullcaps—I was told the case was so old that the file could not be found. Repeated e-mails to a court spokeswoman did not help. "No one here remembers this ancient case," she wrote.

It was around then that I went to see Ezra Kassin at his home in a working-class suburb of Tel Aviv. By this point we had met numerous times. Some of my most informative conversations had taken place on his moped as he wove through Tel Aviv traffic. Each time, I felt he was testing me. He would feed me a scrap of information, hinting there was more where that came from, and then grin and tell me to wait or look for it myself. He had been hoarding material about the Crown for years and was not about to give it all away just because a reporter came and asked.

We went out for lunch at a falafel stand near his house, taking Ezra's two-year-old boy with us. I had already asked him more than once about the trial, eliciting characteristically vague responses. Now, while we ate, he said, "I'm going to show you something you've wanted for a while."

Back in his apartment, he brought out a green binder and handed it to me. I opened it and saw a photocopy of a page written with an old Hebrew typewriter.

The State of Israel
Ministry of Religious Affairs
District Rabbinic Court
Jerusalem
Page 1
File No. 906/5718

It was the transcript from the first day of the trial: March 18, 1958.

The transcript and the other trial documents I eventually obtained were indeed the breakthrough I had been waiting for. They removed the smooth casing constructed around the story of the manuscript's travels in the mid-twentieth century and exposed the carefully concealed gears and levers inside.

Ezra's documents appeared to be copies that someone had made long ago of the transcripts, and as I could not be sure of their accuracy, I still needed the originals. I made another attempt to contact the rabbinic court in Jerusalem. This time I reached a senior clerk who had more important things to do and whom I kept on the phone nonetheless with an enthusiastic explanation of why the Crown and its story were important enough to be worth his time. He agreed to look for the file in the archives, but then weeks went by without word. When I finally called him, he told me he had found it.

"When can I come?" I asked.

The official apologized: he had found the file but did not have permission to let me see it. He gave me the same answer a few more times in the weeks that followed, until I showed up at the court building and knocked unannounced on the door of his office. Distracted, he gestured at his file cabinet as if he had been expecting me. On top was a stack of papers in a disintegrating folder of brown cardboard.

"I'll take it now," I suggested.

"Enjoy," he said. I sat in a corner of a busy waiting room, and within an hour I had photographed the entire file, which included letters, summonses, and other documents pertaining to the trial, as well as the original fifty-year-old transcripts in handwritten Hebrew. With a few exceptions, they matched the typed copies Ezra had shown me.

The court case lasted, on and off, for four years. It was charged and, at times, ugly. Most of the major characters in the story appeared in court. Not all of them told the truth. The trial documents included names, dates, and descriptions of how the Crown traveled from Syria to Israel, and these led me to other documents and people who shed further light on a story that was now quite unrecognizable.

PART THREE

14

The Trial

NEWS OF FAHAM'S arrival in Israel on December 16, 1957, spread quickly within the small community of Aleppo Jews who were already in the country. A few days later, a young teacher named Yitzhak Zaafrani went to pay him a visit. The teacher was the son of one of the two rabbis who had sent the Crown from Aleppo. Because there was no direct communication between Israel and Syria, however, neither he nor anyone else had any inkling that the book that could never be moved had been moved.

Faham was surrounded by other well-wishers when he arrived, according to Zaafrani's testimony in court a few months after this visit—testimony he repeated to me with impressive accuracy more than five decades later. It was the merchant's son who told Zaafrani that the Crown of Aleppo had been sent from Syria and had arrived with his father. Zaafrani could not quite believe that the book had been removed from the synagogue. At the time of his visit, the codex was still held by the customs authorities at the Haifa port, along with the rest of Faham's belongings, and had yet to be transferred to the immigration chief in Jerusalem.

Faham's son said his father had been asking for Rabbi Isaac Dayan, the chief Aleppo rabbi in Israel. Zaafrani took this to mean that Dayan was to be given the Crown, and because Dayan was the head of the local Aleppo community and a colleague of the two rabbis still in Syria, he indeed seemed the most logical recipient. In any case, Faham's son said, the matter was to be kept "completely secret."

More than a month later, on January 22, Zaafrani met Rabbi Dayan at a bar mitzvah celebration and asked him about the Crown, assuming the rabbi had long since received it. But Rabbi Dayan was startled: he did not even know it had arrived. Zaafrani began to understand that something was wrong.

They would go to see Faham the next day, the rabbi declared, and told the young teacher to bring a sheet they could use to wrap up the great book. By this time, more than two weeks had elapsed since the messengers' nighttime arrival at the house of the immigration chief, Shragai, with the brown suitcase, and Faham was no longer in possession of the Crown. But the Aleppo Jews did not know this yet. When they arrived, Zaafrani knocked on the door while the rabbi waited downstairs.

Faham's daughter-in-law came to the door. Faham wasn't there, she said.

"I said that the rabbi of the community was with me and wanted to speak to her father-in-law about an important question," the teacher testified not long afterward. "I said she should come downstairs and speak with him. I told her the rabbi was standing not far away, and that she should take off her apron." She did so. The rabbi asked her about the Crown.

Her father-in-law "did not bring anything old from Aleppo," she said. The two visitors left with their sheet.

Not long afterward, Zaafrani met Faham, who was furious about the way he had behaved with his daughter-in-law. "Why did you come to search as if I've done something wrong?"

Faham asked, in the teacher's recollection. Eventually, Faham revealed what he had done. He had turned the Crown over to Shlomo Zalman Shragai, the head of the Aliya Department—to the Israeli government. Not only had the Crown of Aleppo, the community's treasure and talisman, been moved from its synagogue and city, but it had somehow found its way out of the hands of its guardians and into the hands of strangers.

The Aleppo Jews were suspicious of any government and did not see the largely secular European socialists of the Israeli leadership as representing the entire Jewish people, as they claimed. Indeed, most Aleppo exiles were using Israel as a transit point to the West or bypassing it entirely. The austere socialism of the new state, and its poverty, made it hard for them to do what they knew how to do well—business—and the domination of eastern Europeans, with their condescension toward the Jews of Arab lands, stung. Most of them continued westward, to Panama or São Paulo, or to Brooklyn, where the rows of Lexus SUVs parked along Ocean Parkway decades later would testify to the happy marriage between a people's abilities and a country's possibilities. To them, the idea that the Israeli government had any claim to their book was absurd.

Rabbi Dayan appeared to be under the impression that Faham could still change his mind and get the Crown back. The rabbi took Faham to a new synagogue built by the Aleppo community on the beach in Tel Aviv and showed him a box where he intended to keep the Crown. It was far too flimsy, Faham recalled telling the rabbi. They could build a room of stone, just like the grotto in the Aleppo synagogue, the rabbi suggested, but Faham replied that he did not like the place "in general." The two rabbis in Aleppo told him only to consult with Dayan, Faham informed the rabbi, not to give him the Crown or obey his orders. Those rabbis were in Syria, of course, and could not be contacted for clarification.

While the Aleppo Jews were still struggling to figure out what had happened, the state was swiftly moving to draft a trusteeship document for the Crown that would place the codex permanently under its own control. The trustees were to be President Ben-Zvi, the immigration chief Shragai, and Faham himself; it was now clear Faham's loyalties were no longer with the Aleppo Jews and that he had thrown in his lot with the Israeli authorities. The Aleppo Jews understood they were about to lose the Crown, even if they still did not quite understand how any of this had come about.

Israel, in those years, was a centralized state with one dominant political party: Mapai, the Labor Zionist faction of Ben-Zvi and Ben-Gurion. The party controlled the unions and public housing and nearly everything else, and a signature from an apparatchik often decided who got a job or an apartment. Nonetheless, the Aleppo Jews did not give in, nor did they make do with letters and complaints. In February 1958, two months after the codex had arrived at Haifa, the Aleppo Jews retained a lawyer, went to court, and sued the government.

The court proceedings documented in the long-sought transcripts began the following month at the Jerusalem Rabbinic Court. The hearings were held before three rabbis, instead of judges, but otherwise followed the recognizable formula of a trial. One of the government lawyer's first moves, unopposed by the Aleppo community's attorney, was to ensure that details would not be published in the press. He cited the safety of the Jews still in Syria, who would presumably be in danger if the regime there learned that the Crown had been smuggled to Israel. This was true, but it was also true that the state, as the transcripts make clear, had other reasons not to want details made public. The proceedings were duly kept secret and have remained so for fifty years.

THE COMPLICATED DRAMA that unfolded in the courtroom beginning on March 18, 1958, was, on the surface, a legal dispute between two sides over an object of great worth. But it was more than that. The Jerusalem trial was an argument over who owned the patrimony of the Diaspora, and thus about the nature of Judaism, exile, and the state of Israel.

On one side were the Aleppo Jews, and on the other was the state: President Ben-Zvi, whose institute was now in possession of the book; the immigration chief Shragai; and the cheese merchant Faham, whom the Aleppo Jews saw as a traitor and for whom they reserved much of their fury. For Ben-Zvi and the Israelis, the Jewish state was the rightful heir to the communities of the Diaspora, which were now extinct or would be soon, and was thus the natural owner of Judaism's greatest book. The Aleppo Jews had indeed guarded the book for years in exile and were to be commended, but now the exile was over and the manuscript was home. The codex would be properly cared for and would belong not to a group of rabbis or to one small community but to the entire Jewish people, as embodied by the leaders and scholars of the new state.

The Aleppo Jews, on the other hand, had not subsumed themselves into the Zionist project and its version of history. They were one of the world's oldest Jewish communities, though they might have been humbled, and saw the Crown as the symbol of a place almost none of them had ever considered to be exile. They had not kept it for centuries to turn it over to outsiders. The Crown, the Aleppo rabbis wrote in an angry letter to the court, is "not abandoned property to be won by anyone who so desires." It was theirs, and they wanted it back.

The argument centered on what, exactly, had transpired in the conversation between Faham and the two chief rabbis on the night in Aleppo six months earlier when they had entrusted him with the Crown. The state's claim was based on Faham's account of his instructions: he was told to take the manuscript to Israel and give it to a religious man, and he did precisely that, choosing Shragai, the immigration chief, who passed it on to the president. The state had thus acquired the book legally and could keep it.

The Aleppo Jews, on the other hand, were certain the rabbis would never have willingly let the book out of their hands. They claimed Faham had been instructed to pass it on to the Aleppo community in Israel, in the person of Rabbi Dayan. Ben-Zvi was too respected a personality to attack directly, so most of their antagonism during the trial was directed at Faham and Shragai.

The attorney for the Aleppo Jews, the keen-minded Shlomo Mizrahi, spoke first, beginning his opening remarks with a description of the great synagogue; he recognized that any telling of the story must begin there, with the hidden book and the riot. "During the war of independence, riots erupted in Aleppo and rioters breached the safe, and when they didn't find money, they tore a few pages from the great Crown and threw it to the ground," he told the court. Ten years later, he said, the chief rabbis decided they must send the Crown to the Aleppo community in Israel. The courier whom they trusted had betrayed them. "Faham is only a messenger, and his mission did not render the crowns his property," he charged.

"The crowns were never private property," responded the government lawyer, Shlomo Toussia-Cohen. The merchant, he said, was given "power of attorney" by the Aleppo rabbis to give the Crown to "a religious man of his choosing."

"The power of attorney was oral," he added quickly, heading off what was certain to be the first question from his opponent, "because of the deadly danger involved."

"The value of the crowns," the government lawyer added, "is vast."*

The Aleppo lawyer announced that he would be calling both Faham and the immigration chief to the stand. The government lawyer had no objections, and the court adjourned, to reconvene at noon a week later, on March 25.

When Faham appeared in court, both lawyers insisted on being the first to question him.

"It is my right to question the witness," the Aleppo lawyer told the judges, "as he was called according to my request."

The government attorney objected. "I want to question him first. I represent him," the attorney said. "I want him to recount the events as they took place."

The Aleppo lawyer did not back down. He pulled out the transcript from the first session and read from page 2. "I asked to

---

* There are two notable peculiarities in the transcripts. The trial was also concerned with the ownership of the lesser manuscript that arrived with Faham, the Little Crown, and the protagonists thus sometimes refer to the "crowns." The second book, however, was of far less interest, and references to "crowns" nearly always mean the Crown of Aleppo. Secondly, the transcripts often leave out the attorneys' questions, telling us only what the witness replied. In most places, however, the text allows us to deduce what the questions were, and when possible, I have reconstructed them here. These reconstructed phrases appear without quotation marks.

call him and hear him," he said. The lawyers finally agreed that Faham would first tell his story by himself, without questioning. The merchant began with a plea for sympathy.

"I am a resident of Syria," he began. "I took care of the members of the community coming to Israel and of matters important to the community. The [Syrian] government heard about me through the spy service, and they beat me to make me tell them about my work and about the money from America. I denied everything." He was expelled from Syria but was then allowed back to put his affairs in order before leaving for good, he said. Before the government's deadline was up, he met the community's two chief rabbis, Tawil and Zaafrani.

"Rabbi Tawil said he had secrets to tell me, but was afraid of the authorities," Faham told the court. "I said, 'Do not be afraid. Let us trust in God.' He said, 'The Crown that survived the fire must be taken to Israel, but there is danger in this.' And he told me that if I did not take it, no other man would be able to take it. Our conversation was in the synagogue, and I promised him I would save the Crown."

As for his instructions, he said, "They told me to give it to a religious and God-fearing man," repeating the central point of the government's case. They did mention Rabbi Dayan but said only that he should consult with the rabbi, nothing more. Furthermore, upon arriving in Turkey with the Crown, he received instructions in writing from two of the community's wealthy leaders who were already living abroad. They repeated the rabbis' directive to give the Crown to a "religious man." Faham did not produce the letter, though he said he might still have it; later in the trial, in response to a question from the Aleppo lawyer, he said he could not find it.

In Israel, he went on, the Aleppo Jews heard the Crown had

arrived. They "were surprised by this and alleged that I wanted to sell the crowns. I risked my life to save it, not to sell it, and I did as I was commanded—to give it to a religious man.

"I consulted with Rabbi Dayan," he testified, "and told him about the arrival of the crowns. He took me to the synagogue where he wanted me to put it. I didn't like it, and I told him I was told to consult him, not to give it to him. I told him I had given them to Mr. Shragai."

To the Aleppo community, Faham's act was treason. One of the community's leaders, Meir Laniado, referred to him in a letter as "that crooked messenger, Mr. Faham," who, instructed to give the book to Rabbi Dayan, "betrayed his mission and gave it to other hands." The oral recollections Faham taped twenty years later, which, when compared with his earlier testimony around the time of his arrival in Israel, are exaggerated and unreliable, reflect nonetheless what must have been genuine distress. The Aleppo Jews, he remembered, "would bring six or seven thugs to every hearing of the rabbinic court to scare me." At one hearing, he recalled, "The room was full of thugs, thirty in number. The lawyer for the Aleppo Jews asked me to repeat my testimony from beginning to end. I replied that I am a sick man from all of the blows I was given, my eyesight is bad, and my health is poor, and each time you ask me to repeat things I have already said several times. What do you want from my life?"

A Religious Man

WHEN FAHAM FINISHED his account of the codex's journey, the Aleppo attorney pounced. His first line of questioning was an attempt to discover why the witness had chosen Shragai, the immigration chief, as the recipient of the treasure.

Where did you first hear about Shragai? the lawyer wanted to know.

"I heard about him in Turkey, from a man in Istanbul named Mr. Pessel," the witness replied. Pessel was the Israeli immigration agent who met Faham and notified his superiors of the courier's departure for Israel. Faham said he spent two or three hours at Pessel's home in Istanbul discussing the Crown.

Did the rabbis instruct you to do whatever you wanted with the book?

"They told me to give it to a religious man, not to do with it what I please. Only that I should consult with Rabbi Dayan and do as I see fit," said Faham. He had, in fact, asked Rabbi Dayan what he thought about the immigration chief, he said, and the rabbi agreed that Shragai was indeed a religious man.

What if the rabbi had thought otherwise?

"If Rabbi Dayan had not agreed about Shragai, I would have done what I thought right. I consulted with him out of respect," Faham said.

How much time elapsed between his meeting with the rabbi and the transfer of the manuscript to Shragai?

Faham replied, "Two days passed between the time the books were sent to Shragai and the meeting with Rabbi Dayan." In other words, the merchant had been told to consult with the rabbi but had done so only two days *after* he had already given the Crown to the government. Later in the questioning, he would also admit that he did not go looking for the rabbi, but rather that the rabbi had come looking for him. The Aleppo lawyer was making progress. He continued to grill Faham over the weeks that followed.

When he refused to turn over the Crown to Rabbi Dayan, the merchant said the next time the court convened, the Aleppo community began attacking him, suggesting he had somehow made money from the transaction. He denied this.

"I have not settled in Israel," he testified, "not in housing and not in a job and not in anything else. I borrow money to eat." He suggested he could receive benefits from the government but was purposely not doing so. "I am not demanding an arrangement now so that they won't say I am benefiting from the Crown," he said.

Faham volunteered an interesting piece of information. "Not only did I not make money from the crowns," he told the court, "but because of the crowns I was charged more than five thousand pounds because my possessions were searched." He was referring to a customs bill he received after arriving in Haifa. This clearly drew the Aleppo lawyer's interest, and the attorney repeatedly came back to the customs bill, which, it turned out, had been waived thanks to the intervention of an influential friend.

"Mr. Faham was told to pay customs for the books and with

Mr. Shragai's intervention was released from the customs pay-ment," the lawyer told the court at one point. Then he insin-uated the quid pro quo: "Mr. Faham gave the books to Mr. Shragai for safekeeping." He wasn't quite there, but he was get-ting close.

The lawyer now lunged at a weak link in the merchant's story. You were told to give the Crown to a religious and God-fearing man, he said. Why not Rabbi Dayan himself? Was he not a re-ligious man?

"I had no doubt that Rabbi Dayan was a rabbi, and reli-gious," Faham was forced to admit. Still, he said, "the matter was up to me."

Were there no religious people among the Aleppo Jews in Israel? asked the lawyer.

"I know the people of Aleppo well, and I know that the ones in Israel include people who fear heaven and rabbis and wise men. And I knew that most of the Aleppo Jews in Israel are religious," Faham conceded. But his decision, he suggested, en-joyed the backing of others in the community. After arriving at his son's house in Israel, many visitors came, Aleppo Jews, "and they said Shragai was religious and feared God."

How many of them told you he was religious? asked the lawyer.

"I don't know how many," Faham replied.

And what were their names? the lawyer asked.

"Many people came, and I don't remember the name of any one of them," the witness said.

How many of them did you ask?

"I don't remember how many I asked about Shragai," the witness said.

Are there no religious people in Israel other than Shragai?

"I know that there are many other religious people in Israel, but I don't know them," Faham replied.

The lawyer changed tack. Describe to us again your arrival at Haifa, he said.

"I arrived in Israel on a Monday," Faham said. "I gave the crowns to the Jewish Agency in Haifa, and I told them to send them to Shragai."

What was the name of the clerk at the port?

Faham did not know.

Did you get a receipt?

No, Faham said.

Perhaps the lawyer allowed a moment of silence in the courtroom to let this answer sink in. Handing the Crown over to Israel's president was one thing, but Faham had turned the Crown of Aleppo over to a man whose name he did not know and who gave him nothing in return.

Did you tell the clerk that you were supposed to consult with Rabbi Dayan before ceding the books?

No, Faham said. "I told him to give them to Shragai."

But what was wrong with Rabbi Dayan? the lawyer asked, resuming his previous course of attack. What do you have against him?

"I won't answer what I have against Rabbi Dayan. There are things I won't say to avoid denigrating Rabbi Dayan's honor," the merchant said.

"I ask the court to force the witness to answer what he has against Rabbi Dayan," the Aleppo lawyer demanded, turning to the three judges.

They overruled him, but the lawyer had already done his job.

He had raised doubts about Faham's story and had introduced the court to hints of collusion, forced or voluntary, between the witness and his new allies from the Israeli government.

President Ben-Zvi was not in the courtroom but was following the case closely. Faham's testimony was clearly a matter of some concern. On March 27, the government's lawyer told Ben-Zvi that the merchant had been cross-examined by the Aleppo lawyer two days before. The questioning, he wrote, "reached great levels of tension, but Mr. Faham stood by his story as it was given in writing to Your Honor." A month later, however, after another court session, the lawyer was forced to report that there had been "contradictions in his testimony." Faham, he said, had become "confused" on the stand.

Our Last Drop of Blood

WITH THE ARRIVAL of Shragai, the immigration chief, the atmosphere in the courtroom must have changed. The witness was now an important state official and, unlike Faham, an experienced polemicist fluent in Hebrew. He and Faham were on the same side, but after Shragai had been on the stand for a few minutes and had presented two slips of paper to the court, those present must have realized he was telling a story that contradicted much of what they had heard from the previous witness.

He first heard that the Crown had left Syria, Shragai said, in a letter from the agent Pessel in Turkey. He produced a copy of the letter, dated October 7, 1957, around the time of the Jewish new year.

The Honorable Mr. Shragai,

In the possession of the community in Aleppo (Syria), as is known, is the "Crown of the Torah." All efforts to convince the heads of the community to transfer it to Israel have been met with resistance, and what is also unclear is whose possession it was in, as the fact of its existence was made to disappear after the Syrian authorities came looking for the book.

Recently I succeeded in convincing them to bring the book, and now it has been brought here and is in the possession of the customs authorities, together with one item of cargo, and will be brought to Israel after the holidays by Mr. Faham, who brought it here.

In order to prevent Mr. Faham from having to run around searching for someone to whom to give the book, I would be grateful to you if you would instruct me on the matter of to whom he should give the "Crown of the Torah" upon his arrival in Israel: to the chief rabbis, the president, the university. It is preferable that he should have this upon his arrival in order to prevent others from approaching him in order to take possession of it. I will inform you of the date of his journey.

With holiday blessings,
Y. Pessel

Shragai then produced a copy of his response, dated October 13.

Mr. Y. Pessel
Istanbul

The Honorable Mr. Pessel,

I hereby confirm receipt of your letter of 12 Tishrei [October 7] regarding the "Crown of the Torah," which was brought from Aleppo and will be sent to Israel after the holidays by Mr. Faham.

Mr. Faham should kindly give the "Crown of the Torah" upon his arrival in Haifa to the Aliya Department. Afterward it will be decided where to send it.

With great respect and best holiday wishes,

S. Z. Shragai
Head of the Aliya Dept.

More than two months before the merchant even sailed to Israel, these curious letters suggested, the Israelis, and not Faham, were in charge of the Crown. Whom shall I tell him to give it to? asked the agent in Turkey. To the Aliya Department, replied the head of the Aliya Department. Shragai might have thought it crude to write what he meant, which was: To me. Despite Faham's version of his instructions from the Aleppo rabbis, the letters made no mention of any "religious man." There was no mention at all of Faham's wishes or those of the rabbis.

When Faham sailed into Haifa, the immigration chief testified, he received a call from a port clerk saying the Syrian had arrived with the books. "I instructed them to release them from customs and send them to us," he told the court. In response to a question from the lawyer for the Aleppo Jews, Shragai said he did not believe the Crown had been given to him personally. "Because he is asking about this," Shragai said, "it is clear that it was not given to me to do with as I please." The Crown should be put in the state archive, he said; it was not private property.

The Aleppo lawyer was still hinting, if not stating outright, that Faham's decision to cede the book was related to the customs bill that had been waived thanks to the immigration chief's intervention. Perhaps the lawyer had not yet fully understood the significance of the letters, which indicated that control of the Crown was settled long before it arrived in Israel. Shragai, in any event, brushed this allegation aside. "There are special rights for those who suffered abroad for Zionism and aliya, there are rights for those who bring money, and this is known, and in many cases we ask the government for customs reductions and so forth," he told the court.

The Aleppo lawyer was not done. "In light of Mr. Shragai's testimony, I have questions for Mr. Faham," he said. He had prepared his final offensive against the merchant's credibility. This time, the subject was to be the letter that Faham wrote to the immigration chief soon after his arrival, the one that began, "I am the immigrant Mordechai, son of Ezra Faham."* In it, he described the history of the Crown and, for the first time, put forward the claim that he had been told to give it to a religious man of his own choosing. The letter, the lawyer appeared to have noticed, read like a scholarly exposition on the history of the book, complete with source references; Faham must not have struck him as a likely author. Are you sure that you wrote it yourself? the lawyer asked Faham.

Faham was sure.

Are you certain that the letter was not dictated to you by—for example—the immigration chief? The lawyer was hinting that the "religious man" story originated with none other than Shragai—the "religious man" himself.

"I wrote the letter myself and not according to the request of Mr. Shragai," Faham insisted, at which point the lawyer appeared to abruptly change the subject.

Do you know in what way the Crown was connected to Maimonides? The spectators in court most likely did not understand what the attorney was up to.

No, Faham admitted, I do not. As the lawyer knew, the letter said Maimonides had used the Crown when preparing the laws governing the writing of Torah scrolls.

And do you know anything about the rules governing when scribes must leave blank lines in the columns of a Torah scroll?

No, I do not know what those are, Faham said. Faham's letter said Maimonides used the Crown to draft just those rules.

---

* The text of the letter appears in chapter 13.

Do you know if tradition says the book dates to the time of the first temple in Jerusalem, or the second?

No, Faham said, I do not. Faham's letter cited an Aleppo tradition that it came from the time of the second temple. The attorney's point was made: Faham had not written the letter but had rather signed one written for him.

At a session on May 4, the lawyer asked Shragai about the same letter.

"I did not draft the letter for him," Shragai replied. "You should ask him who wrote the letter for him." The lawyer moved on to other subjects before circling back.

The letter, Shragai said this time, "was the result of my suggestion." Still, he insisted, "It is not true that most of the material in the letter came from me. I told him to write about the crowns and how they arrived."

The lawyer returned to the letter yet again later on. He had noticed that nowhere did it mention any consultation with Rabbi Dayan, which had supposedly been part of Faham's instructions. Had the immigration chief noticed this?

"I did not note to Faham that his letter did not mention Rabbi Dayan at all," the witness said.

The anger in the Aleppo community increased as the proceedings went on. This had partly to do with a sense that they were being treated as inferiors by a European elite. During the trial, one of the community leaders, the lawyer Meir Laniado, wrote a furious letter to Ben-Zvi's secretary accusing the president of trying to cut a deal for the Crown with a wealthy Aleppo Jew in New York—the refrigerator magnate Isaac Shalom—in an attempt to bypass the stubborn community in Israel. "I am amazed by the fact that you approached Isaac Shalom, as this fits arrangements and traditions that were practiced in Eastern communities fifty years ago, in which certain people would try to get the agreement of a rich man or notable of some variety, and thus get the rest of the community to cover their mouths with their hands," Laniado wrote.

That letter was written in 1960, the same year Faham packed up his family and moved to Brooklyn. The trial, which was still going on, was not criminal in nature, and Faham was not suspected of any offense, so he could leave freely. In the oral memoir he recorded two decades later, Faham described how the dispute was finally resolved before his departure. He attended a hearing at the rabbinic court, Faham recalled, and met Tawil, the rabbi from Aleppo, who had by then made it to Israel. Faham confronted him.

> [Tawil] answered before I could finish: "It's true, they tricked me. I met with the president and told him that I never asked you to give the Crown to a specific person." The meeting of the rabbinic court began. They called Rabbi Tawil first, they asked him, and he confirmed what I had said. They took him out a side door. After he left, they called me, asked for my forgiveness, and announced that the trial was postponed.

It had all been a misunderstanding, according to Faham: the trial ended with an admission by his opponents that he had been right all along.

Old men are allowed their stories, but not if they have somehow come to be mistaken for historical truth. In the absence of any serious investigation, this is what has happened here. The merchant's account of this, one of the story's most crucial moments, was quoted uncritically in a scholarly book about the Crown in English, by a professor from New York's Yeshiva University. It is not contradicted in the official version of the

The Aleppo rabbis Moshe Tawil and Salim Zaafrani.

Crown's history in Hebrew, published by the Ben-Zvi Institute. It provides the neat ending many seem to want.

By the time Faham taped his memoirs in the late 1970s, he was elderly. His reminiscences are full of fantastic details and color: He spoke to the Syrian prime minister on an almost daily basis, for example, and single-handedly rescued the Aleppo community from persecution on several occasions. During the riots, he remembered saving no fewer than forty Jewish children in his home, although his son, who was in the house at the time, had no memory of this when I interviewed him. He claimed to have saved the Crown from the synagogue during the riot, though twenty years earlier he had testified that until he was approached by the rabbis about smuggling the manuscript out, he had not even been aware it had survived the fire. His version of the trial's end, the court transcripts show, was another invention.

By 1960, with the trial now two years old, the two Aleppo rabbis who had sent the book with the merchant had both

escaped to Israel. They testified in court together on March 1.
One can almost hear their anger in the old protocols.

"We gave something to a man who betrayed a trust," Rabbi
Moshe Tawil told the court. "We believe the Crown of the
Torah is dedicated to, and belongs to, the Aleppo community,
and that should not be changed at all.

"If Rabbi Dayan had not been in Israel, we would not have
sent the Crown under any circumstances," he said.

"We gave the Crown to Mr. Faham to give it to Rabbi Isaac
Dayan," testified the second rabbi, Salim Zaafrani. "We did not
tell him to give it to someone else at all, and he did not have
permission to do so. We do not want compromises. I want the
Crown to be given to the Aleppo community."

As the Aleppo Jews had insisted all along, the idea that the
rabbis would have willingly handed the Crown to outsiders, or
allowed a member of the community to give it to a person of
his choice, was ludicrous. The Aleppo rabbis had decided that
the Crown could no longer remain in their city, but they never
dreamed of allowing it out of their community.

"We guarded it with our last drop of blood," Rabbi Zaafrani
told the court. "It is the property of the Aleppo community and
not of the state of Israel."

YEARS AFTER THE Crown was brought to Israel, its
new keepers formally added a leaf to the manuscript. On it was
an inscription by a Hebrew calligrapher with the following text:

This Crown of the Torah was given by the chief rabbi of
Aleppo, Rabbi Moshe Tawil, and the judge Rabbi Shlomo
Zaafrani, to Mr. Mordechai ben Ezra Hacohen Faham in the
year 5718, to bring it up to Jerusalem, the holy city.

Mr. Faham had the fortune of receiving this privilege when he agreed to risk his life in order to save it and bring it to Jerusalem, and he gave it to his honor the president, Mr. Itzhak Ben-Zvi.

This is the simple story I knew at the beginning. The one I knew now was very different.

When Faham crossed the border into Turkey with the Crown, Israeli agents were waiting for him on the other side. One was Silo, who ran the Alexandretta immigration station, and one was Pessel. According to Faham, he met with Pessel for several hours in Istanbul in the fall of 1957 and discussed the Crown. The precise content of this meeting is unknown; when I met Pessel's son, he said his late father nearly never spoke of his work and left no written accounts. We do know, however, that the rabbis said they had instructed Faham only weeks before to bring the codex to Rabbi Dayan in Israel, but that by October 7 the Israeli agent was writing to Jerusalem and asking what *he* should instruct Faham to do with it, meaning that the Israelis were now calling the shots. It is possible, therefore, to deduce that at or near the time of the meeting in Istanbul, the Israeli agent persuaded the courier—whether by reason, seduction, or threat—to betray the Aleppo rabbis and yield the book.

It is not difficult to conceive how this was done. Israel was poor, with housing and jobs in short supply, and the government had the means to make life much easier for a refugee and his family. As Faham's port customs bill showed—as it was quite possibly meant to show—the government could also make it harder. Faham was performing a great service to the state: David Bartov, President Ben-Zvi's chief of staff, told me fifty years later that Faham still deserved Israel's gratitude for bringing "the greatest cultural treasure we have" and turning it over to the government, rendering it the property of the Jewish people and not of one community. Faham may have come to agree that the Israelis were right. Or he may have realized that the Crown changed him from just another helpless immigrant, one of thousands who arrived in Israel that month, into a man of consequence: he had something that important people wanted, people who were in a position to help him.

There is written evidence that his powerful new friends did try to help. The state archive preserves a note from October 1958 in which the president's wife, Rachel Yanait Ben-Zvi, wrote to a government clerk about an "important matter": she wanted him to help Faham find an apartment in one of the Tel Aviv suburbs. "The president and Mr. Shragai both know him and told me that he deserves special treatment by your department," she wrote. In a later letter to Faham, the president himself mentioned his efforts to secure an apartment for him. Faham, who spent a little over two years in Israel, always maintained he had not asked for or received anything from the state. With the significant exception of the waiving of his customs bill at Shragai's request, nothing I found in the written record indicates he did. Faham, who died in 1982, left us no clue to his motivations. Instead he spent the rest of his life insisting he had done as he was told.

Agents of the Israeli government were effectively in control of the manuscript shortly after it arrived in Turkey in the early fall of 1957, and Shragai was giving orders from Jerusalem by mid-October. From Alexandretta, Faham continued on the *Marmara* to the Haifa port. There he was greeted by Jewish Agency clerks and exempted from paying the customs tax by Shragai, who had been waiting for the Crown and who ordered his men to bring it directly from the port to his Jerusalem home.

In the first days after his arrival in Israel, Faham's story was still in flux, and he appeared to be trying to give the impression that the codex was still his to dispose of as he pleased. The merchant's claim that he had been told to give the book to a "religious man" of his own choosing appeared only several weeks later and only *after* the book was already in the hands of the "religious man"—the immigration chief Shragai. The story was hatched to justify what had already happened, which was that the book was in the hands of the government. The Israelis knew the story was fiction, and yet they presented it as truth to one of their own courts.

In the end they were forced to concede. The Crown file at the rabbinic court in Jerusalem contains the trusteeship agreement drafted for the codex in 1962, when the long trial finally ended in an out-of-court settlement. The text includes a brief section recounting the Crown's journey. The Aleppo rabbis, it says, sent the Crown and the lesser manuscript with the merchant Faham "in order to give them to Rabbi Isaac Dayan." The document, in other words, explicitly contradicts the story the state had been pushing since the book arrived. It is signed by President Ben-Zvi.

In order to explain how the Crown did not reach its intended address, however, the document follows its admission of the truth with a little convenient fiction: Dayan, it says, was simply out of the country when the book arrived, visiting his children in the United States and Brazil. The fact is that the rabbi was very much in Israel, as Ben-Zvi well knew. A log of the president's meetings shows he met with Dayan himself on two occasions at this time: on January 21, 1958, five weeks after the codex arrived, and then again on February 19.

The Aleppo Jews never got their book back.

The compromise gave the community theoretical part ownership of the manuscript, while effectively ensuring that it would remain in the hands of the state and would never leave Ben-Zvi's institute. The government, faced with evidence that its version was not true, must have realized it had to cede something—though not much, in practical terms—while the Aleppo Jews saw that though they were right, they would not win. Menachem Yadid, a young Aleppo community leader at the time and later a member of Israel's parliament, remembered a feeling of helplessness. "After all, the regime is the regime," he told me. "It was a dirty affair."

The Crown of Aleppo was never given to Israel. It was taken. The government may have believed it was serving the interests of its people and of the book itself, but though those circumstances deserve to be noted, they do not alter the ugly mechanics of the story: the state took the sacred property of people who did not give it voluntarily, with the collusion of a messenger who turned over something that was not his to give. Many of the fictions and evasions that have hidden this story for decades were designed to conceal what was, in effect, the theft of the Crown from the Jews of Aleppo.

With the compromise agreement signed, the trial ended. The intricacies of this phase of the Crown's history have served so far to obscure a rather startling detail: much of the manuscript that everyone was fighting about was not even there.

PART FOUR

The Book

AT THE CENTER of this story is not a diamond, a painting, or a suitcase full of bills, but a book. Some would say it is *the* book: the authoritative copy of a text whose position at the root of more than one civilization has given it bearing on the lives of billions of people, even if they have never read it.

This book begins with the creation of the universe. It tells us about the Garden of Eden, about the expulsion of Adam and Eve for breaking the one rule they were given, and about the murder of their second son by their first. Human beings, the text seems to be saying at the very start, destroy everything good they are given. We read how the world descended so far into corruption that God regretted creating it and obliterated it in a flood survived by one human family, and then we read about Abram, son of idol worshippers, who saw that there was only one God, not many, and that he was invisible and all-powerful. When this God told him to travel to the land of Canaan, Abram was residing in Haran, which is not far from where Alexandretta sits today, and his journey south would have taken him past Aleppo, which is west of the Euphrates, one of the rivers that the text tells us flowed from Eden.

The book tells us how Abram became Abraham, and how he nearly sacrificed his son Isaac. It tells us about his grandson

Jacob, also called Israel, who escaped famine by traveling to Egypt, where his own son Joseph had risen to power in Pharaoh's palace by interpreting dreams. We learn how Israel's descendants were enslaved and how they were redeemed from slavery by Moses after God afflicted the Egyptians with ten plagues and drowned their armies in the Sea of Reeds. Moses led the people into the desert, to a hill in the wilderness of Sinai, where the book becomes frantic with dramatic detail—smoke, fire, shaking mountains, and horn blasts—as if grabbing us by our shoulders and demanding we pay attention to this, the story of its own appearance.

The opening of the Torah's last volume, Deuteronomy, finds the Israelites near the Jordan River, about to enter their land, and Moses near death. In a farewell address, Moses tells his people that if they obey God, they will be blessed.

> Blessed shall be the issue of your womb, the produce of your soil, and the offspring of your cattle, the calving of your herd and the lambing of your flock. Blessed shall be your basket and your kneading bowl. Blessed shall you be in your comings and blessed shall you be in your goings.
>
> The Lord will put to rout before you the enemies who attack you; they will march out against you by a single road, but flee from you by many roads.

But if they do not obey, said Moses, they will be cursed.

> Cursed shall you be in the city and cursed shall you be in the country. Cursed shall be your basket

If you open the Crown of Aleppo, the most important copy of this book, you will find that none of these stories, so familiar to us, are there.

The mutilated codex does not begin, *In the beginning.* It opens instead with Moses about to die, and with the completion of the verse above.

and your kneading bowl.

It continues with a list of curses:

> Cursed shall be the issue of your womb and the produce of your soil, the calving of your herd and the lambing of your flock. Cursed shall you be in your comings, and cursed shall you be in your goings.
>
> The Lord will let loose against you calamity, panic and frustration in all the enterprises you undertake, so that you shall soon be utterly wiped out because of your evildoing in forsaking me.

The Torah, or the Five Books of Moses—the story of creation, of Noah, the Tower of Babel, Abraham's wanderings and Joseph's dreams, the slavery of the Israelites, the plagues, the Exodus, the giving of the book at Mount Sinai, the long trek through the desert to the promised land—are the books at the heart of the Bible, the ones Hebrew scribes need to produce perfect Torah scrolls for use in synagogues, and the most important part of the Crown. Except for the last five leaves, these books are gone. So are the last books of the Bible: the book of Lamentations, mourning the destruction of Jerusalem by the armies of Babylon; the burlesque book of Esther; the hallucinatory Hebrew-Aramaic parables of Daniel; the story of the first return from exile in the book of Ezra; and the despair of Ecclesiastes. Individual pages and sections from the middle of the codex are also gone. And yet while there are many dozens of documents from the months around the time the Crown was spirited to

The first page of the Aleppo Codex as it exists today, from the book
of Deuteronomy. The manuscript's distinctive purplish damage
marks are visible on the bottom left corner.

Israel—the letters exchanged by the Israeli agents and officials,
two transcripts of meetings between Faham and the president,
and records of the court hearings—none of them mentions this.
Reading the documents of the time is akin to listening in on a
conversation among a dozen art critics who are looking at the

Mona Lisa and having an acrimonious discussion of the frame without mentioning that someone has taken scissors and cut out her face.

On February 21, 1958, a month and a half after the book was brought to Shragai's home, three Aleppo rabbis in Israel wrote a letter to the president with an offhand mention of "pages missing from the great Crown." These, they wrote, were "gathered by various people and hidden in a dry hole nearby," and they hoped to recover them soon. On March 2, Rabbi Dayan, who seems to have carefully tried to maintain cordial relations with the president during the trial and thereafter, sent a letter to Ben-Zvi saying he would try to locate the "missing pages." On March 18, at the first court session, the lawyer for the Aleppo Jews described the looting of the synagogue, saying rioters "tore a few pages from the Crown." None of these references makes clear the scope of what was missing, or that the missing sections included the most important one, the Torah; indeed, all three would seem to refer to a small number of leaves.

The first description of the enormous number of pages missing appears only in March, three months after the codex arrived in Israel, in a document drafted by a government lawyer to outline a suggested legal arrangement, with no suggested explanation of why this was so. About two hundred pages were gone, or about 40 percent of the five hundred leaves originally written by the scribe on the Sea of Galilee. This must have weighed on everyone, and one would expect it to be the main topic of discussion. Instead there is only an uncanny silence.

18

The Keepers of the Crown

THE FACT OF the Crown's arrival in Israel had been kept secret for more than two and a half years by the time readers of the *Jerusalem Post* saw the following article on October 28, 1960.

SAGA OF OLDEST BIBLICAL CODEX

President Ben-Zvi Describes 1,000 Year Journey of Recently Recovered Book

"It is my privilege and my pleasure to inform the Jewish public and the world of Biblical scholarship that the precious manuscript of the Codex of Ben Asher has been found and is in safe keeping."

The above words, by President Izhak Ben-Zvi, were uttered in a quiet scholastic fashion, almost in parenthesis, as Mr. Ben-Zvi delivered a paper at the late-night closing session of the Israel Exploration Society conference in Jerusalem during the Succot festival. They probably escaped many in the large audience. Mr. Ben-Zvi's address seemed to be one of those reports of esoteric research . . . The story of this 1,000-year-old book has now come full circle. Details of its latest and last sojourn must for the meantime remain unpublished.

The news was picked up by the foreign press, and a month later a certain M. S. Seale, an Irish Presbyterian missionary, wrote to the *Times* of London.

> Many of your readers will have read with relief your correspondent's report from Tel Aviv on Nov. 16 of the recovery from Aleppo of most of the Ben Asher codex which was feared destroyed in the 1948 [sic] riots. It is to be hoped that the present holders of this great authoritative text will see fit to reveal the mechanics of the "rescue."

The missionary Seale probably did not live to see the mechanics revealed.

The Crown was perhaps the most important book to reach Israel in those years, but there were many thousands more. Accompanying the migration of people was a great migration of books, as Jews returned from the Diaspora with the sacred texts that had helped them survive there as Jews. Legal treatises, tractates of the Talmud, rabbinic expositions and Torah scrolls, printed volumes and handwritten manuscripts arrived in crates at the ports and filled government warehouses. This is a largely untold story, and one key to understanding the story of the Crown.

The president's preoccupation with the Crown of Aleppo reflected a broader appetite for old Hebrew books from the East. In August 1961 he wrote to the Joint Distribution Committee, which sent charitable funds to the Jews of Aleppo, asking that it urge the community to send books to Jerusalem, and specifically "to the institute of which I am head." In July 1962 the president's secretary and the director of his institute, Meir Benayahu—the son of a chief rabbi and scion of a powerful political family with roots in Iraq, who will return later to figure in this story—wrote to Rabbi Dayan, who was now in South America but had left an extensive library in Israel. "It is very unfortunate that these books are touched by no one and have no guarantee of their safety," reads the letter, which requested the rabbi's permission for the institute to take the books it wanted.

The story of the Jews of Yemen, who were airlifted to Israel immediately after Israel's independence, is instructive. The immigration effort, Operation Magic Carpet, saw nearly all of Yemen's Jews, fifty thousand people, leave their cities and villages and make their way to a transit camp outside Aden, where they were put on gleaming white Douglas Skymasters chartered from Alaska Airlines and flown to Israel. They were pulled by an old messianic dream of return to the land of Israel, and pushed by fear: after the partition vote at the United Nations, a mob in Aden killed eighty-two Jews, and there were other outbreaks of violence in the country, as there were in Aleppo and across the Middle East. The transit camp was the scene of terrible suffering; it had been built for five hundred people but for a time held twelve thousand, many of them malnourished and ill after their journey from the interior. These Jews left much behind but brought their books, most of them handwritten codices and scrolls, many of them ancient. At the transit camp, new arrivals were told to deposit them with staffers, who were to transfer them to Israel by sea. Many of the Yemeni Jews never saw their texts again.

Ben-Zvi was particularly enchanted by the Yemenis, with their robes and long side curls and air of biblical authenticity, and he traveled to the Aden camp in 1949. While he was there, he wrote later, he opened two or three crates of belongings that were awaiting shipment. "I intended to check carefully and see if there was any valuable material there which could be purchased for the Institute for the Study of Jewish Communities in the Middle East," he wrote. Ben-Zvi was not the only book enthusiast rummaging through the crates. A large portion of the scrolls and volumes deposited at Aden for transfer to Israel, the Israeli historian Gish Amit has written, ended up in public collections such as those at Ben-Zvi's institute and Israel's national library or in the hands of private dealers and manuscript collectors in Israel and abroad.

One important Yemeni rabbi gave his community's ten Torah scrolls to an Israeli official for safekeeping, but when he came to pick them up from a government warehouse in Tel Aviv, they were gone. "It is a disgrace," he wrote in a furious letter to the immigration authorities of the Jewish Agency, that the holy books "were preserved in the land of the Arabs and stolen in the land of Israel, the land of the Hebrews." Many years later, the same rabbi claimed to have found one of his scrolls in the shop of a Jerusalem bookseller. A different rabbi from the Yemeni city of Sanaa described trying to get his synagogue's books back from a Joint Distribution Committee warehouse at the Jaffa port.

> We would go to the Jaffa port and ask for our books. They would say: Bring evidence that these are books from your synagogue. In Sanaa we had a large synagogue. Before we came to Israel, we put the holy books in crates . . . and on every book we wrote, "Sanctified to the Al-Sheikh synagogue." So I said, "What proof do you want? Our names are on the books." They said: Bring forms from the Ministry of Religious Affairs. Prove to us that you have a place to store them. Afterward I came again, and they said: "There was a fire, the books were burned, don't go in." I didn't believe them.

The Yemenis were seen as primitives, products of a Jewish culture unpolluted by modernity. Their books, as Amit writes, "were presented as sacred relics from the past that should be stored in research institutes for the benefit of science, the state of Israel, and the world." The justification given for taking the books was that their owners were unable to properly care for them; that they had ably done so for centuries was ignored.

One Yemeni Jew who came to Israel with the Magic Carpet airlift left his family's possessions in a crate at the camp in Aden, including two large ram's horns, a five-hundred-year-old prayer book, and a two-part manuscript of the legal text known as the Mishna. The crate arrived several months later, when the family was housed at an immigrant absorption camp near Tel Aviv. When the man, Shalom Ozeri, went to the camp director to ask him to release the package, the director told him to come back the next day. When Ozeri arrived, he wrote many years later, he found that the crate had been opened and looted. The ram's horns, the prayer book, and one of the two books of the Mishna were gone. More than forty years afterward, in 1993, Ozeri happened to see a photograph of a Mishna manuscript kept in Israel's national library, on the campus of Hebrew University in Jerusalem. It seemed familiar. He went to meet with a librarian, bringing along the half of the manuscript that had remained in his possession. It matched. The library returned his property, but according to Amit the stacks there still hold 430 other Yemeni manuscripts. Thousands more simply disappeared.

ON NOVEMBER 1, 1962, with the trial over, the trusteeship agreement signed, and the manuscript secured in his institute, President Ben-Zvi convened a meeting of the new keepers of the Crown. The state had originally suggested three trustees—the president, Shragai, and Faham—but now there were eight, in keeping with the compromise agreement reached in court. Four were from the Aleppo community, and four from the state. The Aleppo representatives included the two rabbis who had sent the Crown and were now in Israel. Faham, spurned by the community and by then residing in Brooklyn, was not included. The government representatives, led by the president himself, were clearly in charge. The rancor of the trial had not subsided.

Ben-Zvi opened the meeting. "For years, we feared for the fate of the Crown," he said, recalling that he had once seen the manuscript in Aleppo long before. "I heard that only once a year, on the Day of Atonement, would they take it out and read the book of Jonah—"

"This was not done in our time," Rabbi Zaafrani cut in. Reading the old transcripts, I could almost hear him snapping in Arabic-accented Hebrew. "Rabbi Intabi says he doesn't know about this custom either."

Ben-Zvi forged ahead. "Mr. Faham of Aleppo had the great honor of being given the Crown by the sages of the community to bring to Jerusalem. He gave it to Mr. Shragai on the second day of Shvat 5718"—January 23, 1958—"and Mr. Shragai brought it to me the next day." The precise date cited by the president was off, in fact, by seventeen days; the nighttime messengers had reached Shragai's apartment on January 6. Shragai, who had also become a trustee, was sitting in the room, but he did not correct the president. This peculiar hiccup in the chronology will be relevant later on.

Rabbi Zaafrani interrupted again. "Faham has no merit at all," he charged. "He is a simple man. He didn't know where the Crown was kept and knew nothing of its value. We gave it to him to give to Rabbi Isaac Dayan in Tel Aviv, and he did not. None of the stories he tells have any truth to them."

The president would not be drawn in. "It has been agreed" to place the book in his institute, he told those present, and he suggested that allowing the Aleppo Jews to participate in the board of trustees at all was an act of generosity. "Because the manuscript once belonged to the Aleppo community, we agreed to appoint eight custodians, half of them from this community," he said.

"Once belonged": this must have stung. One of the other Aleppo representatives interjected that his community should have the majority.

Shragai spoke up: "The document has been made and there is no reason to change it."

"The trust document has been made, and we all approve it, and it was approved by the rabbinic court and it will not be changed," Ben-Zvi summed up. Then he quickly changed the subject to one he may have thought would be more popular. He had received an offer of 20,000 Israeli pounds to photograph the Crown and publish an edition that would be made available to the public.

The sum is too small, the immigration chief said.

It was "close to zero," one of the Aleppo representatives agreed. An expert he spoke to had suggested that a fair price would be $200,000.

At this time, the location of the codex was kept secret. Ben-Zvi, with his scholar's cap on, had already become the first to publish an academic article about the manuscript. Access was limited to a handful of scholars from a special department at Hebrew University, the Bible Project, who were using the Crown to prepare a new edition of the holy text. No one else was allowed to see it.

"I was shocked to hear that Ben-Asher's Crown of the Torah was burned by Arab rioters, and how happy I was to read in *Haaretz* that most of this book is in Israel and was given by the president to the faithful hands of scholars," a certain Mordechai Rigbi wrote to the president after the book's arrival was made public. He had owned an import-export business with a branch in Aleppo and had once been allowed a glimpse of the book in its "underground synagogue."

"I would be happy to be allowed to see this ancient book for a second time and would thank Your Honor if he would instruct the researchers to show it to me for a few moments," he wrote. Other such requests from ordinary people hoping for a glimpse of the great book survive in the archives. They received the same answer Rigbi did.

"For many reasons," the president's secretary wrote, "there is still no possibility of showing the book to the general public." Scholars from Israel and from abroad were similarly turned away. In 1959, Ben-Zvi had decided that photographs of a small number of pages would be published and that other scholars could study them, "but the place of the photographs will be in my articles." The scholars of the Bible Project promised not to remove the Crown from their workroom on campus "and not to let any person not from the project make any use of the manuscript." They would not publish the first book of their new Bible edition for decades.

In his obituary for the Crown a decade and a half before, the Bible scholar Umberto Cassuto had bemoaned the Aleppo rabbis' refusal to allow access or at least to allow photography.

The book, after all, had been created for the express purpose of being copied as much as possible. Now, after Ben-Zvi had been granted his wish and had seen the Crown finally come under the control of modern scholars, the trustees had the following exchange about the proposed publication of a copy.

"If they photograph the Crown, it will be in their possession and they won't need us, and they will be able to make copies and send them to whomever they want," said Israel's chief Sephardic rabbi, Isaac Nissim, who happened also to be the father of Meir Benayahu, the president's close aide and the director of the Ben-Zvi Institute.

They can't possibly put the original on public display, said the immigration chief.

The trusteeship document says it may never leave the Ben-Zvi Institute under any circumstances, added one of the Aleppo trustees.

"The rabbi was right when he said that if we give even one copy, we will lose our rights to it," the president finally agreed. The Crown was to remain hidden, the possession solely of its new owners. A facsimile of the surviving section of the manuscript would be published only fourteen years later, in 1976.

The matter of the missing pages was of great concern to Ben-Zvi in those days, even though there was a ready explanation for their disappearance: they had been consumed in the synagogue fire. Rescue from the flames was a recurring theme in the various stories about the codex, and this notion was supported by its physical appearance: the Crown had purplish marks, burn scars, on the lower corners of its pages. The president, however, appeared to believe that perhaps not all of the missing pages had been burned, and he undertook a worldwide search for surviving pieces.

No one, at that time, knew precisely how much was missing. It was difficult to calculate how many of the original leaves were gone because no one knew how many pages had been in the manuscript in the first place. There were no page numbers. Shortly after the Crown's arrival, Ben-Zvi, scribbling calculations in blue ink on a piece of paper I found in an archived file folder, reached the conclusion that there had originally been 380 pages. Two hundred and ninety-four had arrived, meaning that 86 were missing, or just under a quarter of the manuscript. In fact, as later scholars would show, the original manuscript had nearly 500 pages, and about 200 were missing, or approximately 40 percent of the Crown.

"The president's request is to see if it is possible to salvage pages from those missing from the Crown," Benayahu wrote to an Aleppo rabbi in Buenos Aires. Rumors began to reach Jerusalem: One said pages were stashed "next to the entrance hall" in a certain building known as the House of Olives, near the great synagogue of Aleppo, and Ben-Zvi asked a contact in New York to get someone in Aleppo to check. Another said the pages had been thrown down a dry well in the synagogue's courtyard. The president himself wrote to Aleppo exiles in New York and sent an Israeli diplomat around South America to interview others who might have information about the book.

One exile whom the diplomat tracked down in Rio de Janeiro, a former community treasurer named Yaakov Hazan, gave a perplexing account. He had seen the book after the fire, he claimed, and there were nearly no pages missing at all. "To demonstrate what he meant about the missing part, he pointed at a booklet that was at most five millimeters thick," the diplomat wrote Ben-Zvi from Brazil in November 1961. "He had difficulty estimating the number of pages, but in comparison with the thickness of the Crown, this would be only a few pages, perhaps no more than ten." Ben-Zvi did not believe the treasurer's testimony. A typewritten summary of the diplomat's report survives in the Ben-Zvi Institute's archive, and next to the odd testimony from Rio de Janeiro are the words, "This is an utter error. Close to one hundred pages are missing."

At the same time that the president and his men were tracking the missing pages, there were indications that at least one stone was left unturned. The man who knew precisely in what condition the Crown had been rescued from the synagogue had escaped to Israel years before and was eking out a living making tin dustpans and watering cans in a poor neighborhood of Tel Aviv. This was Bahiyeh's father, Asher Baghdadi. While Aleppo exiles in South American cities were questioned, the old sexton in Tel Aviv never was. He died in 1965.

By that time, Ben-Zvi himself had been dead for two years. With the Crown's indefatigable champion gone, the search petered out.

The Officer and the Scroll

THE LAWYER'S PONTIAC sped through deserted streets toward the old border between Jerusalem's eastern and western sectors, then across it. The rattle of gunfire was audible from the direction of the Old City, where Jordanian troops were holding out. It was June 7, 1967, the third day of the Six-Day War.

The Pontiac was currently in the custody of the Israel Defense Forces, and it had a new driver: Rafi Sutton, originally of Aleppo, last seen just after his arrival on a beach in northern Israel. *Dear soldier,* read a note that the car's owner, an attorney from Haifa, left on the dashboard when the army commandeered his car a few weeks before the outbreak of fighting, *may this vehicle bring you safely to your destination. Please take care of it.*

Sutton, now thirty-five, was an officer in military intelligence. His mission that day, it turned out, would have nearly nothing to do with the war. Instead it would make him a bit player in the saga of a collection of manuscripts far more famous than the one from his own city, and it would serve as an illustration of the importance of ancient texts in the eyes of some in Israel's halls of power—and of the lengths to which they were willing to go to obtain them.

Sutton's sharp mind and native Arabic had helped him work his way up the ranks of the army's intelligence branch, running agents in the Jordanian sector of Jerusalem, compiling dossiers, recruiting informers, and debriefing them in safe houses along the frontier. In the divided Jerusalem of the 1950s, Sutton discovered that useful connections could be made by frequenting Mandelbaum Gate, the crossing point between the two halves of the city, where Israeli and Jordanian officers met for regular talks on the 1949 armistice agreement that had split the city between them. He would come to chat up the Jordanians, changing his Arabic from the Syrian dialect to that of the local Palestinians. One of his early intelligence successes involved a Jordanian official who believed he was passing military secrets to an Arab leader, when in fact the man the officer believed was his liaison with the leader was passing the secrets to Sutton. This network was blown after a few productive years when the Jordanians caught one of Sutton's couriers on his way to a rendezvous along the border. Sutton's deputy around the time of the war, Samuel Nachmias, remembered his commander walking through Jerusalem massaging worry beads like an Arab. The deputy, with the direct style of native-born sabras, would take twenty minutes to debrief an agent, he recalled; Sutton, schooled in the intricate pleasantries of conversation in the Arab world, would take hours. Sutton invariably got better information, Nachmias said. These skills are important to the story of the Aleppo Codex because, much later, Sutton would use them against his own community in an attempt to shed light on the fate of the Crown.

The Syrian Jew was known as a first-rate operator in a business his deputy Nachmias referred to as "sending people to hang themselves" to protect others. More than forty years after the

war, I was in Sutton's apartment when the son of one of his
Palestinian agents from the 1950s called to ask a favor; the old
handler, nearing eighty, was still taking care of his people. Afterward he resumed his story of the conscripted Pontiac, which was
speeding toward east Jerusalem. Columns of Egyptian infantry
and armor were retreating in disarray in Sinai, to the south; in
the north, the air force of Rafi's new country had already obliterated the air force of his old one. Israeli troops now controlled
most of the Jordanian sector of Jerusalem, where Jordan's young
king, Hussein, had attacked two days earlier across the armistice line. Israeli paratroopers were grouped near the Old City's
northeast corner, the same corner where Duke Godfrey's crusaders had encamped nine centuries before, and were preparing
for an assault on the walls. Rafi had been dispatched to link up
with them. He had never been in east Jerusalem, only to the
crossing point at Mandelbaum Gate, but had been running intelligence operations there for so long he believed he knew it
blindfolded. He was speeding in his commandeered car through
the bleak and empty summer streets, exhilarated to be on the
move, when he was abruptly recalled to base and handed new
orders. He was surprised to find a letter signed by the prime
minister and a famous general.

"I awoke in the middle of the night," the general, Yigael
Yadin, wrote later, "and remembered the scroll."

Yadin—soldier, politician, and scholar—was a hero of the independence war and a former chief of staff, an Israeli renaissance
man who embodied a blend of political power and scholarship
in the service of the state. In this he was much like Ben-Zvi. For
these men, the good of Israel, the good of science, and their
own professional prestige were often inextricably muddled; neither hesitated to use the government's power to pursue aims

that often conflated the three. Yadin was famous as an excavator
of the stones and desiccated leather fragments of Israel's ancient
Jewish past, and his image—a fit bald man in shorts, smoking
a pipe, examining a ceramic shard or crouching in a cave—was
familiar to nearly everyone in Israel and to many abroad. He was
behind the excavation of the desert palace at Masada, famous as
the site of a mass suicide of Jewish zealots defying the might of
Rome two thousand years before. The dig was a national project as much as it was an exercise in scholarship. Human remains
found there were declared to be the bodies of Judaean rebels
and buried as Israeli military heroes, their coffins draped in blue
and white flags.

Yadin was also an expert on the Dead Sea Scrolls, which
had come to light two decades earlier after some were found in
Judaean desert caves by Bedouin shepherds and sold to antiquities dealers. The two-thousand-year-old scrolls, thought to have
been written or collected by a Jewish sect that abandoned the
corruption of Jerusalem for the purity of the desert, revealed
much about early Judaism and the roots of Christianity. Yadin's
father, Professor Eliezer Sukenik, had been among the first to
study them and had managed to acquire three from a Jordanian
dealer on November 29, 1947—the day of the partition vote at
Flushing Meadow. There were more scrolls to be obtained, but
Israel's war of independence and the impassable new borders it
created left them out of reach. Sukenik died in 1953, and his son
Yadin—who had taken a new Hebrew family name, in the fashion of those times—continued his investigations.

The scrolls, like Masada, were of more than scholarly importance. "I cannot avoid the feeling," Yadin wrote, "that there is
something symbolic in the discovery of the scrolls and their ac-
quisition at the moment of the creation of the state of Israel. It

is as if these scrolls had been waiting in caves for two thousand years, ever since the destruction of Israel's independence, until the people of Israel had returned to their home and regained their freedom." They were kept at the national museum, in a special building known as the Shrine of the Book, down a dark corridor of rough stone evoking the mouth of a cave, in a circular chamber with the aura of a chapel.

In 1960, seven years before the outbreak of the Six-Day War, Yadin received a letter from a Virginia clergyman offering him a chance to buy another of the Dead Sea Scrolls. The man, whom Yadin referred to in his writings as Mr. Z, sent the Israeli a sample of the merchandise, the remainder of which he said was held by a Jordanian dealer in the West Bank. "And true enough," wrote Yadin, "the envelope contained a fragment of the scroll wrapped in the tinfoil of a cigarette package and set between two pieces of cardboard. The back of the fragment was reinforced with a scrap of a British postal stamp and gummed paper." Yadin judged it to be authentic, and they settled on a price: $130,000. Yadin gave the middleman $1,500 to make the trip to Jordan, plus a $10,000 advance. The middleman Mr. Z then wrote to say that the West Bank dealer now wanted $200,000. "This is the most important discovery in history. Without a doubt this is the book of the beginnings, 'genesis,' " he wrote. The dealer "puts his life on this!" he went on. "The piece you have is the key. Don't lose it." Mr. Z dispatched one more letter in the spring of 1962 before disappearing for good, along with the advance. "From time to time I would check the listings from Jordan to see if it was mentioned," Yadin wrote, referring to the enigmatic scroll, "but no trace of it ever appeared." Like Ben-Zvi, Yadin did not forget, and he, too, would be granted his wish in the end.

When war loomed in 1967, Yadin was called away from his

scholarly pursuits to serve as special military adviser to the prime minister, Levi Eshkol. Fighting, however, was not the only thing on his mind. On the first day of battle, the Jordanians unleashed an artillery barrage on west Jerusalem, and one shell, Yadin noted, just barely missed the Shrine of the Book. That meant the shell had also barely missed Israel's parliament, which sits next to the scrolls' building, but that fact seems to have made less of an impression. When the Israelis fought their way close to the Old City, the army's deputy chief of operations contacted Yadin. The officer was worried that the nearby Rockefeller Museum, which had its own Dead Sea Scrolls collection, might be damaged. Yadin had two Hebrew University professors dispatched in an armored half-track to the museum under artillery fire to ensure the scroll fragments were safe.

With Israeli troops pushing into the West Bank, Yadin remembered the dubious middleman Mr. Z and the scroll and realized that the West Bank dealer was now under Israel's jurisdiction. As Ben-Zvi had done in his quest to acquire the Crown, Yadin went right to the top. "With the approval of the Prime Minister," he wrote, "the General Staff placed a lieutenant colonel of the Military Intelligence at my disposal." It is worth taking a moment to dwell on this sentence: at the height of a war that Israelis saw as a fight for national survival, with thousands of infantrymen, tank crewmen, and pilots from Israel and three of its neighbors dying on the battlefield, the prime minister of Israel spent time, even if it was only a minute or two, dealing with Yadin's book.

The lieutenant colonel was Rafi's commander. The letter Rafi received after being summoned to base in his Pontiac instructed the Jerusalem section of military intelligence—this was Rafi's outfit—to send officers into east Jerusalem and apprehend a man who was in possession of one or more of the Dead Sea Scrolls.

The man was identified only as "Dino." The mission was to be executed immediately, before the fact of the Israeli conquest had sunk in and the man could escape or conceal the scrolls. Rafi remembered still being at headquarters when the paratroopers in the Old City reported that the Temple Mount and the Western Wall had fallen and were in Israeli hands.

Along with the lieutenant colonel, Rafi got back in the Pontiac and, accompanied by another commandeered civilian vehicle, sped back toward Mandelbaum Gate. By now, Jews were thronging the streets, elated at the capture of the Western Wall and determined to get there even though the fighting had not yet subsided. A harried soldier was trying to keep the crowds at bay. Rafi's team turned back and made its way into east Jerusalem through a circuitous and more dangerous route. He found the main commercial thoroughfare of the formerly Jordanian sector, Saladin Street, lined with burnt-out cars and trucks. They went south until they reached the Damascus Gate, leading into the Old City, where Rafi found two paratroop sergeants keeping watch over several hundred Arab men standing with their faces to the stones of the Ottoman wall, their hands up. The men appeared to be Jordanian soldiers or policemen. One, in a neat khaki uniform, caught Rafi's eye. Rafi had the man taken from the lineup and brought to the Pontiac. The man was terrified, and Rafi—sifting coldly in his mind through a list of ways to approach potential sources of information—decided to be friendly, greeting him in the dialect of Jerusalem Palestinians. The man's name was Yunis, and he had been a policeman in the service of the Jordanians.

We're looking for a man called Dino, Rafi said, suggesting that information would be repaid with permission to go home.

Never heard of him, Yunis answered, sitting nervously in the car's leather passenger seat. He asked if Rafi knew the man's profession.

He sells antiquities, Rafi said.

You're looking for Kando, the policeman replied. He took Rafi to an antique store nearby with a sign in Arabic and English. It was, not surprisingly, closed. The policeman said the dealer lived in Bethlehem, which had just fallen to the Israelis, so Rafi sped down the thin strip of asphalt leading south from Jerusalem into the newly conquered territory of the West Bank, past the small dome of Rachel's Tomb, across dry, marbled hills of brown and white. Helmeted Israeli soldiers at a checkpoint stopped them outside Bethlehem—there were still pockets of resistance inside, they said—but soon the Pontiac was allowed to pass. Rafi followed the policeman's directions to a neighborhood not far from the Church of the Nativity and stopped. Yunis pointed to the house. The man who opened the door was about seventy and had, in Rafi's recollection, a friendly face and clever eyes.

We've come to drink a cup of coffee with you, Rafi said.

Tfadalu, said the man, faced with his city's new masters: Come in. The dealer known as Kando—an Assyrian Christian and a cobbler by trade, whose real name was Khalil Iskander Shahin—was joined by his adult son.

We know you have in your possession some of the hidden scrolls of Qumran, Rafi said, and as representatives of the government of Israel we are interested in receiving them in return for full payment.

The dealer denied it. Over the next hour, Rafi tried the various techniques in his repertoire: he tried friendly, and implicitly threatening, and then overtly threatening. Kando would not budge.

Get dressed and come with me, Rafi said, his patience exhausted, and, citing martial law, he placed both the man and his son under arrest, bringing them out to the Pontiac as the women of the house wailed.

In Jerusalem the interrogators got nowhere: the man and his son knew nothing of any Dead Sea Scrolls. With their bag of tricks nearly exhausted, the interrogators tried an old one: Kando, they told his son, had just broken under questioning and had revealed that he did have the scrolls, and the Israelis were already on their way to Bethlehem to pick them up. The son still did not break, and the interrogators put him in a cell with his father, who was already asleep, and left them alone. The night passed.

How could you have told the Jews about the scrolls? the dealer's son said when they woke up.

Don't be stupid, Kando said. I revealed nothing.

The Israelis then entered the cell, Rafi remembered, took Kando to another room, and replayed the conversation on tape. The dealer betrayed no emotion. He would give them the scrolls on two conditions, he said, as if this had been the plan all along. The government of Israel must pay him full price, and he would not be identified as having collaborated. The Israelis agreed—he would eventually be paid $105,000—and the scroll-seeking convoy sped back toward Bethlehem.

In his bedroom, Kando started at the doorframe and walked forward, counting floor tiles. Then he stopped, turned right, and counted several more. He took off one of his shoes, stooped down, placed it across two tiles, walked over to a closet, and took out a toilet plunger. He stuck it to the tiles and pulled. Underneath the floor, Rafi saw a little niche lined with straw. Inside was a shoe box; photographs show one that is yellow, white, and red with the word *Bata* on the lid. Inside the box

Israeli intelligence officers take possession of the Temple Scroll in
Bethlehem. From left to right: Rafi Sutton; Kando; Rafi's commander,
Shmuel Goren; and Rafi's deputy, Samuel Nachmias.

was an ordinary white towel, and under the towel, wrapped in
cellophane, was an ancient parchment scroll. It would later be
identified as the Temple Scroll, one of the most important of
the Dead Sea collection. Other scroll fragments were later discovered behind family photos in the dealer's home and in an old
box of Karel I Elegant cigars.

On the evening of Thursday, June 8, the ministers of Israel's cabinet convened to decide whether to launch an assault
against Syrian forces in the Golan Heights. The defense minister, Moshe Dayan, was opposed. The argument, Yadin wrote,
"became heated." Dayan eventually came around, and the next
day Israeli troops would be sent into battle on the Heights. In
the middle of the meeting, Yadin was called out. "I waited until
I had heard the major arguments on both sides, offered my own

judgment, and then left quietly," he wrote. Outside he found a lieutenant colonel holding a Bata shoe box.

"Well, I don't know," the officer said. "I hope this was the scroll you meant."

THE TEMPLE SCROLL eventually joined the other Dead Sea manuscripts in the Shrine of the Book at the national museum, where they enjoyed temperature and humidity controls and stringent security measures. The story of the scrolls was exciting, and they were remnants of a period of Jewish history that Israel was very much interested in remembering, because it served to emphasize the new state's ties to the land and self-image in the present. The scrolls riveted the world's attention and drew thousands of visitors.

At the same time, the Crown of Aleppo was decaying in a filing cabinet.

20

Exodus

OF ALL THE scenarios that might have befallen the codex after the failed attempts to obtain it, the operation to extract it from Syria, and the charged legal battle over its ownership, perhaps the most unlikely one had befallen the book: it had been quickly and almost completely forgotten.

The Aleppo Jews, now spread across the world, were busy building new communities; Aleppo was history, and the book was no longer theirs to care for. President Ben-Zvi had died in 1963. The trustees would not allow the manuscript to be exhibited or copied, and the university scholars studying it continued to keep it to themselves. The unpleasant details of the story seem to have convinced those involved that it would be best simply not to tell it, and the lie that the Aleppo Jews had given their book to the state became accepted as truth outside the small circle of people who knew the real story, to the extent that anyone gave it any thought at all. The search for the missing pages, driven by Ben-Zvi, had been called off, with a few exceptions—one of them particularly unusual, I discovered—and the uncomplicated belief in their loss in the synagogue fire had come to be largely accepted as fact.

Like the Dead Sea Scrolls, the Crown was an ancient manuscript of immense value, but it had no connection to Jewish sovereignty in the land of Israel two millennia ago—a period to which the new state explicitly linked itself, glossing over the intervening centuries—and so it was of less interest to the government and the general public. Feelings were far more ambivalent about the Crown's world, that of the Jews of Islam, which was quickly vanishing, mourned by few besides the refugees themselves. The codex represented nothing that most people seemed inclined to remember, and though it, too, had an exciting story, it was not one that the people who knew it wanted to recount.

One of the state's justifications for holding the Crown was that only academic scholars could properly care for it. The manner in which the Ben-Zvi Institute tended to its hard-won manuscript is evident from letters I found in its own archive and that of Hebrew University, of which the institute is a part. After work hours ended at the university at two in the afternoon, "there is of course no one guarding the Crown, which is kept only behind locked doors," scholars studying the Crown wrote to the university's president in 1963. Not much had changed by 1971, when two of the scholars with access to the manuscript wrote another letter. "The Crown of Aleppo is kept today in a regular locked office cabinet in one of the rooms of the Ben-Zvi Institute at Hebrew University, wrapped in fabric," they wrote. Years of this treatment had "damaged the remains of this precious manuscript, and today there are places in the manuscript that are not legible, though they were several years ago." The same year, the head of the conservation labs at Israel's national museum was given special permission to view the manuscript. "I found," he informed a meeting of the Crown trustees, "that photographs taken ten years ago show more than the original does today."

The first evidence of a visit from outside conservators comes from 1970, twelve years after the Crown arrived in Israel. "It would seem," the two experts informed the institute, "that there have been years of neglect."

Four years after that report, and three years after the scholars' warning that the book was being ruined, the Ben-Zvi Institute, the manuscript's trustees, and scholars at Hebrew University were still arguing about whether to transfer the book across town to the vaults of the national library, where it would enjoy adequate conditions for the first time. The proposal included a complicated legal agreement—one inspired by the extraterritorial arrangements governing foreign embassies—that would transform the corner of the national library that became home to the Crown to a zone that was technically under the jurisdiction of the Ben-Zvi Institute.

At a meeting of the institute's directorate, the late president's elderly widow, Rachel Yanait Ben-Zvi, rebuffed the implication that the institute had been neglectful in its handling of the manuscript and said they should not be "hasty" in moving it. She demanded that the president of Hebrew University "visit the Crown and see that we made sure there was maximum security." Her comments are preserved in a typed transcript of the meeting kept in the archive at the Ben-Zvi Institute. Referring with sarcasm to a university professor who was urging that the book be moved to the national library, she suggested he was doing so because this would "be easier for his work."

"The institute has value with the Crown in its possession," the president's widow insisted, inadvertently channeling the Aleppo rabbis of long ago. "This is the essence of the institute and its prestige."

In Aleppo, the community that had once guarded the Crown had been reduced by those years to several hundred people. In 1972, Moshe Cohen's turn came to leave. Cohen was from the family of the Crown's last keepers in Aleppo: he was the great-nephew of the late Ibrahim Effendi Cohen and the son of Edmond Cohen, the man who had removed the treasure from its hiding place in the fall of 1957.

Cohen's parents were among the few well-off Jews still in the city. He had been raised by an Armenian nanny and educated at a Catholic private school, where he and his Jewish friends passed around a contraband French copy of *Exodus,* the best-selling Zionist fantasy from America, which a foreign acquaintance had smuggled into Syria. In 1972, Cohen was a student at the University of Aleppo, majoring in Arabic literature; Jews were largely barred from a list of other subjects he would have preferred, including medicine and pharmacology.

At about this time, Cohen traveled to Damascus with his father for a memorial service for a recently deceased kabbalist rabbi. The young Cohen delivered a speech in literary Arabic to an audience in the synagogue that included, inevitably, several members of the *mukhabarat,* the secret police. Not long afterward, he was summoned to the top floor of the *mukhabarat's* headquarters in Aleppo. He entered the well-appointed room of an officer whose epaulets indicated high rank.

Thank you for accepting our invitation, the officer said, smiling.

Cohen said he had been summoned, not invited.

Who forced you to come? I'll punish him. I asked them to invite you with respect, said the officer.

These were the usual games of the *mukhabarat.*

Listen, the officer said. I see that you are an educated person, that you are on the honor roll at university, and that you spoke in Damascus at the synagogue. We liked your speech very much.

Then the officer dispensed with the pleasantries: The government wanted Cohen to begin doing radio broadcasts once a week. Both of them knew he meant that the regime wanted a Jew willing to serve as a propaganda mouthpiece.

General, Cohen said, I might be good at literature and eulogies for rabbis and academic studies, but this is politics. I don't understand politics.

That's not a problem, the officer replied, still friendly. We'll prepare material for you, and you'll speak, because you have a good voice for radio.

Cohen equivocated some more, and the officer's temperament became progressively less sunny. You're making a laughingstock of us, he growled. Cohen understood that he was now officially in trouble. His father pulled a few strings with the authorities, buying him a reprieve, but this was temporary. Cohen realized he had to get out.

The route was as risky as it had always been. Escapees were entirely at the mercy of smugglers, and some had vanished on the way. Others had been turned over to the authorities. Two years later, in 1974, four Jewish girls, three of them sisters, would be raped and murdered as they tried to escape, their bodies thrown in a cave.

One evening, Cohen went to a prearranged meeting point amid the bustle of the clubs on Baron Street, near the Cinéma Roxy. He was accompanied by a close friend, Reuven Dayo, and a girl whose name he would not reveal. When he recounted this story to me, he left other names and details of his story purposely vague; nearly thirty years later, he retained the instincts of someone raised with the *mukhabarat* listening. Parked amid the taxis along the curb was the smuggler's black Mercedes. Pretend you're asleep, the smuggler told them as they sped out of Aleppo. They did. This was so they would not have to speak if the car was stopped, since the Jews' Arabic accents, like those of

Christians and upper-class Muslims, replaced the throaty *qah* of most Syrians with a more refined glottal stop, *ah,* which would draw attention. The Mercedes took them south, finally stopping around midnight. Cohen saw barbed wire and what appeared to be an army camp and concluded they were at a border crossing. The smuggler opened the car door and disappeared. A few minutes later he returned with two armed and jumpy soldiers who gave the passengers back their identity cards. This was odd, as they had not given the cards in the first place. Cohen was so frightened that he stuffed the card into his pocket without looking to see whose name and photograph appeared on it. They drove for another hour, until he saw the outskirts of a city. This was Beirut. The smuggler stopped at a house, tapped out some kind of rhythm on the door, stepped back, watched it open, saw his three charges ushered inside, and disappeared.

The three ate breakfast. Cohen took off his extra layers of clothes, which were the only things he had brought from Aleppo, other than $200 in cash and the honor roll certificate he had snatched from the wall at the university the night before. That day they were split among different families. Lebanon was still enjoying the heady years before its colorful jumble of ethnicities descended into the nightmare of civil war, and Cohen's host family took him skiing in the hills, to the shops on Hamra Street, to the casino. After a few days of this, he received a phone call.

Walk down Hamra Street, the voice said, then down to the seaside promenade. Carry today's edition of *L'Orient–Le Jour* under your arm.

On the promenade, Cohen met Reuven and the girl, and they walked down the beach until they reached a small, ramshackle building. Inside were three rooms furnished with old beds and dressers. They were greeted by a number of men who spoke with musical Lebanese accents and wore jackets that Cohen thought concealed weapons. Cohen did not know if he was a guest or a captive, and when he tried to inquire who the men were and what they planned to do with them, he was instructed to shut up. Night fell. A small fishing boat arrived on the beach, piloted by a man in an Australian bush hat. With the escapees and the Lebanese men onboard, the boat motored back out into the Mediterranean. Cohen, who had seen the sea for the first time in his life only days before, was terrified, and to keep his spirits up he pretended he was not a scared kid from an Arab city but the Zionist poster boy Ari Ben-Canaan, the Paul Newman character from the movie version of *Exodus*.

This went on for more than an hour, the small boat cutting through the dark Mediterranean waves, the passengers' backs to the lights of the Beirut shoreline and their faces to the open sea, the Lebanese men saying nothing. These men were smugglers like the ones who had taken the Jews who vanished, Cohen began to think. They had already been paid, and now they would dump their cargo in the sea. First they would rape the girl. Or perhaps this was a trap: Syrian boats would pick them up and take them to prison back home.

One of the men produced a flashlight, pointed it out to sea, and began flicking it on and off. There was no response, just blackness and the weak glimmer of the beam reflecting off the water, vanishing and reappearing. Cohen lost hope. A light blinked back from some distance away. The man in the Australian hat cut the engine, and the boat bobbed in silence as a black silhouette hove into view. Cohen, who had never seen a warship except in photographs, first thought he might be looking at a submarine. The ship drew alongside the fishing boat, dwarfing it, and a rope ladder unfurled down the hull.

Up, one of the Lebanese men ordered.

Almost paralyzed with apprehension, Cohen watched Reuven grip the ladder and begin to climb out of the boat. When his friend was halfway up, he began climbing himself.

The first thing Reuven saw when his head peeked over the hull was a metal box mounted on a wall; later he would understand that it was a first-aid kit. A tiny lightbulb illuminated a red star with six points. He turned back down the ladder to Cohen and said, They're Jews.

PART FIVE

Aspergillus

WITH COW INTESTINES, tweezers, microscopes, air guns, and gelatin, Michael Maggen wages war against rot and age, an endless defensive action meant to save the paper and parchment of old books. I found Maggen standing by a few humidifiers that emitted a cold mist into air tinged with the scent of chemicals, peering through a microscope, and using goldbeater's skin—a transparent tissue from a cow's digestive tract, so named because it has long been used as a film in the production of gold leaf—to repair minute tears in a page with a square of brilliant blue and four golden Hebrew letters taken from an exquisite fifteenth-century copy of Maimonides's *Mishneh Torah*. It was in this laboratory at Israel's national museum in Jerusalem that a layer of myth obscuring the truth about the codex was removed.

The unadorned pages of the Crown were enough to intimidate the young Maggen when the manuscript arrived in a Brink's truck one day in 1986, when restoration work finally began. A museum official scrawled a makeshift receipt on a piece of paper and handed it to the man who brought the book from the Ben-Zvi Institute: "I have received the Crown of Aleppo." Maggen was thirty-six, with a red beard and a new degree from Italy. He had treated manuscripts from the eighteenth century, and even from the seventeenth, but never anything like this. He felt, he recalled, "like a pilot who is told, 'Next week you're flying to the moon.'"

The ancient knowledge contained in a book is of little consequence to Maggen when he works. He sees parts of animals and plants, fibers, fats, and sugars, in various arrangements and states of decay, and deploys different parts of animals and plants to repair the damage. Looking at the Crown, he saw parchment folios made from the skin of cows or goats—the expert work of the Tiberias leatherworkers a millennium before had made it impossible to tell which—covered in ink markings.

First he surveyed the manuscript page by page, marking each rip, smudge, and fold on a facsimile. This took six months. Rips were represented by green lines. Black lines indicated smudges from ash. In some places there were black stains, and in others, entire chunks of pages were missing. This was to be expected. More surprising, perhaps, were the rectangular glue marks that could only have been left by an adhesive from the 1950s or later and that informed Maggen's expert eye that someone under the auspices of the Ben-Zvi Institute had tried to mend one of the world's most precious manuscripts with Scotch tape.

The difference between the sides of the parchment was clear: the hair side, which had been covered with the fur of tenth-century livestock, was hardier, while the flesh side was more susceptible to damage. The Tiberias scribe had used iron gall ink of the type developed in Rome, not the kind used in earlier books like the Dead Sea Scrolls, which was made by mixing ash with something sticky, like honey or sap, and could easily be erased. Iron gall ink could not, at least not without leaving telltale scrape marks, a key advantage for contracts or holy texts, which were meant to be unalterable. But the ink was also acidic, and in some places it had eaten through the parchment and caused letters to disappear.

Maggen and his team removed a clumsy binding that had been attached to the book after its arrival in Israel, cleaned the glue off the spine, and undid the threads holding the thirty-two folios together. To remove centuries of accumulated grease that had become attached to the pages, Maggen used the substance he found to be most effective: his own saliva. He wet cotton swabs in his mouth, then rolled them gently on the pages until the parchment was clean. One day, in the midst of the restoration, one of Israel's chief rabbis paid a visit to see how work was coming along. With some trepidation, Maggen told him how he was cleaning the pages. "Imagine me going up to the chief rabbi and saying, 'Listen, I'm spitting on your manuscript, the one Maimonides used to study,'" Maggen told me. The rabbi praised his work and wished him a long life. When the pages were clean, the museum's restoration team sprayed them with a gelatin mist to stabilize the brittle ink, then moistened each one to relax the fibers of the parchment. After that, the pages were stretched, dried, and flattened. The restoration project went on for six years.

Maggen was puzzled by one aspect of the codex: the purplish marks on the damaged lower corners of the pages, traces of the flames that had consumed much of the book. It was not just common wisdom that had identified these as burn marks; previous experts had believed the same. "Microscopic and microchemical methods have found no biotic agent that caused the books to change color or the brittle nature of the corners of the Crown," one specialist wrote after examining the book sixteen years before. "The damage is without a doubt *chemical* and was the result of hydrolysis of collagen when the fire was extinguished." Maggen, however, thought the marks looked strange. Fire warps, blackens, and hardens parchment, but the damaged corners of the Crown were soft and brittle.

Maggen collected a few purplish corner fragments and sent them across town to the clinical microbiology lab on the second floor of the Hadassah Medical Center. The head of the hospital's mycology lab, Izhack Polacheck, treating the one-thousand-year-old pieces of parchment like infected human skin obtained in a biopsy, placed the fragments in an alkaline solution that melted the parchment's proteins and then examined the remains under a phase-contrast microscope. Across the globe, in Albany, New York, two scientists then ran fluorescence tests on the same fragments. These were methods unavailable to the earlier experts who had examined the Crown. The results were sent to the museum.

In his office off the restoration lab, Maggen looked at the photographs taken of the microscope slides. They showed sausage-like structures with dark dividers in the middle. The scientific explanation: "Specific fluorescent-antibody staining identifies the filaments as *Aspergillus* hyphae." Maggen remembered actually leaping from his chair.

The subsequent headline in the international scientific journal *Nature* read, FUNGI NOT FIRE DAMAGED ALEPPO CODEX. The Crown, read the article, "was damaged by a fungus of the genus *Aspergillus*, rather than by fire as was previously assumed." The "burn marks" were not burn marks at all.

The widely circulated stories of the Crown's rescue from the flames, combined with the marks on the corners of the parchment, had helped create the conviction that the manuscript had been burned. Conveniently, this account also explained why so much of it was gone. But nothing Maggen saw in six years of studying the manuscript suggested it was harmed by fire in the 1947 riot. The damage was a fungus, one that had taken hold, the scientists theorized, on the corner of the leaves that would have been touched repeatedly with saliva from fingers licked as readers turned the page. (If this theory was true, human saliva had helped to both damage and repair the Crown.)

Simple stories tend to be hard to kill, and the myth that fire consumed part of the Crown lives on even today. A *Jerusalem Post* article from 2010, for example, referred to the "parts of the once complete manuscript lost in a fire set by Syrian rioters in Aleppo on the eve of Israel's establishment." Other such references still crop up with some frequency.

Maggen's discovery, though, was not just a minor alteration of the manuscript's history. It resurrected a question to which nearly no one had paid any serious thought in decades. If the two hundred missing pages of the Crown had not been consumed by fire, then where were they?

Brooklyn

THE ASSUMPTION THAT the Crown's missing pieces had been burned gave way to a new theory that changed the method, but not the time, of the pages' disappearance. The pages, it was now said, were taken by Aleppo Jews during or immediately after the riot. This belief remains in force today, and at first it largely guided my own research, when most of what I knew still came from the Ben-Zvi Institute. "The key to finding the pages," I wrote in my first article about the manuscript in 2008, lies with "Jews originating in Aleppo, Syria, where the manuscript resided in a synagogue's iron chest for centuries." Past efforts to locate them "came up against a wall of silence in the Aleppo community." This idea dates to the 1980s, when two Crown fragments surfaced, four decades after the riot in Aleppo, among the brick homes and kosher pizzerias of Brooklyn.

The first piece materialized with a man named Leon Tawil. When I tracked Tawil down in the Aleppo Jews' New York colony, I found a storyteller in possession of a sarcastic sense of humor that seemed only mildly marred by the broken hip that had imprisoned him in his armchair. He was looking out at the traffic going up and down Ocean Parkway.

In 1981, a woman brought an old parchment leaf to a scholar at Israel's national library in Jerusalem. It came, she said, from her aunt in Brooklyn, who was originally from Aleppo. One side began as follows:

and are incorporated into the laments. The other events of Josiah's reign and his faithful deeds, in accord with the teachings of the Lord, and his acts, early and late, are recorded in the book of the kings of Israel and Judah.

The text, from the book of Chronicles, described the meddling of two ancient superpowers, Egypt and Babylon, in the politics of the little land sandwiched between them where people worshipped one God, or were, at least, supposed to. The page went on to recount a string of kings whose behavior was "displeasing to the Lord," who then unleashed a catastrophe in the form of Babylonian armies that slaughtered old men and virgins and condemned the survivors to exile. The time of the first temple in Jerusalem was coming to a close. The page ended as it began, in midsentence:

They burned the house of God and tore down the wall of Jerusalem, burned down all of its mansions, and consigned all of its precious objects

The concluding words of the verse are *to destruction*. The writing was that of the scribe Ben-Buya'a; the notes across the top and down the margins were those of Ben-Asher. In one corner of the page was the telltale purplish "burn" mark. Thirty-four years after the riot in Aleppo, the first missing piece of the Crown had reappeared. It sent a frisson of excitement through the Aleppo Codex Underground.

Leon Tawil was fifteen years old when he found the page, and seventy-eight when I found him. Sitting in his living room, eating nuts and apricots, he returned to Aleppo and to late 1947.

The young Tawil—who was not related to Moshe Tawil, the chief rabbi—was a Sherlock Holmes enthusiast and a collector of British gold sovereigns, which he kept in a secret drawer in his room. He spent hours wandering around Aleppo on foot, beginning at his home in the Jamiliyeh neighborhood and ending up in the markets of the Old City. Every year on the Day of Atonement his father took him to the great synagogue, where he remembered dark rooms and one small grotto. "You walk in. It's very dark, lit up by the candles that people brought, by the oil, and right next to it, a big safe. What's in it?" He paused for dramatic effect: "The *Crown*," he breathed, his eyes widening.

When Aleppo erupted, the rioters stalking his neighborhood climbed the outer staircase of the family's three-story building, but before the men could reach the Tawils' apartment, a Muslim neighbor told them there were no Jews inside. The men turned back. That night, Leon's mother sent him to sleep at the home of the Armenian maid. By the next afternoon the rage seemed to have dissipated, and the city felt bleary and exhausted. He set out toward the Old City. Muslim boys, like Jewish boys, wore short pants until they turned sixteen, but the Muslim shorts were longer, so when Tawil left the Jewish area he pulled his own shorts lower so that he wouldn't stand out. He passed the Cinéma Roxy, and then a Jewish-owned clothing store that had been gutted by the looters. He passed the *manzul*, the brothel—a grin accompanied this memory—and followed the alleys to the synagogue. The gate was open.

Inside, everything under the arched ceilings was "shadowy from the flame," he remembered. There were a few other people around, Jews who had also heard of the synagogue's destruction and had come to see for themselves. They were clicking their tongues and shaking their heads. No one paid much attention to him. The walls of books that he remembered from the visits with his father were now bare, and in the courtyard he saw a heap of parchment a yard high. "Right next to it I saw a paper, and I picked it up and put it in my pocket," he said.

Tawil knew only that it was a page from an old Hebrew book. At home, his father told him it must be from the Crown of Aleppo and began reading the passages. This tells of cities burning, of an evil time like this one, the elder Tawil told his son, and handed the page back. Adults in Aleppo were preoccupied with other matters.

Two years later, Leon escaped to Lebanon, and in 1950 he stood on the deck of an ocean liner with his family and watched the Statue of Liberty glide by. When they joined the other Aleppo Jews in Brooklyn, the Tawils stayed with Leon's aunt, Mary Hedaya. Leon showed her his page, and she kept it. Leon did not think much about it after that.

When I met Mary Hedaya's daughter and son-in-law, Renee and Isadore Shamah, in an apartment high above the doormen and dog-walking women on Central Park South, Isadore remembered that Mary hid the page in a cupboard between two stiff panels, wrapped in fabric. It was her talisman, he said. Hedaya had died and her daughter did not remember much. She had been vaguely aware of the page's presence in their home but wasn't sure if her mother knew how many people were looking for it or that it was valuable at all. To an American kid it must have seemed like an inexplicable and slightly embarrassing relic of some unknowable world.

The page remained in Mary Hedaya's home for three decades. Her daughter did not remember why she decided to send it to Jerusalem; according to one account, Hedaya was caring for a sick relative when a visiting rabbi counseled her that the page was bringing bad luck and should be sent to join the rest of the Crown. Hedaya gave the page to her niece, who brought it to the national library. The page completed the book of Chronicles and brought the number of Crown pages in Jerusalem to 295. At this time the fire theory was widely accepted, but still some thought that if there was one page in Brooklyn, there might well be more.

Six years later, in 1987, Steve Shalom, one of the prominent leaders of the Aleppo Jews in New York,* gave the Ben-Zvi Institute a rare and surprising piece of information: he knew someone who kept a piece of the codex in his pocket. He produced a name and a phone number. Not long afterward, the institute dispatched one of its staffers, Dallas-born Michael Glatzer, to New York. After landing at John F. Kennedy International Airport, the envoy from Jerusalem dialed the number Shalom had provided. Samuel Sabbagh answered the phone.

The visitor found Sabbagh, a thin man in his seventies, at a Brooklyn community center amid other old Syrian Jews playing cards and waiting for lunch. Sabbagh pulled out his wallet and removed a plastic slip a bit bigger than a credit card. Inside was a mangled piece of parchment. On one side were the words

and they piled them up in heaps and the land stank

This was from the book of Exodus. After the Nile ran red with blood, Moses's brother Aaron raised his staff again, and this time frogs descended on Egypt. When Pharaoh appeared to relent, Moses asked God to stop. *And God did according to the word of Moses,* the text tells us, *and the frogs died out of the houses*

* Steve Shalom's father was Isaac Shalom, President Ben-Zvi's old New York contact from the 1950s.

*and yards and fields, and they piled them up in heaps and the land
stank.*

On the other side were these words:

upon your servants and upon your people and into your
homes

The frogs did not convince Pharaoh to release the Israelites,
and neither did the lice he sent next. Go to Pharaoh again, God
told Moses, and say, *If you will not let my people go, I will send
swarms of insects upon you and upon your servants and upon your
people and into your homes, and all the houses of Egypt will be full
of swarms of insects and also the ground upon which they stand.*

After the fire, Sabbagh told the visitor, he set out toward the
great synagogue in old Aleppo. He found the fragment on the
floor and took it.

He would not part with the fragment for any sum of money,
Sabbagh said: it had protected him for years in his new home
and helped him survive open-heart surgery. Sabbagh did let
the visitor take the fragment to the community center's office,
where there was a Xerox machine. Using the photocopies, a researcher back in Israel judged the fragment to be genuine. The
second missing fragment of the Crown had surfaced.

Sabbagh, true to his word, did not give it up as long as he
lived. Twenty years later, after his death, his family sent the piece
to Jerusalem. "There were all sorts of miraculous properties attached to the piece," his daughter, Rachel Magen, told me. "My
father was a believing man. He held it in his hand and he knew
its worth—it had spiritual value." Though the Sabbaghs, she
said, "are not people who keep magic amulets," her father nonetheless "believed it protected him."

The Aleppo Jews had always thought the codex safeguarded

them. This belief, it seemed, had been transferred to pieces of the book that were circulating in the exile communities. When the fire story was disproved by the Israel Museum restorer, the scholars on the trail of the Crown decided that other fragments, pages, or larger sections of the manuscript were being held by Aleppo Jews. If two pieces had surfaced within a few years of each other between the Atlantic and the East River, the thinking went, surely more would turn up—if not in Brooklyn, then in São Paulo, Panama City, or another of the Aleppo Jews' international outposts. And yet none did.

ONE OTHER ATTEMPT to solve the mystery of the missing pages in those years deserves to be told, its failure notwithstanding.

On June 4, 1978, the professor then in charge of the Ben-Zvi Institute posted a letter to Zurich, addressed to a certain Gavriel Gavrieli.

> I am sending you maps of south Lebanon as per the request from Ms. Miriam Gromb. I would be grateful if you kept the maps to yourself and then returned them to us as quickly as possible because of their classified nature.

Among the rumors about the fate of the missing pieces was one suggesting that refugees fleeing Aleppo had buried them in southern Lebanon en route to Israel. Such a possibility, it appears, was behind this unusual letter. The maps were not intended for an intelligence expert or a diplomat, but for an expert in the art of divining secrets using a pendulum: a psychic. The professor's contacts in Switzerland, Gavrieli and Gromb, arranged the session with the man, who is not named in the correspondence.

Miriam Gromb posted a reply from Zurich on June 15. The psychic had come the day before, she wrote, and used the classified military maps sent by the institute. The missing pages could be found next to the village of Ein Ata in south Lebanon, near the intersection of latitudinal line 315 and longitudinal line 154 on the military grid, possibly "in a nearby grove of trees" or "down the hill."

"I paid him fifty francs," Gromb wrote, adding that it was "not worth risking human lives for this matter." This was stating the obvious: Lebanon was an enemy country, and the areas close to the border with Israel were controlled by the Palestinian guerrillas of Fatah and its various armed affiliates. There is no indication that anything was done with the information at first. In 1982, however, Israel invaded Lebanon and took over a swath of land close to the border. The occupied area, which Israel called the "security zone," included Ein Ata.

In 1985, a new professor heading the institute sent a letter to a friend in northern Israel.

Subject: Locating missing pages from the "Crown of Aleppo" in the security zone

We have information indicating there is a certain possibility that additional pages from the Crown of Aleppo are located in the security zone next to the village of Ein Ata. We will send you the exact locations of the possible sites in the next few days. These pages have great importance to the study of Bible traditions and to many other subjects.

Please do what you can in order to convince IDF commanders in the area to look for these pages. We will address a letter to the relevant authorities at the right time.

The professor's friend contacted an officer in the military's Northern Command and even showed him the maps with the locations pinpointed by the psychic, but army forces were unable to help. The letters documenting this episode were duly archived by the Ben-Zvi Institute.

23

The Fog Grows

PERPLEXED BY ASPECTS of the story that seemed more and more peculiar, I returned on more than one occasion to the only book that had existed on the subject of the Crown at the time I embarked on my own investigation: *The Crown,* a Hebrew volume published in 1987 by the Ben-Zvi Institute. Each time I became more confused.

I first began reading the book expecting to find a clear account of what had befallen the Crown after 1947 and of how it had reached Israel. This was a reasonable thing to expect: behind the book was the institute that was the Crown's custodian and that held all the relevant documentation. I did not find what I was looking for. Though ostensibly aimed at a general audience, the book opened with an almost impenetrable discussion of a debate among scholars over an obscure point related to the Crown's connection to Maimonides, and a casual reader would find it hard to survive the first twenty pages. The book was exacting, often tedious, in its attention to matters relating to the Crown's history before 1947, and markedly vague and hurried in its attention to everything thereafter. The examination of the debate over Maimonides, for example, stretched over six pages. A description of how the book traveled from Aleppo to Israel lasted two sentences:

In the month of Elul 5717 the Crown left Syria for Turkey. In
the month of Shvat 5718 it reached Jerusalem.*

Elsewhere the story is summed up as follows:

In the riots in Aleppo's Jewish neighborhoods in December
1947, after the United Nations declaration of the founding of
a Jewish state in the land of Israel, riots that centered on the
burning of synagogues, the Crown was damaged. Most of it
survived in the hands of members of the community and was
hidden for about ten years in various places. In the year 5717
(1957) the rabbis Moshe Tawil and Shlomo Zaafrani gave it to
Mordechai ben Ezra Faham, who took it secretly to Turkey.
From there he brought it on January 23, 1958, to Jerusalem,
and it came full circle.

This is the official version with which we are familiar, and the
closest thing to a coherent narrative the book provided. It
erased the role of Shragai, the immigration chief, and made
no mention of the Israeli agents in Turkey. What sparse details
of the story were included were broken up, scrambled, and inserted piecemeal into different chapters, rendering them all but
incomprehensible.

The book laid out the dispute between the Aleppo community and the state only in the briefest terms and skimmed over
the trial in three sentences:

The trial took place in the district rabbinic court in Jerusalem
in 5718—1958. The transcripts of the trial have enough material for a whole book, if not for a drama centering on the

* The first Hebrew month corresponds to August–September 1957.
The second corresponds to January–February 1958.

character of [Murad] Faham. In the end, not least because of the respect commanded by Israel's president, Itzhak Ben-Zvi, the Sephardic chief rabbi, and the Aleppo sages, the sides reached a compromise agreement.

The writer, clearly sensing the peculiarity of this omission, offered an unusual explanation in the next paragraph: "I prefer not to open old wounds." With my own research making progress, I sought out the author, hoping to clarify the more bewildering aspects of his account. I was presumably going over many of the same documents he had. Why had I found a more complicated story?

The author of the Ben-Zvi Institute's book was not an academic but an important Hebrew novelist, Amnon Shamosh, who was born in Aleppo and came to Israel as a child. At the time he took on the Crown project, under contract with the institute, he was at the height of his fame, thanks largely to the success of *Michel Ezra Safra and Sons,* a multigenerational epic about a fictional Aleppo family that was made into a popular TV miniseries. The writer had a longtime interest in the Crown, as well as a family connection to the story: Isaac Shamosh, who had been sent from Jerusalem to Aleppo in 1943 to bring back the Crown, was his older brother.

I interviewed Amnon Shamosh, who is now nearly blind, during a fierce rainstorm at his tiny home on a kibbutz along the Israel-Lebanon frontier. He told me of arriving in Tel Aviv from Aleppo in 1937: "It was a city of wonders," he said. "Everything was written in Hebrew. People were speaking Hebrew. I thought, This is redemption. This is the city of the Messiah." Uniquely, for a first-generation Aleppo Jew, he found his way to the secular, socialist wing of the Zionist movement, marrying a

Viennese woman and settling on this communal farm as a young man. For years, Shamosh put all his royalties into the members' joint bank account, which left him with nearly nothing when the kibbutz's finances failed. Our exchange, which lasted several hours, was interrupted once by an air raid siren—"They're testing," said his wife—and once when the writer rose to help make tea, which he and his wife do together because his hands are still steady and she can still see.

When he began work on his Crown history, he told me, he felt that time was slipping away: "I kept calling widows who said, 'Thanks for calling, but he died two months ago.'" Researching the more distant history of the manuscript was relatively easy, he said. Anything after the riot in 1947 was not. On more than one occasion he knew he was being stymied, especially when he began looking into what happened after the codex arrived in Israel. "I encountered a closed wall," he said. "No one knew anything. Nothing." Shragai, the immigration chief, was "evasive." Meir Benayahu, the director of the Ben-Zvi Institute at the time of the codex's arrival, agreed to talk; the writer found him "polite" but felt he was not telling the truth.

"You felt that you were touching something unpleasant, something people didn't want to talk about," Shamosh said. "The feeling was that everyone wanted me to leave them alone, not to write about them."

Why was that? I asked.

"Because two hundred pages are missing, every one worth . . ." His voice trailed off. "I was not given the authority of a policeman," he said. "I was given only the authority to interview people and ask them questions."

The officials in charge of the Crown were concerned about what Shamosh might write. In 1985, as Shamosh worked on the book, the Crown trustees convened. One of the trustees was Shlomo Toussia-Cohen, the attorney who had represented the government at the trial years before. "Amnon Shamosh must be warned that there are serious disagreements about the matter of the Crown's removal from Syria and its transfer to Israel, and we shouldn't walk into this entanglement," the attorney told those present, according to a transcript of the meeting. The trustees decided that they would vet the book before it was published.

Shamosh was a novelist, and a respected one, but he did not have a journalist's nose for confrontation and dirt. He had the opportunity to read the trial transcripts—the key to understanding the whole story—but claimed he did not do so. I asked him why. "I said, I don't have the energy, I don't have the time, I don't think it's important what every rabbi said about what he thinks about who it belongs to," he replied. He knew that the book he had written did not include the real story. Faham was a teller of tall tales, he told me, who had disobeyed his orders from the rabbis and turned the book over to the state. "From the Aleppo community he would have got merely a thank-you, while the Aliya Department, through Shragai and Ben-Zvi, received him with the best conditions that immigrants could get, on the condition that he did not agree to the version saying he had been told to bring it to the Aleppo rabbis in Israel." Shamosh knew all this but did not write it.

The manuscript Shamosh submitted did include references to Faham's inventions, which he understood were muddying crucial details of the story. The Ben-Zvi Institute refused to publish most of them, the writer told me, arguing that the cheese merchant, who had died by then, deserved to be portrayed in a positive light for his two "good deeds": he had brought the book to Israel at considerable personal risk, and he "gave it to the state and not to the Aleppo Jews." A few remaining critical references to the cheese merchant were left in, but when Faham's children got wind of the unpublished text and threatened to sue, the institute removed those, too.

Shamosh had come to feel protective of the Crown, taking its neglect personally, and he wrote sections on the deterioration of the manuscript over the years in the institute's care, quoting from the same experts' reports I found later. Those sections do not appear in the book, however, because the institute cut them out. The scholars told Shamosh, he remembered, that they "would not put out a book that makes us look like criminals." He put up a fight, he said, but finally agreed to go ahead with publication when he realized that his contract left him powerless and after the institute promised to expedite the physical restoration of the Crown. I found the writer's original pages in the institute's archive with X marks through the offending paragraphs. The book that was finally published included no overt indication that anything was amiss, that anyone had been less than perfectly honest, or that any facts had been left out.

One of the scholars involved in editing the book was Menahem Ben-Sasson, a professor who went on to serve as a member of the Knesset and then as president of Hebrew University. In an interview, he said he could not recall what information had been removed from Shamosh's history of the Crown. Another of the book's editors was the institute's longtime administrative director, Zvi Zameret, who left in 2009 after twenty-six years to take a senior position at the Ministry of Education. When I presented him with the writer's account, he unapologetically confirmed it. The reports of the book's neglect "did not appear to us to be central," he told me, suggesting that the fact that the institute paid for the Crown's restoration more than made up for any mistreatment in the past. "It seemed to us like kicking our-selves," he said. "We restored the Crown, and we should make ourselves look bad—for what?"

For his part, Shamosh wrote proudly of his own connection to the Crown's story through his brother, Isaac, but chose not to mention a second, more complicated family link. It will be noted here later on.

If *The Crown* was meant to cripple independent inquiry into the manuscript's recent history, it worked: for twenty-three years, it remained the only book on the subject. In 2010, when I was already involved in my own investigation, a new book appeared in the United States. This one, *The Crown of Aleppo*, was printed by the venerable Jewish Publication Society. One of its two authors was Hayim Tawil, an expert on Semitic languages from Yeshiva University in New York. (He is not of Aleppo descent and is not related to any of this story's other Tawils.) The book included rich historical material and scholarly analysis, but on the events after 1947 it was no less confounding than the first. As in the Ben-Zvi Institute's account, this one also accepted at face value the idea that the Crown had been "returned" or "restored" to Israel. It quoted extensively and uncritically from Faham's taped oral recollections from the late 1970s, which are contradicted by information available elsewhere; this information appeared to have been either missed or ignored. The book's brief description of the trial was drawn solely from Faham's account, ending with the merchant's assertion that the legal proceedings in Jerusalem ended with an admission by the Aleppo rabbis that he had been right all along. The book referred to Faham's "heroic efforts," and while it acknowledged some kind of "controversy" around his actions, it attributed the Aleppo rabbis' anger toward him to a "grudge." Faham was the vehicle of the state's seizure of the manuscript, as anyone who carefully went over the documentary record would know, and yet here, too, those truths were covered up; instead, the book perpetuated the same story that had been in circulation for years.

The explanation for this is not complicated: if the first book was put out by Ben-Zvi's executors, the scholars of his institute, this one was put out with the support of descendants of the man who turned the codex over to Israel. Though this is not explicitly noted anywhere in the book, one of Faham's grandchildren, a New York businessman, partially funded it. His condition—according to the author Tawil and the donor himself, both of whom I interviewed—was that he be allowed to see the manuscript before publication to ensure there was nothing the family would find damaging.

In an interview, Tawil acknowledged that some funding had come from Faham's family, but he said he had not been pressured to make any changes to the text. The book's account of Faham's role dovetailed with Faham's own account of his role simply because it was based entirely on Faham's oral testimony and on interviews with his sons, Tawil said. "I didn't want to get into controversy," the author said. The Israeli government's official version supported Faham's, he noted, and nothing he found in the Ben-Zvi Institute, which helped him with his research, contradicted it. That being the case, he said, "who am I to argue against it?"

Having concluded that the Ben-Zvi Institute's book, the one written by Amnon Shamosh, was less an example of historical inquiry than a carefully engineered smoke screen, I combed through it again to analyze its treatment of the missing pages. Here, I thought, the institute would have little to hide. If pages had survived the riot, they were held by Aleppo Jews, and the codex had arrived in Jerusalem incomplete only a decade later. And yet here, too, the book was not forthcoming. "Surprisingly, as we get closer to our own times, the fog grows, and there are more and more differing accounts of the Crown's journeys," read one typical sentence, without elaborating. The codex's travels "are cloaked in mystery, and it is doubtful that the truth will ever be known," read another. The book ventured no hypothesis about what might have happened, and most of the sections about the missing pages read like this: "The question that arises, one we must never tire of asking, is what happened to those books [of the Bible] and missing pages? Are they lost and gone? Every last one of them? Or, perhaps, do some of them exist in the hands of different people in different places, waiting to be redeemed?"

At his home, Shamosh told me he believed most of the pages had been taken by people in Aleppo. Of the Aleppo community, he said, "If it's possible not to tell the truth, why tell the truth? The truth is a dangerous thing."

The Agent's Investigation

IT WAS 1989, and Channel 1 TV, Israel's public television station, was planning a documentary about the Crown's missing pages. The production team asked Rafi Sutton, the Aleppo Jew with years of spying behind him, to put his skills at their disposal.

By now, Sutton had completed a successful spying career, including a stint with the Mossad in Europe beginning in 1969, at a time when the intelligence service had agents building networks among Palestinians and other Arabs abroad. Many of the Israeli agents were, like Sutton, Jews from Arab countries. He served in Europe in the aftermath of the killing of Israeli athletes at the 1972 Munich Olympics, when Mossad teams hunted down and assassinated members of the Palestine Liberation Organization in Rome, Paris, Cyprus, and elsewhere. I once asked him about a book I had read documenting the details of that merciless campaign, and he told me brusquely that it was "accurate." But in all, Sutton revealed almost nothing about his Mossad work, except that it was similar to his work in Jerusalem; that meant running agents. An old friend of his told me that Sutton had spent much of his time in Europe living under an assumed identity as an Arab, showing up occasionally to visit his wife and children, who were parked discreetly elsewhere on the continent. He returned to Israel in 1975. After we had known each other for some time, Sutton confided to me that the memory of one prolonged stint undercover in an Arab country still woke him in dread in the middle of the night.

Sutton's interest in his roots in Aleppo had grown as he aged, and he immediately agreed to the request from Channel 1. He saw the job, he said, as an intelligence mission, though it happened to come from a TV station and not from the Mossad, and though the goal this time was not secrecy but maximum publicity. The result—about forty minutes of low-budget television, resembling an extended segment of *60 Minutes*—was the closest thing to a methodical investigation of the Crown's fate attempted up to that time. Though the results of the investigation were inconclusive, to this day the program is one of the most crucial troves of information available to anyone interested in the story. Nearly all the people interviewed have since died.

I first saw the program, which I subsequently watched at least a dozen times, in Sutton's living room. When he tried to show it to me, he couldn't get his DVD player to work, and stood stooped, in flip-flops, staring with uncomprehending hatred at the remote.

"Didn't you operate technology back in the Mossad?" I ribbed him. By this time we were friends. He didn't look up.

"I operated people," he muttered.

Sutton's objective was to nail down the chronology of the Crown's history after the riot—at which time, it was assumed, the pages had gone missing—and to determine when, exactly, it was recognized to be incomplete. Going through his memory and his contacts in the Aleppo community, he submitted a list of targets, noting with impatience how many of the central players were already gone: the cheese merchant Faham was dead, and so were the sexton and the two Aleppo rabbis, Tawil and Zaafrani.

Sutton, like other old spies I have met, is torn between a tendency toward secrecy drilled into him over decades and an urge
to tell his stories, which he knows are very good. He clearly loved
the spotlight, the TV footage showed: he played up the role of
the Mossad man, crossing streets and hotel lobbies in a black
trench coat and sunglasses, impaling his subjects with interrogator's eyes from behind the large frames perched on his nose.

One of his on-air interviews was with a man identified in
the program only as "the tourist" and filmed from the back so
that his face could not be seen. A voice-over at the beginning
announced that Sutton and his subject were in "a European
country." They were, in fact, in Tel Aviv. The man was Edmond
Cohen, whose family had hidden the Crown and who was the
one to personally bring it to the courier Faham as he prepared
to leave. Cohen had stayed in Aleppo until almost all the other
Jews were gone and had finally left only a short time before, and
his anonymity and the false location were meant to address his
fear that he might endanger relatives still in Syria if it became
known that he was in Israel. Like nearly everyone in the Aleppo
community connected to the manuscript's rescue from the synagogue and transfer to Israel, Cohen was evasive. They spoke in
Syrian Arabic.

> SUTTON. From the day of the fires until the Crown was found,
> can you tell me who had it and where?
> COHEN. For a time, not a long time afterward, I don't remem-
> ber exactly, they said they brought the Crown. A certain
> person had it and hid it in his store, in his storeroom. I had
> the privilege of seeing it.

The "certain person" whom Cohen would not name was his
uncle, Ibrahim Effendi Cohen.

SUTTON. When you say they brought it, who brought it?

COHEN. I don't quite remember. They hid it with him, and I saw it. It arrived incomplete.

SUTTON. It was incomplete.

COHEN. This man wrapped it up. It was in his storeroom, in a room within a room, a dark room.

SUTTON. When you say it arrived incomplete, is it known how much was missing?

COHEN. I don't remember.

SUTTON. But you saw it was incomplete. Did people speak among themselves about how much—

COHEN. It was missing mostly from the Torah.

SUTTON. From the Pentateuch.

COHEN. Yes. That's what I remember.

SUTTON. When they brought it to this man, was this a long time after the fires, or immediately afterward?

COHEN. I don't remember exactly.

SUTTON. You don't remember. What was the state of the Crown when you saw it?

COHEN. It was a big, thick book.

SUTTON. I'm asking about its condition, if it was whole . . . You said it was incomplete.

COHEN. It was incomplete and taken apart a bit at the beginning. I don't remember exactly after thirty years.

SUTTON. Was it damaged? Was it burned?

COHEN. I don't remember exactly. I don't remember.

Cohen believed the book was missing pages when it reached his uncle, but he wasn't sure how many. Sutton noted that in a few short minutes of filmed footage, the subject had said "I don't remember" no fewer than eight times, which made him suspicious, though he granted that the man was worried about relatives in Syria and had only recently escaped the grip of the *mukhabarat* himself.

Sutton also interviewed the sexton's son, Shahoud Baghdadi, who was then in his late sixties and had long been a grave digger in a cemetery near Tel Aviv. People who knew him described him to me as charitable and scrupulously honest. Baghdadi, dressed in his best clothes and visibly nervous in front of the camera, sat opposite the old Mossad man.

In the riot's aftermath, the sexton's son recounted, his father took him to the synagogue and they began searching amid the rubble and scattered pages of other books for pieces of the Crown.

> BAGHDADI. I saw my father crying like a baby. I said, *Abba*, what happened? Get up, why are you sitting there? In the place where he was sitting there was no fire, just damage . . . My father is sitting, I'm picking through the piles to try to find the pieces of the Crown, page by page.
>
> SUTTON. Maybe you remember how much you sorted through.
>
> BAGHDADI. Believe me, I sorted through a lot. A big pile. More than I can count.
>
> SUTTON. But how much did you find after sorting through it all?
>
> BAGHDADI. I found the whole Crown.
>
> SUTTON. All of the Crown? All of it, in its entirety?
>
> BAGHDADI. All of the Crown, in its entirety, page after page.
>
> SUTTON. What did you do with what you found?
>
> BAGHDADI. What I found I gave to my father.
>
> SUTTON. Immediately.
>
> BAGHDADI. Immediately. My father was sitting there, looking.

SUTTON. How do you know you found it all?

BAGHDADI. When it was done, my father put it in order: Genesis, Exodus. Deuteronomy was incomplete. I said, It's all right—

SUTTON. Wait, you're saying Genesis, Exodus—

BAGHDADI. Numbers, Leviticus. Deuteronomy was incomplete, I remember well.

SUTTON. The book of Deuteronomy was missing?

BAGHDADI. Not the whole book. Pieces. And there were parts missing from the book of Isaiah.

Sutton stopped him to make sure he was hearing right. "One minute," he said.

SUTTON. You're saying this: The books of Genesis, Exodus, Leviticus, and Numbers were there.

BAGHDADI. Were almost there.

SUTTON. What do you mean by "almost"?

BAGHDADI. I remember that they were there. They were there.

SUTTON. Whole.

BAGHDADI. Whole.

SUTTON. And burned at the edge.

Sutton asked this question to ensure the subject was talking about the Crown, with its trademark purple "burn" marks, and not one of the other manuscripts from the synagogue.

BAGHDADI. Everything was burned at the edge.

SUTTON. And the book of Deuteronomy, you say, was not whole.

BAGHDADI. It was not whole, it was incomplete. And from Prophets, Isaiah was incomplete.

The sexton's son appeared to have said that all the missing books of the Crown, with the exception of part of Deuteronomy and Isaiah, were rescued after the fire. This contradicted what nearly everyone believed. But the testimony of one simple man, especially one who seemed confused about some details, was not enough to turn the accepted story on its head. That would require Sutton's next target, the most respected Aleppo rabbi of that time and a man who had been involved in the Crown's rescue and preservation in Aleppo years before. This was Itzjak Chehebar, who had left Aleppo in 1952 and now led the exile community in Buenos Aires. Sutton had no doubt that the rabbi could help if he so chose; he also knew that Chehebar was in his eighties and that no time could be wasted.

The agent carefully considered his approach. He remembered the rabbi's wedding in Aleppo, which he had attended as a child, and knew that his own uncles, the Beirut jewelers, had taken care of the rabbi when he arrived in Lebanon after fleeing Aleppo. He decided to mention both details in his request for an audience, which he sent through a relative in Buenos Aires. The rabbi agreed to see him.

With an embroidered skullcap perched on his head, Sutton went to the Aleppo synagogue in the Argentinian capital. It was December 1989. He entered the rabbi's office, which was lined with Hebrew books in glass-fronted cupboards, bent over, and kissed Chehebar's hand, in keeping with a tradition he had not observed since leaving Aleppo. Chehebar was clean shaven, lucid, and personable. They reminisced about Aleppo in Arabic and Hebrew. The ice broken, Sutton came back the next day wearing a powder-blue suit and trailed by a TV crew. It was fortunate for those interested in the Crown's history that the subsequent interview—the only time one of the Aleppo community leaders from the period in question has ever spoken candidly and publicly on the subject—was recorded. The rabbi died ten months later.

Chehebar, who was among those responsible for the Crown in its hiding place, went to see the book in 1952, just before he left the city for good, he said. At the time, it was in Ibrahim Effendi Cohen's storeroom in one of the Aleppo souks.

"I opened it in the storeroom of Ibrahim Effendi Cohen, and I saw it," the rabbi said. "It was missing a few pages that perhaps fell to the ground or were burned, but not to this extent. Not hundreds of pages."

> SUTTON. Missing are Genesis, Exodus, Leviticus, Numbers, and half the book of Deuteronomy. And parts of other books are missing.
>
> CHEHEBAR. I saw that it was missing a few pages. Not that many pages.
>
> SUTTON. You mean individual pages?
>
> CHEHEBAR. Individual pages. Not even dozens were missing.

This matched the testimony from the sexton's son. We may also remember that it matched what the exile in Rio de Janeiro, the treasurer Yaakov Hazan, told Ben-Zvi's envoy three decades before. "To demonstrate what he meant about the missing part, he pointed at a booklet that was at most five millimeters thick," the diplomat wrote to the president in 1961. "He had difficulty estimating the number of pages, but in comparison with the thickness of the Crown, this would be only a few pages, perhaps no more than ten." This was dismissed at the time as an "utter error." Now came the third eyewitness testimony to this effect. In 1952, five years after the riot, the Crown was seen to be intact except for a small number of pages. By March 1958, as we know, with the book already in Israel, nearly two hundred pages, including the Torah, were gone.

What of the missing pages? Sutton asked. Two hundred have vanished.

"That was not the case," the rabbi answered. "Perhaps a hand . . ." He tapped the table, looking for a word.

"Played with it," suggested Sutton.

"Played with it," agreed the rabbi, weighing his words, "and stole it."

FOUR EYEWITNESS TESTIMONIES had now been collected.

The testimony of Edmond Cohen, who claimed not to remember, was inconclusive. The other three witnesses—the treasurer in Rio de Janeiro, the sexton's son, and the rabbi in Buenos Aires—were in agreement that the Crown had in fact been complete after the riot, except for a small number of pages. The sexton's son saw the codex on the day after the riot, the treasurer saw it several weeks later, and the rabbi saw it five years later.

The accumulation of evidence amassed by Rafi Sutton pointed to a conclusion that was explosive. If the Crown was intact in Aleppo in 1952 but was no longer intact in Israel in 1958, it meant the missing pages had disappeared while the book was in the hands of supposedly trustworthy guardians. It meant the missing pages of the Crown were not "lost." They were not burned, looted by rioters, or picked up as souvenirs and spirited to New York. The missing pages were missing because one or more of the keepers of the codex had stolen them.

At this point the TV channel's money ran out and Sutton's assignment was terminated. The ex-agent, feeling he was on the cusp of breaking the case, wrote up a new report urging that the investigation be continued even after the show was aired. "The broadcast of the program, even though we did not succeed in discovering the missing pieces, is very important and will certainly lead to unexpected developments," he wrote. But then the reels sat in the vaults at Channel 1 for three years because the producers had not used union TV crews when they filmed abroad and the union technicians refused to edit the footage. When the show finally aired in 1993, Sutton tried to drum up support for renewing the search. He wrote letters to foundations. He approached the famous Edmond Safra, a global financier originally from Aleppo. He met the mayor of Jerusalem. He sent more copies of his report to the Ben-Zvi Institute and to the Aleppo community's heritage center in Tel Aviv, thinking they would certainly want the truth uncovered. "In order to strengthen our hypothesis and collect additional evidence," he wrote, "we must continue the investigation and interview people who are the sons of those who were involved in saving the Crown in Aleppo." In addition, he wrote, "We must find a fitting person abroad"—he had in mind a private investigator— "who can help in gathering and obtaining evidence and additional proof." Rafi figured he needed about $50,000 but could make do with less. No one was interested.

At one of our meetings in his living room, I asked him why.

"I present a situation, and it must be interpreted," he said. He looked at me. Many of our conversations went like this.

Was it because no one was interested in seeing you get further? I asked.

"Correct," he said.

Talking vaguely about "lost" pages was safe. Talking about

"stolen" pages was not, because it meant that someone must have stolen them—that a crime had been committed. It meant that something might actually have to be done about it. After sparking a brief flurry of newspaper articles, the program was forgotten. The Mossad man put his unwanted report on his bookshelf and watched the trail go cold.

The Collector

I ENTERED THE opulent and charmless lobby of the hotel, took the elevator to the top floor, the fourteenth, and pressed the buzzer next to one of the doors. I imagined that inside I would see a glamorous penthouse with a view of lights sparkling down the coast toward Tel Aviv, but when the door swung open I found myself in a room resembling a dark cave. The suite might have been tiny or huge; in the gloom, it was impossible to tell. A circle a few paces from the doorway was illuminated, and in the fading light on its edges I made out an Ali Baba's trove of jugs, oil lamps, and candelabra. Sitting at a table in the circle of light was a frail man with watery and unsettling blue eyes.

When I walked into the hotel, a decade and a half had passed since Sutton's investigation. There had been no breakthroughs in the case since then. No pages of the codex had been found since the fragment from Samuel Sabbagh's wallet surfaced in 1987. If the pages were indeed stolen, I reasoned, they might have appeared by now, and yet there was no proof that they had. The traffic in ancient manuscripts, and certainly in ancient manuscripts acquired in a questionable fashion, is almost completely opaque, and looking for the pages would be like looking for gold by staring intently at the ground. But there were, I found, indications that some of the pages had indeed turned up, only to disappear again. In this search there were no certain answers, only brief flashes of lightning that illuminated the story for a moment before I was left in the dark again.

In my first months of sniffing around the story of the Crown, several people I spoke to mentioned someone who might be holding a large number of pages. They would not give me a name, but eventually I realized that they were all talking about the same person. It took a while longer before I discovered that the person was Shlomo Moussaieff: mysterious tycoon, jeweler to the oil sheikhs of the Persian Gulf, father-in-law of the president of Iceland, and owner of one of the world's most extensive private collections of Jewish and biblical antiquities. Moussaieff was eighty-seven years old. I decided that I would try to induce him to tell me what he had and that I would get it on tape.

Expecting someone aloof and refined, I found a figure far more interesting, even baffling: a merchant of the East, a master of the dance between seller and buyer, a dropper of hints, and a teller of stories. I felt that I had met him before in the carpet bazaars of Cairo or Istanbul. The perfect carpet, you believe, is kept hidden in the back, but the seller does not know you well enough, or respect you enough, to let you see it. If you play your cards right, you think, he might, and he might even sell it to you for a good price. But there is always the suspicion that the perfect carpet does not, in fact, exist. The dance is not just about profit; it is also about honor and social interaction, and it is not untouched by comedy. Moussaieff was a human hall of mirrors. I spent hours and hours with him and cannot say for sure if behind his stories lay something amazing or nothing at all.

An inquiry into the fate of the pages must begin with a consideration of what we are looking for. A significant piece of the codex is missing from the beginning: this is the Torah, the Five

Books of Moses. A piece of similar size, consisting mainly of books of the Prophets, is missing from the end, and there are individual pages and sections missing from the middle. The pages might be together, or they might be circulating separately. It is also possible that individual pages have been cut up and sold as charms. Most books lose value if they are not whole, but there are some manuscripts—chiefly those seen to have talismanic qualities—that are worth more in pieces. A book of mysticism written by the kabbalist rabbi Haim Vital four hundred years ago, for example, was dismembered by its owners and put on sale page by page in recent years, to the futile fury of scholars. The book business is a business, and the profit margin was simply better that way.

Anyone looking into the fate of the Crown's missing pieces will hear numerous stories about pages circulating among Aleppo Jews. These stories share a formula and are all impossible to confirm. I heard a typical example from a book dealer named Moshe Rosenfeld, who works out of a cluttered office in downtown Jerusalem. In 1990, Rosenfeld told me, he was in New York, walking down Broadway as the office buildings emptied their workers onto the street, when he heard someone shouting his name. He turned to see a man of about thirty-five who had been a student of his twenty years before, when he taught high school. The man, whose family was from Aleppo, said he had since moved from Israel to New York, where he had relatives who ran a business importing merchandise from China.

What are you up to now? the man asked.

I'm in old books, Rosenfeld answered, and he saw a light switch on in the man's eyes.

Have you heard of the Crown of Aleppo? asked the man.

That's the book that was burned, the dealer said. The man

laughed. Nothing was burned, he said. He reached into his
pocket, pulled out his wallet, and showed the dealer a small
piece of folded parchment in a protective plastic slip. This is from
the Crown, he said. Rosenfeld was new in the book business at
the time, he said, and only later understood the significance of
what he had purportedly been shown. Later he heard another
report: an Israeli who worked as a security guard for an Aleppo
banking family in São Paulo told him the family had two pages
of the Crown.

Michael Maggen, the paper conservator at Israel's national
museum, and Adolfo Roitman, the curator in charge of the
Crown and the Dead Sea Scrolls at the museum, both said they
had received tips about people holding pages, but the leads invariably ended with people who were not willing to talk. Beyond
these fragmentary hints at the existence of small pieces, however,
there are rumors of a large portion of the Crown that has been
kept together. In the Aleppo Codex Underground, this is the
grail.

William Gross, a collector who lives in Tel Aviv, offered me
a rapid beginner's course on the world of rare Hebrew books,
where he is well known but not representative: he is open, and
happy to talk, and sees himself less as a collector than as a custodian. Gross was born in Minneapolis. The walls of his living
room are lined with pieces of antique metalwork: menorahs,
spice boxes, pomegranate-shaped decorations for Torah scrolls
from Jewish communities in Europe and the Islamic world that
are now, with few exceptions, gone. "I'm very aware of what's
behind my collection," Gross told me. "The Holocaust, the
movement of Jews from the East. A great sadness accompanies
these things." He collects many different kinds of artifacts but

sees books as special: "When a man writes a manuscript, he invests part of his soul in it," he said.

Hebrew manuscripts move through the book market, from seller to buyer, through dealers or at auction, openly or secretly. It is often unclear who is buying what. For years, some of the most beautiful and expensive Hebrew manuscripts on the market simply disappeared without a trace, until René Braginsky, a little-known Zurich collector, went public with a collection now considered one of the world's finest. As a rule, the oldest books are the most expensive, and books the Crown's age almost never go on sale. Sometime before we met, Gross followed an auction where two spectacular pieces went on the block: a scroll of the book of Esther from the sixteenth century, written by a woman scribe, which sold for about $600,000, and a Torah scroll from before the Spanish expulsion in 1492, which sold for $350,000. On the black market, a part of the Crown would be worth far more, even taking into account the reduction in its value because it had been illicitly obtained and could not be exhibited or easily resold. One biblical codex not as old and far less important than the Crown, Gross said, sold in the 1990s for $3 million.

If it is sometimes unclear where objects are going, it is often impossible to discern where they came from. Sacred Jewish manuscripts invariably originated in Jewish communities—in homes, seminaries, and synagogues—and moved from place to place with their owners. As a result, there are almost never good records of their provenance. This is a symptom of Jewish history: a powerless and transient people had no royal libraries or endowed monasteries. A significant part of the Hebrew manuscript market is made up of books that were stolen, slipping through the grate dividing the forthright world of synagogues and libraries from the unseen world of the black market. Thefts from synagogues, religious seminaries, and public libraries still happen with frequency. Many go unnoticed, as synagogues usually have no formal records of what they have. The sexton might know, but sometimes the sexton is the thief. Inside jobs are common: in one of the most notorious recent cases, the curator in charge of Hebrew books at the Bibliothèque nationale in Paris was arrested in 2004, and later convicted, for stealing and selling a precious Bible manuscript from his own collection. "Most collectors would not knowingly buy a stolen item," Gross told me, "but there are those who will."

The market is made up of a small number of wealthy collectors, perhaps fifty, Gross said. Within that number is an elite of a dozen men rich enough to buy any book they want, no matter what the cost. One of them is Shlomo Moussaieff.

Moussaieff was born in a poor Jerusalem neighborhood populated by people who, like his family, had origins in Bukhara, on the central Asian steppe. In his telling, he was thrown out of his home as a rebellious young teenager by an exactingly religious father, joined the British army at the beginning of World War II, fought Rommel in North Africa, fled the British debacle at Tobruk in 1942 on camelback, and eventually returned home to Palestine, where he participated in the Jews' doomed attempt to fight off the Arab Legion in Jerusalem's Old City during the independence war and then spent a year in a Jordanian prison camp. Moussaieff's father was a collector of old books himself, and his son continued the tradition, amassing a collection of manuscripts and antiquities as he built a fortune in the jewelry business. In the 1960s, as he went from rich to fabulously rich, he left Israel for London.

The idea that Moussaieff was somehow connected to the

story of the Crown originated with the same TV documentary
that Rafi Sutton helped produce. Another member of the investigative team, a former police detective, acting on a tip from a
small-time antiquities dealer, interviewed Moussaieff at his London apartment.

A few years before, the collector told him, he was at a book fair
in Jerusalem when he was approached by two ultra-Orthodox
men who wanted to show him something they had in a suitcase.
This was not uncommon: at every auction and fair, the legitimate activity going on in the busy conference room downstairs
is accompanied by deals taking place behind closed doors and
DO NOT DISTURB signs on the floors above. The hidden deals,
not surprisingly, are often more lucrative and intriguing.

Inside the suitcase, Moussaieff told the investigator, was a
stack of parchment pages with three columns of Hebrew text.
The lines did not end precisely at the margin but instead ended
where the scribe finished a particular word. This was the way
the scribe Ben-Buya'a wrote, and the description matched the
Crown of Aleppo. Moussaieff offered no further details of any
importance. The investigator said on camera that the collector
told him he had not purchased the pages, though Moussaieff is
not seen making this statement himself. It appeared little had
been done with the information. In the years that had passed,
there had been sporadic rumors and secondhand reports about
comments Moussaieff had supposedly made about parts of the
Crown that he did, or did not, have.

MOUSSAIEFF WAS NOW said to be ailing but lucid and
splitting his time between a London apartment and a five-star
hotel in Herzliya, a town north of Tel Aviv. One acquaintance
who had been at the hotel suite not long before told me he had

watched Moussaieff glance at a diamond someone wanted to sell him, evaluate its worth, and order a $1 million bank transfer over the phone. The collector was famously shrewd, but I hoped he might just be old enough now to care less about keeping his secrets.

I found his number and called, expecting to speak with a secretary or an aide, and was startled to find myself on the line with Moussaieff himself. I explained why I was calling.

"What do you want with the Crown of Aleppo?" he asked, and I told him. By this time I was used to people who were unwilling to talk, and I was expecting him to put me off. There was silence on the other end of the line. "Come at five," he said, and he hung up. Five was in three hours.

I set out from Jerusalem on the highway down to the coast. When I was buzzed into the suite and found the old collector surrounded by his hoard in the pool of light, there were two other people there, a woman in black and a burly man with a ponytail, both of whom shot me dark glances. I was interfering with something. The collector was preoccupied, and the mood in the room was sinister. I reminded him that I had come to talk about the Crown of Aleppo. He looked at me with suspicion.

"Are you from Aleppo?" he asked.

No, I said, I'm an Ashkenazi—a European Jew. He said nothing and seemed to be waiting for me to leave. I did, and then went back the next day, making the two-hour drive from Jerusalem without calling in advance. When I rang the buzzer, the same nasal voice from the day before asked from a speaker, "Who is it?"

I introduced myself again: I'm here about the Crown of Aleppo, I said.

There was a moment of silence. "I'm sick today," said the voice. The speaker went dead.

Convinced that I had missed my chance, I nonetheless made a third attempt a few days later, passing again through the revolving door and the perfumed air of the hotel lobby and riding the elevator to the fourteenth floor. I rang the doorbell and eyed the speaker, expecting to be turned away again, but then the door made a sound like a trapped hornet and I was in.

26

The Magicians

THE ALI BABA effect was gone. Instead, the daylight pouring through the windows illuminated the blue velvet case of a Torah scroll, Aladdin's lamps, and other ancient detritus cluttering the vast living room. Two small bronze lions glared at my knees with eyeballs of ivory. At the same table a few paces from the doorway, Moussaieff sat where I had left him days before. The same watery blue eyes fixed themselves on me.

This time he seemed to be holding court. At the table were a young man in jeans and a T-shirt, a pretty woman in a leather jacket, an older man who sounded French and was holding a vase, and another man dressed, improbably, in the traditional garb of the Jews of Yemen: a robe, a turban, and curly side locks hanging down to his jaw. The young man in jeans took control.

"Who are you?" he asked, his voice curt. I explained, yet again, that I was here about the Crown of Aleppo.

"He wants to sell me something?" Moussaieff asked, turning to the man in jeans. No, he replied, he's a journalist—he made the word sound like a common but nonetheless painful strain of syphilis—writing about something called the Crown of Aleppo.

"And he comes to me, of all people?" Moussaieff asked, feigning amazement, and I knew he wanted to talk.

"Sorry," the Frenchman with the vase said in English, "but what is the Crown of Aleppo?"

As Moussaieff answered him, the woman in the leather jacket engaged me in a brief and friendly conversation, explaining the cast of characters around the table. She and the Frenchman were collectors, the robed Yemeni—who spoke Hebrew like the Israeli city kid he clearly was—was a manuscript scholar, and the young man in jeans was Moussaieff's aide.

"The Aleppo Jews, they cut out pieces and put them in their prayer book for good luck," Moussaieff was saying, in a voice loud enough to reach my ears and the small digital recorder I had running in the chest pocket of my shirt. The following record, and those of most of my subsequent conversations with the collector, come from recorded transcripts.*

The Frenchman thought the vase in his hand was more interesting. How old is it? he wanted to know.

"Ummayad. One thousand years," the elderly collector said. The woman in the leather jacket asked Moussaieff about some rubies she was apparently trying to sell him. He was not interested, he apologized, because they were heat-treated to bring out their colors—he didn't touch jewels like that. She and the Frenchman took their leave, but not before she planted a kiss on Moussaieff's cheek.

"Oy!" said the collector, clutching his heart. "Now I'm pregnant."

His aide looked at me and indicated that my time was up. "Leave me a business card with a cell phone number," he ordered.

---

* Fortunately for journalists, surreptitiously taping conversations to which you are party is legal in Israel.

"No problem," I said, scrambling to think of a way to buy time. Moussaieff was leaving for London the next day, the aide informed me, so I might be able to catch him upon his return in a month. Or, he was implying, I might not.

"Maybe it's possible to do it later today? I don't want to push," I said, pushing.

"Today there won't be time at all. You"—he looked at his boss—"have a doctor's appointment and a few other things. No, today won't be possible."

"Maybe ten minutes?" I pleaded. Then I addressed Moussaieff directly. He told a fascinating story on TV twenty years ago, I reminded him, speaking quickly before the aide could interrupt, about two ultra-Orthodox men who approached him at the King David Hotel in Jerusalem—

"Not the King David," Moussaieff said. "The hotel was the Hilton."

His aide was miraculously silent.

The men approached him at a book fair at the hotel, Moussaieff went on. This was in the mid-1980s. They showed him a suitcase. "I saw ninety pages and realized it was the Crown of Aleppo," he said. They wanted $1 million. He offered $300,000.

"They said, OK, we'll get back to you," he went on, and then, in the same breath: "Do you want to see a piece? I have one here—"

It felt as if the air had been sucked out of the room. The aide cut in urgently like the ringing of a telephone in a dream. I thought I might not have heard him correctly.

"One minute, Shlomo, let's do it like this, because today you don't have time and no one has time. Today's busy. I took the phone number," the aide said, turning to me, "and in three weeks you'll come and we'll talk."

I tried to buy more time, explaining that an article I wrote about the manuscript for the AP had appeared in hundreds of newspapers. I thought this might impress him.

"Send me the article with your contact details, and when we get back to Israel, we'll invite you if I think the article is good. Send the article. Thank you," said the aide.

"There's nothing left to write about it," Moussaieff said. He seemed to mean that there was much left to write about it.

"Of course there is," I said, which I felt sure was what he wanted me to say.

"Do you want to see a piece?" he asked again.

"Yes, if your assistant—I'd like to see one," I stammered, trying to sound as if this was not at all a big deal.

The aide cut in again. "Shlomo, let's not—he'll send that article that he wrote . . ."

"Show him the piece," the collector ordered, now not sounding old at all, "so that he'll enjoy himself, so that he won't have come for nothing."

The aide got up and walked unhappily over to a cabinet set in one corner of the living room. "He wants to be the ruler," the collector confided in me, "and what's nice is that— "

"Shlomo!" protested the aide from the other side of the room. The collector laughed.

"Come and see something interesting," Moussaieff said as the aide returned to the table. The younger man's fingers framed the edges of a piece of old parchment cropped on two sides. It was about the size of a small paperback book—Aleppo Jews, the collector had said a few minutes earlier, "cut out pieces and put them in their prayer book for good luck."

On the piece of parchment were two columns of text and the beginning of a third. It was the top right-hand corner of a page,

with notes in tiny letters visible in the margins. On the parchment's flesh side, nearly all the letters had flaked off, leaving only
some of the vowel signs. On the hardier hair side, the text was in
perfect condition. Before the aide whisked it back to its hiding
place a few seconds later, I managed to read and remember the
following sentence:

The magicians did the like with their spells to produce lice

With Egypt infested with the insects of the third plague,
Pharaoh's court magicians tried to replicate the feat with their
own spells and failed: it was a passage from the book of Exodus. This fragment, the product of centuries of scholarship
and a millennium of safekeeping, had been sliced to pieces and
reduced to a rich man's bauble, something produced to impress
a guest.

I could now count myself among a handful of people on earth
who had seen one of the missing pieces of the Crown of Aleppo.

Moussaieff seemed to lose interest in me after that, so I took
my leave, reluctant but also relieved to be out of the unnerving
suite. I rode the elevator down fourteen floors, still elated by
what I had seen—or rather by what I thought I had seen, because, it would turn out, I hadn't seen the Crown at all.

In the week after the meeting, I repeatedly went over the details of our conversation. Though I had discovered more than
I had hoped, it was still not enough. I needed to know where
the collector had acquired his fragment. I needed to know more
about the attempted sale of the Crown at the Hilton, and especially the identity of the two would-be sellers, so that I could
locate them and trace the pages back to their source. I needed
to know why Moussaieff hadn't bought the pages—or whether,

perhaps, he had. Moussiaeff was back in London. He was eighty-seven years old. So much information about the Crown had already been lost; the prospect of watching more slip away when it was so close was unbearable. Perhaps a change of scene could shake more information out of him. I booked a flight to Heathrow and set off in pursuit.

27

A Deal at the Hilton

THE GLOWING NUMBERS of the hotel clock insisted it was 7:00 a.m., but out the window the sun was nowhere to be seen. A disheartening drizzle descended on the figures trudging under umbrellas through the December gloom to the Tube station at Belsize Park.

By the time I reached Grosvenor Square in central London a few hours later, the sky had cleared and brightened. Dwight Eisenhower, from his perch on a pedestal by the US Embassy, directed a bronze gaze across the green rectangle hemmed in by some of the earth's most exclusive real estate. A different elevator, a different door, and a different room on the other side—this one dominated by a nineteenth-century landscape of Jerusalem in a gilt frame—but the same watery blue eyes. Moussaieff was in a white bathrobe. He appraised me, then left and reappeared wearing trousers and a shirt with pink stripes. He settled into an armchair, a hearing aid in each ear. I sat opposite him on a couch.

After some initial small talk, I mentioned the Crown fragment he had shown me and asked if he had any more. He had only that one, he told me. He had purchased it thirdhand in the United States, he said, suggesting this was not a big deal. When

I asked the price, he shrugged. "Even today there are more in America—you can buy them," he said.

They must cost tens of thousands of dollars or more, I said. He shrugged again. "Each person according to his face," he said.

He stopped to take a phone call in Arabic, and after he signed off — "Allah ma'ak," he said, God be with you—he complained that his Gulf clients were becoming more and more religious, so much so that he had arranged to have prayer rugs brought to his London jewelry showroom. Today was very different from the freewheeling 1970s, he said, but the upside was that many of his richest customers now had multiple wives. This was good for the jewelry business.

The Crown, I reminded him.

"You don't understand," he said. "There are things that are secret."

When I saw he had no intention of continuing, I told him I was writing a book that I hoped would tell the story of the Crown.

"The story of the Crown isn't over, it's only beginning," he said. At one point he gave me a suspicious glance, as if he had just thought of something.

"How do you know so much?" he said.

"I've done my homework. I've been busy with this story for months," I replied.

He snorted. "You need years," he said, and then he began to talk.

Moussaieff was in the lobby of the Hilton in Jerusalem, where he had flown from London with his daughter Tammy, who had been educated at English boarding schools and was then in her

twenties. This was in the mid-1980s, probably in the summer of
1985.* Two men in the black garb of ultra-Orthodox Jews approached them. One of them, a fat man with a long beard and
side locks, was someone the collector and his daughter knew
well: Haim Schneebalg, one of the most prominent dealers in
rare Hebrew manuscripts.

Collectors of Hebrew books were serviced by several dozen
dealers, most of them ultra-Orthodox Jews with knowledge they
brought with them from lives spent studying ancient texts. These
men moved around the globe with their valuable wares—an illuminated work of mysticism, an early printed Bible, a prayer
book from sixteenth-century Venice—not in titanium briefcases
handcuffed to their wrists but in tattered shopping bags that
might have held their lunch. This was to avoid the unwanted attention of thieves and customs agents. Schneebalg, considered
one of the most knowledgeable of the dealers, was known for
keeping small books tucked into his high white stockings.

As a young man in Jerusalem, Schneebalg had been a follower
of the Hasidic Rebbe of Vizhnitz and had learned much of what
he knew about books in the Rebbe's library. He later rejected
the sect as too moderate and joined the more extreme Satmar
Hasidim, moving to the sect's stronghold in the Brooklyn neighborhood of Williamsburg. Schneebalg was "good-hearted, a

---

* Neither Moussaieff nor his daughter Tammy Moussaieff, whom I
later interviewed, remembered the precise year of the Hilton auction.
There were three such book shows in the 1980s: in 1985, 1987, and 1988.
Tammy Moussaieff pointed to the 1985 show as the most likely and remembered seeing "Yemeni artifacts" on display; catalogues show that
Yemeni pieces were on display only in 1985. This also matches Moussaieff's
claim in his 1989 TV interview that the attempted sale had been "four or
five" years earlier.

man of charity and compassion, who fed the hungry and helped brides and grooms to marry," according to one newspaperman's description of him. "He always spoke in a loud voice, he was stormy and never rested for a moment." The collector William Gross remembered that the dealer would invariably show up at his apartment between midnight and one: these were his business hours. The Hasid was working, at the time, with an Israeli who lived in Vienna and whose other businesses, according to press reports, included brothels and slot machines. In the book partnership, the businessman brought the money; Schneebalg, the expertise. They split the profits.

Schneebalg was said to have a photographic memory that enabled him to glance at a manuscript and immediately identify the scribe. In the unregulated world of rare books, where deals tend to be conducted in cash, far from the prying eyes of onlookers and income tax officials, trust is crucial. The Hasid was trusted. He dealt not in midrange books but in those that were rare and expensive and also, according to two prominent collectors I interviewed, occasionally of uncertain provenance. When he had something good to sell, he would make the rounds, pulling the book out of his shopping bag in a collector's living room, leaving it there if he made a sale or putting it back and disappearing into the night.

When they approached the collector and his daughter at the Jerusalem Hilton, Schneebalg and his partner had a simple briefcase that appeared to be made of straw, Tammy Moussaieff told me when I interviewed her later at her father's hotel suite in Israel.

Shlomo, come quick, we have something for you, the dealer said, in the elderly collector's recollection.

What do you have? Moussaieff asked.

Quiet, the Hasid said. We know that you'll be quiet and won't tell anyone.

The four of them ascended to a room upstairs, where the dealer opened the briefcase. Inside was a stack of parchment pages. Tammy, who was standing off to one side, heard Schneebalg say the words "Crown of Aleppo." Her father, she remembered, was impressed.

Moussaieff counted the pages, he told me in London, by measuring them between his thumb and forefinger. He estimated their number at about ninety. On top of the pile he saw the book of Genesis, which appeared to mean that what he was seeing was the most valuable part of all: the missing Torah.

How much? Moussaieff asked.

A million, the Hasid replied.

The collector told me he believed this was too much. This was before the Crown became well known in Israel with the publication of the Ben-Zvi Institute's book and the broadcast of the Channel 1 TV show. He offered $300,000. The dealer refused. The collector offered to take just part of the manuscript. The dealer said it was all or nothing. Moussaieff walked away, or so he told me.

When I later spoke to Tammy Moussaieff, she said, "I think my father was very silly not to have bought it."

When Moussaieff's story first became public, in abbreviated form, in the TV segment aired in the early nineties, the scholars involved with the Crown brushed it aside. This might have been because they did not believe that Moussaieff, who had no academic training, could have had the expertise necessary to identify the Crown. It might also have been because if the pages were indeed on the market, it meant someone had put them there. It was easier to continue to believe they had simply evaporated.

Moussaieff's version of events was backed up and elaborated

on by his middle-aged daughter, who seemed to have an entirely reasonable attitude of fond and detached exasperation with many of her father's stories. And the story, I discovered, also has support from an unrelated source: Amnon Shamosh, the writer behind the Ben-Zvi Institute's book about the Crown.

Shortly after the book came out in 1987, Shamosh told me, he received a call from a man in the leadership of the ultra-Orthodox community in Jerusalem. The man told Shamosh he was sitting just then in his office with two book dealers who were offering pages of the Crown of Aleppo. The man knew Shamosh had written a book about the Crown and wanted his help in ascertaining the authenticity of the pages. Based on the man's description, Shamosh believed the manuscript they were selling was not the Crown, and he told them so. In our conversation, though, he admitted he was not an expert and could not remember why he had decided this was the case or how he could have made that assessment over the telephone. One of the dealers was Haim Schneebalg.

With three witness testimonies, it is possible to conclude with some certainty that in the mid-1980s the dealer Haim Schneebalg was offering for sale a manuscript that he claimed was part of the Crown of Aleppo. It is impossible to know if it really was, of course, though two points give some credence to his claim. The first was Schneebalg's prominence as a dealer, which would have been undermined were he found to be peddling a lesser manuscript or a fake. The second is the existence since 1976 of a facsimile edition of the surviving pages of the Crown; this meant a potential buyer could check the authenticity of the pages against the facsimile before putting down the considerable sum of money the seller wanted.

In Moussaieff's London apartment, I asked him how much

the part of the manuscript he had been offered would be worth today.

"It has no price," he said.

We spoke some more, and he turned to me with a thoughtful look. "The problem with this story," he said, "is that it could damage your health."

What happened to the pages after Schneebalg offered them to you? I asked.

Moussaieff said he did not know—that was the last he heard of the Crown. Or at least that is what he told me in London. There would be one more meeting, and one more version of the story, after that. "What was pushing me afterward was only curiosity," the collector said. "And for curiosity you don't go deep. You understand?" I nodded.

Exiting back onto Grosvenor Square, I sat on a wooden bench in the park. The sky was overcast again. I had found what I came for—a detailed version of the attempted sale at the Hilton, including the name of the dealer. Now, it would seem, all I had to do was track him down.

28

Room 915

ON AUGUST 16, 1989, four years after the book fair at the Hilton, the phone rang in the modest apartment Haim Schneebalg kept in the Jerusalem neighborhood of Mea She'arim. It was a Wednesday. The lively streets were full of bespectacled men in black and their severely dressed wives and daughters. The dealer had arrived with his wife from Brooklyn two weeks earlier. He spent some of his time with contacts from the world of manuscripts—one of them was Meir Benayahu, a well-known collector and the former director of the Ben-Zvi Institute—as well as with friends and relatives.

On the line was a man named Dan Cohen, who wanted to meet Schneebalg at the Plaza Hotel downtown. Cohen had checked in earlier that day accompanied by a woman and had given the reception clerk an ID card number and an address in the city of Herzliya: 2 Hatchelet Street. The investigation file kept by the Jerusalem District police remains classified, but a few writers for Israeli dailies at the time obtained leaked material and tracked down the friends and associates of the protagonists; it is thanks to these reporters that we know the details of the story.

Cohen wanted to meet the dealer immediately. Schneebalg's wife, who was in the kitchen, warned him not to go, though later she would not tell investigators why. A few of Schneebalg's associates told reporters that he seemed more nervous than usual in the days leading up to the phone call, and they thought this was connected to substantial debts he had incurred, some of them to black-market lenders. One recounted that Schneebalg had told him, in speaking of his debts, "Ich mach in meine hoisen"—Yiddish for "I'm peeing in my pants." At the time, he and his partner from Vienna were running a book business worth millions of dollars. In his own community, the Hasid was known for walking around with rolls of cash in his pockets, but also for living modestly and making prodigious contributions to charity.

That evening, Schneebalg caught a cab from his apartment to the Plaza, a ten-minute ride. He told his wife he would be back by 9:30 p.m. He walked over to the bank of elevators in the lobby, rode one up to the ninth floor, turned left down the corridor, then turned left again into room 915.

The next day, a maid coming to clean the room after Dan Cohen's scheduled checkout time saw a DO NOT DISTURB sign hanging from the doorknob. She opened the door anyway. A window looked north over a park and the low stone buildings of downtown Jerusalem. Next to the window was a chair, and on the chair was a black hat. On the floor was the body of an obese man with a beard and side-locks, a thick, bloody liquid oozing from his nose.

Police from the Jerusalem station arrived quickly with a pathologist in tow, but the news spread just as fast in the city's ultra-Orthodox precincts, and soon dozens of men were mobbing the hotel and interfering with the investigation. Jews of the ultra-Orthodox sects are often opposed to autopsies; this is partly because of a belief that the dead have dignity and that damaging their bodies harms their chances of resurrection at the End of Days, and partly because of a closed society's conviction that the truth in matters like untimely death might best be left to God. There have been riots in Jerusalem when police insist on going ahead. The pathologist managed only a superficial external check of Schneebalg's corpse before the dealer was buried in the old cemetery on the Mount of Olives the next day. "The ultra-Orthodox world and the world of Judaica dealers are buzzing, inventing theories," a reporter wrote two weeks later. "Murder is a possibility. A natural death is a possibility. The scenarios are generating fear. The Judaica market has never known a murder, at least as far as we know."

Investigators checking the hotel's records found, unsurprisingly, that Dan Cohen did not exist. The address he had given was on a street that did not exist, and the ID number matched someone by the name of Shohat from one of the southern suburbs of Tel Aviv. The pathologist found no clear signs of violence on the dealer's body but noted in his report, "Without an autopsy it is impossible to determine a cause of death." An acquaintance of the dealer told police that the day before, Schneebalg had complained to him of chest pains. Based on that testimony and on the fact that the pathologist had seen no evidence of violence—and influenced, certainly, by reluctance to inflame thousands of ultra-Orthodox Jews—the police attributed the death to a heart attack and closed the case.

The complications that began to emerge later on were reported by several aggressive Israeli newspaper reporters, chiefly Ben Caspit of *Maariv* and Amos Nevo of *Yediot Ahronot*. The Hasid's business partner in Vienna, the reporters found, had taken out an insurance policy on the dealer worth $6 million and had tried to cash in on the premium immediately after his death. The German insurance company, the Cologne-based Gothaer Finanzholding,

sensed foul play and refused to pay, instead dispatching investigators to pick up where the Jerusalem police had left off.

The insurance company's lawyer in Israel began fighting to
get the investigation reopened and to have the body exhumed.
Meanwhile, the company's investigators in Europe obtained details of the two physical checkups the dealer had undergone in
order to have the policy approved, one in Vienna and one in
Jerusalem. The Vienna checkup gave his height as 174 centimeters and his weight as 95 kilograms. The Jerusalem checkup
gave his height as 170 centimeters and his weight as 90 kilograms. In reality, according to the insurance company, the dead
man had been 180 centimeters tall and weighed 125 kilograms.
In all likelihood he had never appeared for a physical, and it was
possible, the company asserted, that he had not even known he
was insured. The investigators concluded that the policy had
been fraudulently obtained and linked the Hasid's death to a
possible injection of poison; they believed the hurried pathologist probably missed the needle prick. The Vienna businessman,
they suggested, might have been involved.

The businessman denied the charge and petitioned the court
to allow an autopsy to prove his innocence. The case made its
way through courts in Israel and Germany for a few years, but
the body was never exhumed and the premium was never paid.*
"Any detective novel would pale next to this story," Michael
Pappe, the insurance company's lawyer, said in court. One

* The Israeli lawyer for the insurance company, Michael Pappe, de-
clined requests for an interview but told me that the details reported by
the two newsmen were accurate. A spokeswoman for Gothaer Finanz-
holding in Cologne would confirm only that a German court ruled in
favor of the company in 1997 because of "irregularities" in the policy, and
that the $6 million policy was indeed not paid.

reporter quipped that the story could have been written by Agatha Christie, if Agatha Christie were an ultra-Orthodox Jew. The case was never solved. Officially, in fact, there was no case, as the Hasid had died of a heart attack, in a hotel room that happened to have been rented by someone using an alias, who had then disappeared without a trace. More than two decades later, the death of the dealer at the Plaza Hotel remains the perfect symbol of the dark convergence of holy books and money.

29

Money

FOR WEEKS, I had been keeping it a secret that I had seen one
of the missing pieces of the Crown. But I needn't have bothered;
I hadn't seen one.

Back in Israel, I met the scholar Raphael Zer, a white-bearded
researcher with a knitted skullcap. Zer, who works for Hebrew
University's Bible Project, has encyclopedic knowledge of the
biblical text, and because he is engaged in using the Crown to
create the most perfect scientific edition of the Bible, he has better knowledge of the codex than nearly anyone else alive. Zer,
too, had once carried out an independent investigation into the
disappearance of the Crown's pages, and he showed me a chart
he had compiled with names, dates, and pieces of information.
In 2006 he even managed to arrange a meeting with Israel's
president in an attempt to enlist him in the search, but nothing came of it. A decade before that, in 1997, he had contacted
a private investigation company about taking the case, and the
company agreed; for $50,000, they told Zer, they could locate
at least one page. Using connections in the Ministry of Education and Culture, Zer was given a meeting with the minister
himself, the Orthodox politician Zevulun Hammer, who was
interested in the story and approved the expense from his own
budget—on the condition that the Ben-Zvi Institute sign off

on it. But when Zer called the institute's director, he was not interested. Zer found this infuriating.

My conversation with Zer followed the usual pattern for exchanges with people in the Aleppo Codex Underground: they would float vague pieces of information to see if I knew more than they did, and I did the same. Zer mentioned that there was someone he believed had pieces of the manuscript, but he would not tell me who the person was. When pressed, he said this person split his time between Israel and a foreign country.

"Shlomo Moussaieff," I said, used to this by now, and Zer grinned. I confided that I had visited the collector and that I had seen one of the missing pieces. Zer was visibly impressed, as I hoped he would be. After I left, Zer, displaying a rather journalistic forcefulness and speed rare in a university scholar, called the collector himself, found that he was back in Israel, and set up a meeting. He arrived at the hotel suite and chatted with Moussaieff for a while. Zer was not sure if Moussaieff understood that he was an academic expert; the collector, Zer said, seemed to have decided, based on Zer's appearance, that he was simply a rabbi. When Zer asked to see the piece, the collector produced it. The scholar knew immediately that it was not from the Crown.

The parchment and the script indicated that the page was indeed from a valuable medieval manuscript, Zer said, but the notes of the Masora—the ones written by Ben-Asher in the Crown—did not match. Furthermore, the parchment was not the same and the writing was not that of Ben-Buya'a; it was sloppier, with letters that varied in size. Ben-Buya'a's script was so precise it might have been run off on a laser printer.

"Are you sure?" I asked.

"There is no question," he said.

My first reaction was to conclude that Moussaieff was un-
aware of what he had and must know less as a collector than he
thought he did. But when I suggested this to Ezra Kassin, the
amateur sleuth upon whom I had come to rely in navigating
the more bewildering patches of the Crown's story, he laughed
at me. "You don't get that rich by being stupid," he said.
"Moussaieff knows exactly what he has." The collector would
not keep a priceless fragment of the Crown in his living room
cabinet, Kassin said: "He has it around to impress people who
don't know any better." I was looking for the Crown, and
Moussaieff was looking at me. I now felt that he had known
what I wanted, and what I knew, and gave me something I was
too ignorant to see was not that at all. I bought it. In the bazaar
this would have been a merchant's triumph.

I called Moussaieff's hotel suite in Israel, determined that
he was in town, and drove there again. I found him wearing
oversize Gucci sunglasses and a pinky ring, surrounded by his
stockpile of lamps and jugs and bronze lions. His aide was there
but no longer seemed interested in me. The collector's daughter
Dorit, the one married to the president of Iceland, was coming in and out of the living room, maneuvering nonchalantly
around the jumble of priceless antiquities. It seemed for a split
second that the collector was happy to see me.

We talked for a long time. He showed me some of his collection, moving a poster that was leaning against a wall to reveal
an ancient stela that he said was from the biblical land of Sheba.
The president of Yemen, a personal friend of his, helped him
obtain it, he said. His purchases, he explained, were driven by a
desire to prove the historical accuracy of the Bible.

I asked to see the manuscript fragment again, and when he
brought it out, I asked why it seemed so different from the rest

of the Crown. He did not blink. The Crown was written by several different scribes, he explained, and then he changed the subject.

There was no longer any point in going in circles; I was tiring of Moussaieff and his kaleidoscope of facts and was not sure I was making progress. I thought I might be familiar enough by now for him to reveal more of the truth. While I had come to believe it likely that he had indeed been offered pages of the Crown, I did not believe he had turned them down. A million dollars was not too high—a million dollars was nothing for Moussaieff. This part of the story did not ring true.

Where, I asked, are the missing pieces of the Crown?

Now his aide was paying attention. "He's writing a book about this, you know," he warned the collector.

"What do I care?" Moussaieff said. "I'm eighty-seven, what do I care? What are they going to do, put me in jail?" The aide wandered away.

"Today there is only a small part of the book of Deuteronomy," the collector told me, accurately. And then he said, "The rest—I know where it is." He said this as if it were perfectly natural, as if he had not told me in London that he had no idea where the rest of the pages might be.

"And I am prepared to tell you everything," he went on. There was just one condition. "Take out a million dollars and show it to me. Without a million dollars, don't waste my time. You just want to write a book. Book, no book—do you have a million dollars?"

I confessed that I did not.

"In front of my eyes," he said. "I'll show you, I'll introduce you, everything. They are all robbers," he added. I wasn't sure whom he meant, but I agreed that he was probably right.

"Today, only I know where it is," he said.

"How many pages can be bought for a million?" I asked.

"About sixty or seventy," he said, and then he distanced himself somewhat. "I have to give them a million dollars, and afterward they'll give it to me." He would not say who "they" were, and I was left to conclude that "they" were people close to Moussaieff, if not simply Moussaieff himself, ensuring deniability and throwing a bit of sand in my eyes. The money, he was saying, was not for him—he hardly needed it—but for "them," the mysterious holders of a large section of the Aleppo Codex, from whom he could easily obtain it if only I came up with a sum he knew I did not have.

If I understand correctly, I said, there are individual pages circulating on the market, as well as a large piece of the manuscript. That was the Torah, the part offered to him in the 1980s.

Correct, he said. "Come with a million dollars. No one is going to do you a favor."

That seems clear, I said.

"Then I'll open the door for you. Otherwise nothing can be done. They won't even talk to you if you don't have a million dollars in your hand. I don't just mean saying you'll pay. *In your hand.*"

A few sentences later he returned to the same theme, in case I still had not understood what the Crown of Aleppo had become. "Money," he growled, thumping on the table. He said no more on the matter.

Without a million dollars, a court order, or a clear sense of whether I was being given a glimpse of the solution to a great mystery or being taken for a fool, I saw no further use in pursuing the collector after that.

PART SIX

30

The Missing Pieces

DURING NIGHT MANEUVERS in the desert as a young infantryman, I was taught that if I could not find Polaris, the North Star, I was to look for a group of bright stars, the belt and sword of the constellation Orion, which together formed an arrow pointing north.

Facing the questions raised by this inquiry—what befell the Aleppo Codex, and if a theft occurred, who was the thief, and when did he act?—I was forced to come to grips with the fact that the story's main characters were dead and didn't talk when they were alive, and that the opportunities that might have existed to discover the truth were squandered by those who chose instead to replace the story with half-truths and vague formulations designed to raise as few questions as possible. No criminal investigation was ever launched into the Crown's fate. Authoritative answers to all the questions raised by this story will, as a result, remain elusive. And yet, by the end, I found myself in possession of hard-won pieces of information that, like the stars I remembered from nights spent crossing hills and riverbeds on foot, were not themselves the answer but pointed to an answer, or to several possible answers. These were very different from the ones I expected at the beginning.

Rewind past the octogenarian collector and the dead dealer,

past the museum restoration lab, the exiles on Ocean Parkway, the trial in Jerusalem, the disintegration of one of Jewry's most venerable outposts, the escapes by sea from the Lebanese coast, and the founding of a Jewish state, to the very beginning of this story—to November 1947 and to the great synagogue in the heart of old Aleppo. All previous attempts to look at the question of the missing pages have been based on a narrative that was false. Now, having stripped away the layers of wishful thinking and trickery coating the story of the Crown, we are left with the following account of what happened.

On the day of the riot in Aleppo, looters ransacked the synagogue, breached the Crown's safe, and threw the codex on the ground. Many of the pages scattered. The looters considered them worthless and seem to have ignored them as they torched the synagogue. Contrary to what was long believed, there is no evidence that any significant portion of the Crown was lost in the fire.

Early the next day, the synagogue's sexton, Asher Baghdadi, arrived with his son. They collected the pages they found and removed them from the synagogue. But they did not find all of them. A small number of pages, perhaps a dozen out of a total of nearly five hundred, either were gone already or were left behind.* Some were picked up later that day or in the days that followed by Jews who came to the synagogue, like Samuel Sabbagh, who kept an Exodus fragment in his wallet, and Leon Tawil, who took a page from Chronicles to Brooklyn. These two

* When the fragment kept by Samuel Sabbagh was sent to Israel in 2007, it was thought to have evidence of fire damage, unlike the rest of the manuscript. Subsequent tests, however, led experts at the Israel Museum to conclude that the damage to the piece of parchment was caused not by the 1947 fire but by the heat of the machine Sabbagh later used to laminate it.

Asher Baghdadi in Israel, sometime
before his death in 1965.

pieces have long been thought to point to the location of the
rest of the missing pages, but it is safe to say they do not. The
Brooklyn fragments are exceptions.

The sexton turned the nearly intact codex over to the community leaders, who placed it in the care of a Christian merchant
and spread the story of its supposed loss. The codex remained
in the merchant's custody for several months before it was

transferred to the Jewish textile trader Ibrahim Effendi Cohen. The Buenos Aires rabbi saw the book—whole but for a small number of pages—in Cohen's storeroom in 1952, five years after the riot. Five years after that, in the fall of 1957, the Crown was sent with the courier Faham out of Syria to Turkey, where it remained for approximately three months before arriving at Haifa on December 16 of that year. It was released from customs and sent to Shlomo Zalman Shragai, the Israeli immigration chief, on January 6, 1958, and reached President Ben-Zvi and his institute on January 24. No one who touched the codex between the date of the riot in 1947 and March 1958 came forward to say that a huge part of the book was missing. No one, including the academics of the Ben-Zvi Institute, appears to have left any record of the state of the book when they received it or when they passed it on. Only three months after the codex's arrival in Israel do we find documentation indicating that significant parts were gone, including the Five Books of Moses.

Whatever happened to the book, then, happened between 1952, when the rabbi saw it nearly whole, and March 1958. Anyone who touched it in these six years is, at least in theory, a suspect. Because the missing pieces include a large section from the beginning, a large section from the end, and individual pieces from the middle, it is possible that there was not one theft, but several thefts. In the period in question, the book was hidden in Aleppo, moved to Turkey, brought to Israel, and kept in the Ben-Zvi Institute.

The first station was Aleppo.

"LAU KAN EL-KALAM min fida, as-skoot min dahab," goes an old saying of the Jews of Aleppo. If words are of silver, silence is of gold.

An Aleppo-born bookseller in Jerusalem described a "conspiracy of silence" about the Crown in the Aleppo community. This is true. The silence began with the riot and continued through the late 1950s and the Jerusalem trial, where there is no record of any of the Aleppo representatives—or of anyone else—mentioning the fact that approximately 40 percent of the Crown's pages, including the most important ones, were now gone. The silence among the Aleppo rabbis involved in hiding the book and smuggling it out of Syria appears to have been violated just once, by the rabbi in Buenos Aires, who spoke to Rafi Sutton on camera four decades after the riot and shortly before his own death.

A close look at the existing testimonies about the Crown's sojourn in Aleppo in the years after the riot reveals contradictory descriptions of the state of the manuscript. The rabbi in Buenos Aires, the global Aleppo community's most respected religious authority at the time of the interview in 1989, said that almost none of the pages were missing when he saw the Crown in 1952 in the keeping of the Cohen family. But Edmond Cohen has given different accounts. Cohen seems to have been the person most responsible for the Crown while it was in his family's care—his uncle, Ibrahim Effendi Cohen, the official guardian, was already an elderly man—and it was Edmond who removed the Crown from its hiding place and brought it to Faham for its journey out of Syria. When Rafi Sutton interviewed him on camera, also in 1989, Cohen said he could not remember exactly what had been missing, only that part of the Torah was gone. The phrase "I don't remember," as Sutton noticed, recurred in the brief recorded segment no fewer than eight times.

I found another version in a profile of Cohen that appeared in an ultra-Orthodox paper in Israel in 1994. According to this

article, which was based on an interview with Cohen, after the
riot the manuscript was missing up to the Torah portion of Ki
Tissa in the book of Exodus. That is a striking departure from all
other accounts, because it would mean that one and a half books
were missing from the beginning of the manuscript—perhaps
several dozen leaves, more than the handful of pages mentioned
by other witnesses, but far less than the two hundred leaves that
were missing by 1958. Yet another account came from Edmond
Cohen's son, Moshe Cohen, who told me he understood from
his father that all the pieces missing today had been missing
since the riot. In other words, the Buenos Aires rabbi said explicitly that the Crown was nearly intact when it was in the Cohen
family's care, but Edmond Cohen said it was not.

In his report summing up his Crown investigation in the
early 1990s, Rafi Sutton listed the people who had access to the
manuscript in Aleppo in the years in question: Ibrahim Effendi
Cohen, the rabbis Tawil and Zaafrani, the Christian merchant
who cared for it briefly after the riot, and Edmond Cohen himself. "The question is," Sutton wrote, "is it possible to point to
one of them as the person who took or helped take the parts of
the Crown? The answer is absolutely not. We cannot suspect one
of them because they did not give testimony before their death."
Still, he went on, and here it is possible to see his spy's mind
at work, "It must be said that of all five mentioned here, only
Edmond Cohen is still alive (may he be granted long life), and
in the interview with him it could be felt that he was not freely
and openly recounting the story of the Crown."

The Mossad man's language was cautious, but his reasoning
was apparent. Edmond Cohen would certainly have known if
the manuscript was nearly whole when it was in his care, or if

it was already missing large sections. He thus knew if the pages had disappeared before he received it or after he gave it to the cheese merchant—or possibly while he had it. In any case, he had to know more than he had volunteered. Later in his report, Sutton returned, again, to Cohen.

> In light of the above conclusions, it is necessary to try to persuade Edmond Cohen to agree to another interview in order to try to clarify points that were revealed and raised in this attempt. If he is opposed to an on-camera interview, we must conduct a recorded interview. Because Mr. Edmond Cohen is now becoming a key player in the whole matter.

Sutton did not get a chance to interview Cohen again before Cohen's death.

Anyone looking at the spotty record from the period after the riot, when the Crown was still in Aleppo but no longer in the synagogue, cannot help noticing the differing descriptions of the book given by some of the men who hid it, as well as an unwillingness to talk on the part of others. If the Aleppo Jews were certain they sent a nearly complete manuscript to Israel, it is logical to expect that they would have said so publicly. They never did, and one explanation for the silence could be a suspicion or certainty that one of their own was responsible for the theft. If this is true, the fictional account of the Crown's fate in *Michel Ezra Safra and Sons,* Amnon Shamosh's novel about an Aleppo family, might not be so far from the truth. In the book, the dying patriarch of a fictional Aleppo clan leaves his firstborn son a mysterious safe that he is to open only three years later; in the meantime, the son knows only that the safe contains a treasure linked to a "terrible secret."

In the car, on the long way home, Rahmo closed his eyes, leaned his head back, and thought of the terrible secret bequeathed him by his father. He would not have been more afraid had he known that a monster awaited him in that safe. The worst was that he would have to bear the burden of the terrible secret and the sin for three whole years . . .

Now it was clear to him that the feeling of sin was what had slowly destroyed Michel, from the day he left his city and took with him that holy object. What that object was, Michel had not wanted to say. He said only that it was holy and valuable, and millions could be had for it. It was not to be sold except in a time of crisis. He had not stolen it, he said, he had saved it. And yet his conscience had not given him rest for all those years and his hidden treasure dimmed the light of his life.

When I interviewed him, Shamosh said he believed Aleppo Jews were responsible for taking most of the Crown's missing pages. "It was passed among merchants," he said. "And a merchant, if such a treasure falls into his hands, won't he put aside a piece for himself?"

In the fall of 1957, after a decade in hiding, the Crown was removed on the orders of the chief rabbis and given to Murad Faham, who was preparing to leave Syria. The merchant packed it along with his possessions and smuggled it across the Turkish border.

Silo

FAHAM ARRIVED IN the frontier town of Alexandretta in or around September 1957. The Israeli agents running the immigration route through Turkey knew who Faham was and what he was carrying. Faham remained in Turkey until he sailed for Israel in mid-December.

When Faham arrived, he contacted a local shopkeeper and kosher butcher who worked for the Israeli government as an agent in charge of arranging the escape of Syrian Jews. Here I have referred to this man by the pseudonym of Isaac Silo. Silo, the Jewish Agency's archive makes clear, was a crucial agent on an important smuggling route, entrusted with secret information about the identities of smugglers and with large sums of money, some of it intended to bribe border guards and customs agents. He was a middle-aged man at the time and died in the 1970s.

During this investigation, I learned to note not only what was said by the story's protagonists but also what was not; on occasion, the latter was more important. The strange silence about the missing pieces that I noticed in the letters and transcripts of the time appears to have been observed not just by the Aleppo Jews but by the Israelis as well. The silence began immediately after Faham's arrival in Israel, when he twice gave testimony

to President Ben-Zvi about the Crown and also wrote a letter about the manuscript to the immigration chief Shragai. Nowhere is there any sign that the Israelis asked for information
about the missing pieces or that Faham volunteered any. At the
trial in Jerusalem, the witnesses hashed and rehashed the story
of how the Crown was given to Faham and taken to Israel. But
like Faham himself, not one of them mentioned the fact that
the world's most famous Hebrew Bible had somehow arrived in
Israel with its most important part missing. The silence in the
archives fifty years after the fact most likely does not reflect an
actual silence at the time: the matter, it is safe to assume, was
discussed, but these discussions were not written down, or if
records did exist, they were subsequently destroyed or stored
out of reach.

Along with what was not said or recorded, an observer might
also notice what was not done. The man who knew for a fact
that the Crown had been rescued nearly intact from the synagogue and had not, in fact, been significantly damaged in the
riot—Asher Baghdadi, the sexton—was never questioned, even
several years later, when Israel's president was supposedly turning the world upside down in the search for the missing pages
and Baghdadi was living just down the road in Tel Aviv.

This silence is one of the most striking characteristics of the
Crown's first months in Israel. Another is the unusual behavior
of Shlomo Zalman Shragai, the head of the Aliya Department.
In the official version of the story, Shragai received the Crown
on January 23, 1958, and brought it to the president the next day.
Both men explicitly put forward that amended chronology later
on, and it was enshrined as fact in the book published by the
Ben-Zvi Institute. But while it is true that the codex reached
Ben-Zvi on January 24, it is not true that it reached Shragai

only the day before. According to his own testimony in court, Shragai was given the manuscript not on January 23 but on January 6, seventeen days earlier.

The president had been trying to obtain the Crown for years, but Shragai testified that he kept the manuscript for two weeks without even telling Ben-Zvi that it had arrived. Four more days went by before he turned it over. The story was soon neatened up, as we have seen, and Shragai was eventually airbrushed out altogether; the book published by the Ben-Zvi Institute mentions him only in passing and without explaining his role. Shragai's removal allowed a simple narrative: the Aleppo Jews sent their book to Israel and gave it to the president. This became the official story, allowing the keepers of the Crown's history to sidestep the embarrassing "religious man" episode and the trial and to obscure the way they had obtained the book. It also erased the mysterious seventeen-day period in which Israel's immigration chief kept the Crown from the country's president.

The documentary record gives us a strong indication that Shragai, along with other high-ranking government officials, knew something they were not telling. "There are complications in the matter of the Crown of the Torah," Shragai wrote in a 1964 letter to the president of Hebrew University, with a copy to the president of Israel.* "The man who brought the book of the Torah, and who is in the United States, can no longer control himself despite all my calming letters and despite my oral conversations with him." The man in the United States was Faham, and he was threatening to go public with something he knew. "I am very afraid that the matter will be made known and turn

* This was Zalman Shazar, who had replaced Ben-Zvi after the latter's death the previous year.

into a worldwide public scandal," the immigration chief wrote, adding that his letter was driven by "desperation."

There are no details in the letter, no explicit indication of what he means. Shragai was too canny for that, and the recipients of the letter obviously did not need to be told. Shragai, who had spent decades immersed in Israel's full-contact politics and who had helped engineer the immigration of hundreds of thousands of people, was no amateur and was not easily rattled; he would not have used words like "worldwide public scandal" and "desperation" lightly. Something had happened to the codex while the cheese merchant had it, something that was of enough concern to warrant the attention of the most important figure in Israeli academia, the president of Hebrew University, and the president of the country. It was something that could not become known, and people at the highest levels were involved in ensuring that it did not. They were successful, which leaves us to guess what they were talking about.

It may be that Faham's secret was one we know already: his collusion in the seizure of the book by the government. It is hard to believe, though, that the merchant would have implicated himself by drawing attention to his actions, and though this story was successfully covered up in subsequent decades, it was not really a secret at the time, certainly not in the Aleppo community. It is more likely, I believe, that Shragai was referring to something that happened to the book while it was in Faham's care—that is, in the three months that elapsed from the time it was handed to him in Aleppo to the time he gave it to the Israelis at the Haifa port. We may also deduce that whatever happened somehow involved Shragai: why else would the immigration chief be the one trying to calm Faham down, and the one writing the letter? Shragai's responsibilty for the codex, we now know, effectively began shortly after it crossed into Turkey.

Going through a dusty file in the state archive in Jerusalem, I found three pages of handwritten notes. The document was unsigned, but its contents showed it to be the first testimony given by Faham to President Ben-Zvi after his arrival. I had not seen a reference to this testimony elsewhere. Before Faham related anything about the codex, or about Aleppo, or about his treacherous journey, according to the notes, he wanted to tell the president something else.

"What is known about Qamisli," the document opens, referring to one of the towns on the Syria-Turkey border, "and about the robbery of immigrants by a Jew named [Silo] and by a Jewish Agency worker." Silo, it goes on, "took 11,000 Turkish pounds from Faham, in addition to what he took from the others."

The man who carried the treasure to Israel claimed to have been robbed en route by an Israeli agent. There was nothing Faham deemed more important to tell the president when they first met. Whoever wrote the minutes drew a line under those brief phrases, and Faham's testimony continued for another two and a half pages with no further mention of this incident. There was no reference to any theft of a part of the codex. None of the documents suggest that Faham ever brought this up again.

I began making queries about Silo. Yitzhak Zaafrani, the son of one of the Aleppo rabbis who had sent the Crown to Israel, identified him as a kosher butcher trained in Aleppo and sent to serve as a ritual slaughterer for the Jews of Alexandretta. There were questions about his religious observance, Zaafrani said, and about the sharpness of his blade—a crucial matter for a kosher butcher, who is supposed to kill animals painlessly—and some would not agree to eat animals he had slaughtered. An elderly Aleppo woman who fled Syria in 1956 and now lives in Tel Aviv told me the same thing. Silo had helped many Aleppo Jews escape, and yet the community seemed not to remember him with the appreciation one might expect. Among traditional people, it seemed to me, talk of his religious observance was a way of saying he was a man with a bad reputation.

One evening I was on a street corner in Tel Aviv with Ezra Kassin, the amateur Crown sleuth. We were in the habit of spending hours constructing scenarios for the disappearance of the pages and then trying to poke holes in them, and on this occasion we happened to be talking about Alexandretta. The passersby were the usual Tel Aviv gallery of young men with goatees and flip-flops and women in tank tops. The elderly man who passed us in an old blue suit and a little black hat looked like a visitor from another world. He was from Aleppo, and Ezra knew him from synagogue. The man's name was Leon Naftali. He was seventy-four years old and came up to my shoulders.

"Remind me how you got out of Aleppo," Ezra said after the man stopped to talk. Through Alexandretta, he replied, at the end of 1949.

Did you encounter a man called Silo? Ezra asked.

"Of course," Naftali answered.

Naftali and his mother were relatively well off and managed to get passports allowing them to leave Syria legally, he told me when I later interviewed him at his apartment. His brothers had already escaped, and his father was dead. The two of them took a bus in December 1949 from Aleppo to the Syria-Turkey border and then on to Alexandretta, where they asked for Silo's store.

They had been told the Israeli representative would put them up for a few days and book their passage to Haifa. Naftali's mother was carrying a bag with her gold jewelry and several silver kiddush cups, used on the Sabbath for the blessing over the wine, which had long been in their family. Silo told them they risked having the valuables seized by Turkish officials and suggested leaving the bag with him, saying he would bring it when they were onboard ship at the port and ready to leave for Haifa. They agreed, Naftali recounted, and they waited for Silo as the ship prepared to sail. He never showed up. Neither Naftali nor his mother ever forgot it.

"There wasn't a Jew who passed through Alexandretta who did not complain about him," Naftali said. He and his mother never filed an official complaint after arriving in Israel, assuming there was no chance of anything being done.

There appear to have been more reports of this sort in the years after Faham's passage. One, which reached the Jewish Agency in 1962, is mentioned in a letter from an Israeli immigration agent in Turkey dated November 29 of that year: an immigrant who passed through Alexandretta had complained of the loss of two pieces of luggage and clearly blamed Silo. The agent wrote to his superiors defending Silo, saying he did not have access to baggage in transit and thus could not be responsible.

These stories, if true, would hardly be surprising. After all, refugees fleeing across borders, carrying their valuables, are vulnerable to robbery. And as any experienced spy handler will tell you, the best agents are often people without the scruples that would prevent them from operating comfortably on both sides of the law.

Silo continued to serve as the Jewish Agency's man in Alexandretta for years afterward, transferring several thousand

Jews to Israel, according to a tally kept by a close relative, whom I interviewed in the United States. He was clearly useful, and this must have trumped other considerations. It might also have trumped the disappearance of part of an old manuscript that passed through his hands and that he, an Aleppo Jew himself, would certainly have recognized as an object of immense value.

There is no indication in the archives that Ben-Zvi did anything with the information from Faham, but he must have been asking around. In the summer of 1960, in one of his notebooks, now in the state archive, Ben-Zvi scrawled the following brief sentence:

> From David Sasson: [Silo] has several parchment pages from the Crown of Aleppo.

"Silo" is written without explanation, indicating that Ben-Zvi now knew who he was. The identity of David Sasson is not clear; it is a common name. That sentence is the only surviving contemporary indication, however fragmentary, that one of the people through whose hands the Crown passed was thought to be in possession of some of its missing pieces.

Silo's relative denied that Silo had ever taken money or belongings from refugees, and he said he did not know what the "David Sasson" note might refer to. Faham's complaint against Silo was rooted, he said, in a business dispute between the two men involving the purchase of textiles; Faham's son, whom I interviewed in Israel, remembered a similar disagreement. Both denied the possibility that Silo had taken part of the codex from Faham.

The Silo theory presents one way of explaining why the Israelis were so eager to cast a fog over where and when the pages went missing. Making the story public would have reflected badly on the Jewish Agency—causing, perhaps, "a worldwide public scandal"—and endangered one of its key operations, exposing an agent who was a citizen of a foreign country and who knew a great deal. The theory would explain the involvement of Shragai, the immigration chief, who was directly responsible for Silo and the Syria-Turkey-Israel smuggling route. The missing seventeen days might also fit into this scenario: the immigration chief received the manuscript from Faham, along with a report of what had happened, and perhaps needed time to investigate and decide how to proceed before bringing the book to Ben-Zvi. Written records from Shragai might help clarify these suspicions, but he appears to have left none on this subject. The Jewish Agency's archive in Jerusalem preserves records from his office at the Aliya Department, but the records from the years around the Crown's arrival are missing.

When Amnon Shamosh wrote the official history of the Crown in the mid-1980s, his research assistant was Yosef Ofer, a young university student who later went on to be a Bible professor and one of the foremost experts on the Crown. Ofer spent months in the archives. He found Ben-Zvi's note about Silo and the pages of the Crown, and the other references to the Alexandretta agent. He passed them on to Shamosh, who left them out of the book. Silo is not mentioned in its pages at all.

When I asked the elderly Shamosh about this, he said he did not remember seeing any such documents pertaining to Silo. But he knew exactly who Silo was. The Alexandretta agent was his first cousin.

Up to this point, my examination of the record had raised

questions about the codex's time in Aleppo and offered indications that it might have been tampered with in Turkey—though judging from Ben-Zvi's note, even the source of his information believed Silo was holding no more than "several pages" of the Crown and not, it would seem, all the missing pieces.

From Alexandretta, the manuscript traveled to the final station of its journey in Jerusalem.

32

The Institute

IT HAS LONG been accepted as truth by those interested in the extraordinary history of the Crown of Aleppo that the book was safe once it reached the hands of scholars in Israel and that anyone seeking to solve the mystery of the missing pages should look elsewhere. I found no reason to believe that assumption is true, and one good reason to believe it is not. Here lies, perhaps, the most potent secret at the heart of the case of the Crown, and the reason for much of the ambiguity and obfuscation I encountered.

I came upon the key that unlocked this part of the story one morning, quite by chance, in a Manhattan synagogue a few steps from Central Park.

The Ben-Zvi Institute has always insisted the pages were lost during or immediately after the 1947 Aleppo riot. This is unsupported by the evidence; indeed, it is contradicted by the evidence. When I interviewed Amnon Shamosh—who, after the institute's book about the codex was published, had gone on a high-profile tour of Aleppo communities worldwide looking for the missing pages, sponsored by the institute—I asked him why he believed the missing pages disappeared before the Crown reached Israel. He thought for a second. "Out of politeness," he said, "and caution." There was, he admitted, no proof to support this supposition. I found no documentation of the parts missing from the Crown dating from before March 1958, by which time the book had been in Israel for three months and at the Ben-Zvi Institute for much of that time.

When the Crown arrived, the day-to-day running of the institute was in the hands not of the president, who was preoccupied with matters of state, but of his secretary and the institute's director, Meir Benayahu. It was Benayahu, not the president, who was directly in charge of the Crown. Benayahu, whom I have mentioned earlier, was from a well-connected family, the son of a chief rabbi and the brother of a future cabinet minister. A remarkable scholar by all accounts, he died in 2009 after a long and prominent academic career. Parallel to his university pursuits, Benayahu bought, sold, and collected rare books. He left behind an important private collection of around one thousand Hebrew manuscripts, now kept by his family in Jerusalem.

One day in May 2010, I attended morning prayers at an Aleppo synagogue just off Fifth Avenue in New York. The synagogue had a striking sanctuary of wood and stone for Sabbaths and festivals, and a simpler room downstairs for daily use. There I found a few dozen men conducting the weekday service in the old Aleppo style and sipping black coffee from little china cups, savoring a bit of Syria in the morning before heading out into America. Afterward I met Maurice Silvera, the son of a prominent Aleppo family, a businessman in his seventies who had spent twenty years of his life in Japan, where Aleppo Jews have established a small outpost. He had heard I was researching the story of the Crown and thought I might be able to help him.

In 1961, he told me, his father, the banker and trader David Silvera, brought a valuable biblical manuscript from Aleppo to Israel and entrusted it to the Ben-Zvi Institute. This codex, which was also known as a crown, appeared to have been written in the fifteenth century, or about five hundred years after the Crown of Aleppo. The family was not sure where it was now, he said, though he thought it might have been sent on loan to Israel's national museum. He wondered if I might be able to locate it. When we met again later that day at a coffee bar a few blocks away from the synagogue, he produced two photocopies of receipts that the family had preserved for fifty years. The first, dated May 15, 1961, was signed by President Ben-Zvi himself.

I was happy to receive you today in my office and to meet you. You came bearing a book, an ancient "crown of the Torah" on parchment, which was written, it seems, in Corfu by Rabbi Yitzhak Zahalon, may his memory be blessed, and which includes the five books of the Torah and the first books of the Prophets.

I am very grateful to you for turning this important manuscript over to me so it may be kept under excellent guard along with the archived manuscripts kept in the Ben-Zvi Institute, which I founded and expanded.

The ancient and important community of Aleppo is disappearing. The sons of the Silvera family have been known in this community for their deeds over many generations. You, a scion of this great family, performed a great deed when you gave this beautiful and important piece from the Silvera library in Aleppo to a scientific institution in Jerusalem, the holy city. We will guard this manuscript well, and we will allow sages and scholars to read it and study matters of Torah and the textual traditions.

The second receipt, in a similar vein and from the same day, was signed by David Silvera and Meir Benayahu.

I took the receipts back to Jerusalem and called a veteran

manuscript expert who has spent decades working for the national library's vast microfilm project, which aims to photograph every Hebrew manuscript on earth. The project's staff put the entire collection at the Ben-Zvi Institute on microfilm beginning in the late 1970s, and their records would be the quickest way to find Silvera's book. But when the expert, Benjamin Richler, ran the details through the database, nothing came up. He tweaked the spelling of the scribe's name, Yitzhak Zahalon, and again came up with nothing. Next I went across town to the Ben-Zvi Institute, where by this time I was a familiar face, and showed the receipts to an official there. He confirmed what I suspected: the manuscript that Ben-Zvi had promised would be kept forever "under excellent guard" had vanished without a trace.

The disappearance of the Silvera manuscript from the Ben-Zvi Institute did not appear to be recent; had it been in the institute's collection in the late 1970s, it would have been photographed by the national library's microfilm staff. It must have disappeared before that time. At the same time, I found a document in the institute's archive containing an oblique reference to the termination of Benayahu's employment in October 1970. This was surprising, since academics of his rank are rarely fired, and it would have been highly unusual for an institute to dismiss its founding director.

When I interviewed David Bartov, Ben-Zvi's old chief of staff, I asked why Benayahu had left the institute.

He paused. "Perhaps we'll put a period here," he said.

Ezra Kassin, the Crown sleuth, who was with me, said, "Maybe not, Mr. Bartov. We want to know the truth."

"May he rest in peace," Bartov said, "and we'll say, Amen."

I set up a meeting with Professor Yom-Tov Assis, the head of the Ben-Zvi Institute.

The professor hesitated when I asked about Benayahu's termination. The institute had a "fat file" on this, he conceded, but he said he had never read it. He would check, he said, and then ceased all communication with me. I never heard back from him, despite repeated requests over several months.

In the meantime, while poring over a hoard of several hundred documents gathered by Ezra Kassin, I discovered a second missing manuscript. A piece of paper from the Ben-Zvi Institute, unsigned but seemingly written by Ben-Zvi himself, recorded the receipt of a damaged book of Esther that had been rescued after the Aleppo synagogue fire by a Jewish family, the Lerners, who brought it to him on February 18, 1955. Using the computerized manuscript database at the national library, I searched for this book in the institute's collection. It wasn't there. I e-mailed an inquiry to Professor Assis at the institute and received no reply.

Finally, I filed an official request for the details of Benayahu's dismissal under Israel's Freedom of Information law, which applies to the Ben-Zvi Institute because it is a public, taxpayer-funded research institution. Three months had gone by since my meeting with the professor by the time the institute finally sent me a curt letter that seemed to have been written by a lawyer. The institute's scholars had rejected my request, the letter informed me, because the information I wanted could violate Benayahu's privacy and that of his family. A loophole in the law allowed them to withhold information on those grounds.

But by this time I already had information from another source.

Armed with the Silvera receipts, I had gone to the Ministry

of Education, to the office of Zvi Zameret, who was the administrative director of the Ben-Zvi Institute for twenty-six years,
until 2009. Where is this book? I asked.

Zameret read the receipts, his expression darkening. When
he was done, he said, "May I tell you something in the clearest
way possible?"

Please, I said, and then, speaking in measured, forceful words,
he told me Benayahu was responsible for the disappearance of
"dozens" of manuscripts from the Ben-Zvi Institute.

THE INSTITUTE'S DIRECTOR, Zameret told me, was
found to have transferred manuscripts from the institute's collection to his own. Israel's president at the time, Zalman Shazar,
personally intervened on Benayahu's behalf as the contentious
and potentially explosive affair unfolded, thus ensuring that it
did not become the subject of a legal inquiry, Zameret told me.
Benayahu's father was one of the country's chief rabbis at the
time and a trial would have been too embarrassing for the state.
The missing books came to light during a broader affair that saw
Benayahu leave amid a bitter legal battle with other academics
over control of the institute. The books were not returned, he
said. Their absence was never made public.

Several years later, a young scholar named Joseph Hacker was
brought in to serve as deputy director of the institute, which was
still reeling. Hacker, today a professor emeritus of Jewish history at Hebrew University, was charged with helping to rehabili-
tate the institute and had access to all relevant documentation.
Hacker agreed to speak on record when I contacted him, and he
carefully confirmed and elaborated upon Zameret's account. He
had seen, and still remembered, a list of rare books the director

had taken, Hacker said, and knew of more. "I told those who needed to be told," he said, but nothing was done.

"It seems that all of the sides wanted to finish this matter and swept these things under the carpet," he said.

When I presented the Silvera receipts to a veteran official still at the Ben-Zvi Institute, he, too, confirmed the details. I cannot claim to establish precisely what happened at the Ben-Zvi Institute, but one cannot hear these testimonies without concluding that people with direct knowledge of the institute's internal workings had grave concerns about the safety of the books there at the time in question.

Benayahu continued his career at a different institution, Tel Aviv University. He went on to win one of the country's top academic prizes in 2004, and when he died five years later, an obituary in the daily *Haaretz* praised him as a combination of a traditional Jewish scholar and a modern academic.

Benayahu was the man in charge of the Crown of Aleppo from the moment it arrived at the institute in 1958 until his departure twelve years later.

It is not difficult to understand why the Ben-Zvi Institute would have desperately wanted to keep this incident quiet, and why it is still trying to do so. It was potentially devastating, not least because it would have raised questions about the mysteriously missing parts of the jewel of the institute's collection. The institute's archive, as we have seen, preserves no evidence of how many pages the Crown had when it arrived.

When I sent a list of questions to Benayahu's brother, Moshe Nissim, a former cabinet minister and a prominent Tel Aviv lawyer, I expected a threatening, lawyerly response or none at all. Instead, I received a five-page defense of Benayahu in typed, angry

Hebrew. The charges against his brother were "lies" and a "pathetic conspiracy," Nissim wrote. "I find it difficult to understand how you did not understand this fact and questioned me about this."

Benayahu could not have taken pages from the Crown because none had gone missing after the manuscript arrived in Israel, Nissim wrote. He seemed to have researched his answer, referring me for a proof to a 1958 article by Ben-Zvi and to specific pages in Amnon Shamosh's book, which, he informed me, "includes important information backed up by solid facts."

My questions, he wrote, "gave off an evil odor," but he had nonetheless decided to answer in the hope that I had made an honest error and was not driven by "impure motives," and also "because of the honor of the deceased, who cannot stand and rebuff the conspiracies put forward in his absence." He attached documents showing that the legal fight at the institute ended with his brother leaving voluntarily, called those making the charges "people of perjury," and suggested Benayahu's accusers were trying to cover up other instances of manuscript theft or might have stolen books themselves.

"Why, for forty years, have they not gone to law enforcement authorities and complained?" he wrote, and he had a point.

The institute's approach to the possibility of a link between its missing books and the missing pages of the codex seems to rest largely on denial. In our interview, Zameret insisted that the pages of the Crown had gone missing before the manuscript arrived at the institute, meaning that no one there could be responsible for their disappearance. My investigation turned up no proof for this assertion, and we are left with this fact: In late January 1958, before the absence of any significant part of the manuscript was recorded, the Crown of Aleppo came under the care of a library in which books were not safe. By March, two hundred pages were known to be missing.

Over the decades, the scholars of the Ben-Zvi Institute let it be known that they were searching the world for the missing pieces. They looked in old Aleppo, Brooklyn, São Paulo, and Rio de Janeiro. They asked a psychic in Switzerland to look at maps of south Lebanon. They looked everywhere, it seems, but in the mirror.

33

Bahiyeh

"I WAS BORN in 1936, in Aleppo, which is in Syria," the sexton's daughter told me. "Mind if I smoke?" She leaned forward and inhaled.

"There are two doors to the synagogue," she said, speaking of her childhood in the present tense, her eyes on a point somewhere in the air of her living room. One door is enormous: "The bolt is like this"—she held her hands a few feet apart—"and the key is like this." She tapped her elbow and then her fingertips. "We come in through the small door," she said.

"I can't even describe the aura to you. Something gives you a sense of calm, a kind of divine beauty that you can't—" Her voice caught. Her cigarette smoldered forgotten on the side of the ashtray. "It is impossible to describe how beautiful it was. You look at everything—the blessings, all in gold embroidery, the chandeliers, all of crystal and silver," she said. Now her eyes were closed. "You go up three stairs, then come down another two stairs, and there's a dark place, and then you're in the cave where the safe is kept."

We were in a weathered block of apartments in a town south of Tel Aviv. The sexton's daughter was seventy-four. She hadn't seen her birthplace in more than six decades, and yet she spoke as if all of this still existed: She and her brothers and sisters lived at home. Their father tended to the synagogue. Inside, the great book was where it had been for six centuries, hidden and whole.

The sexton's daughter was the first person I interviewed for this project. I was taken with her story, with her memories of the great synagogue and its treasure. I expected to write a heartening story about the rescue of this book, but instead found myself like a person who innocently opens a cupboard and finds himself buried under a pile of forgotten things.

As my inquiry stretched on and grew more complicated, I read and reread what is perhaps the classic account of the passions a book can elicit in men: the Italian medievalist Umberto Eco's *The Name of the Rose*. In this story, strange and violent events at a hilltop monastery are found to be connected to the existence of a forbidden volume in the library. It is the only copy of a work by Aristotle on comedy, hidden because the church considers the knowledge inside to be dangerous to its own teachings. The book becomes the focal point for the emotions and desires of the monks, some of whom understand what is written in it, and some of whom do not. When the story ends, the human actions unleashed by the contents of the book have destroyed it and have burned the monastery to the ground.

The Crown was brought to Aleppo in the fourteenth century AD. It was kept in a secluded room in the great synagogue and was safe as long as it remained there. Over the years, in the care of its keepers, it became less a source of knowledge for the improvement of man, as its creators had intended, than a holy relic of great value, like a cathedral's fragment of saintly bone or hair. After the riot that followed the United Nations vote at Flushing Meadow on November 29, 1947, the codex was removed from its hiding place by a mob. The synagogue was burned. The core of the book was lost, and the ancient community that guarded it was soon dispersed.

Had the mob destroyed the codex, my story would have been simpler. It would have ended, perhaps, with an allusion to the crusaders' attack on Jerusalem at the end of the eleventh century and to their theft of the Crown from its owners: in Jerusalem, the marauders were Christians bent on cleansing the holy city of infidels, while in Aleppo they were Muslims taking out their anger at their own weakness on a defenseless native community far older than their own. But if the analysis presented in these pages is correct, the destruction of this magnificent book was an inside job.

The hunger for old and beautiful things is not new. Paintings and other works of art are routinely stolen and fenced for large sums. But here the object stolen is not a thing of beauty but a book that condemns theft. The page with the passage *Thou shalt not steal* was stolen. Also missing are the commandments not to bear false witness, covet another's property, or commit murder, all of which have been violated in these chapters.

The Hebrew Bible, of which our codex was the most perfect copy, the one used by Maimonides himself, was meant to serve humans as a moral compass. Its story is a tragedy of human weakness. The book was the result of generations of scholarship in Tiberias, of the attempt to arrive at a perfect edition of the divine word. It was a singular accomplishment and a testimony to the faith of the men who created it. It was desecrated. Maimonides would have reacted with dismay to this story, no doubt, but perhaps also with a sad smile of recognition: this is what men do. The story of this book, he might say, should come as no surprise to any who have read it. *There is nothing new under the sun,* reads the book of Ecclesiastes. *Sometimes there is a phenomenon of which they say, "Look, this one is new"—it occurred long since, in ages that went by before us.* Those passages, too, are among those that have disappeared.

Those who understand the book's meaning and those who do not; those who would protect it and those who would destroy it; and those who seek it for the right reasons and those whose desire for it is base and dark—the book contained all these people and their conflicting motivations before it succumbed to them. We might file this tale between Cain and Abel and the golden calf, parables about the many ways we fail: A volume that survived one thousand years of turbulent history was betrayed in our times by the people charged with guarding it. It fell victim to the instincts it was created to temper and was devoured by the creatures it was meant to save.

ACKNOWLEDGMENTS

I BENEFITED WHILE writing this book from the assistance of many people, including some who appear in its pages and others who played crucial roles behind the scenes.

I am indebted to the inimitable Rafi Sutton, who agreed to share his files, thoughts, stories, and suspicions with me, and who pointed me in the right direction. And I owe a great deal to Ezra Kassin, who walked me through some of the more complicated parts of the story, served as a partner and a sounding board, and told me, quite rightly as it turned out, to be less naïve. And thanks to all of those who agreed to share their memories with me—their names, too numerous to mention here, appear in the text and source notes.

Thanks also to the scholars who lent their expertise as I navigated unfamiliar territory, including my friend Jonathan Rubin of Hebrew University, on the Crusades; Rafael Zer of Hebrew University's Bible Project, on the Masora and the creation of the Hebrew Bible; Yosef Ofer of Bar-Ilan University, on the Masora and the travels of the codex; Gish Amit of Ben-Gurion University, on the arrival of ancient manuscripts in the young state of Israel; and Benjamin Richler at the National Library in Jerusalem and Angelo Piatelli, book expert and dealer extraordinaire, on the world of rare Hebrew books. I learned much about Maimonides from the work of Joel Kraemer of the University of Chicago. Any mistakes, of course, are mine alone.

This book would never have been written without my agent, Deborah Harris, whose encouragement and expertise propelled me forward through an endeavor that turned out to be far more interesting and complex than either of us anticipated. Thanks also to Judy Heiblum of Sterling Lord Literistic in New York for her work on the project and her keen reading eye. Very special thanks to Amy Gash, my editor at Algonquin Books of Chapel Hill, whose steady hand shaped the book and guided it to publication. I am grateful to Amy and the rest of the staff at Algonquin for their belief in this project and their willingness to gamble on a first-time author at a time of uncertainty in the book business. Whether it was Rachel Careau's peerless copy editing or Kelly Bowen's promotional energies, I could not have worked with more capable, professional, or pleasant people.

I am also indebted to those who agreed to read the manuscript and who contributed suggestions and encouragement: George Eltman; my journalistic mentors David Horovitz and Gershom Gorenberg; Rabbi Shimon Felix; Mitchell Ginsburg; Tali Ginsburg; Aliza Raz-Meltzer; Amiad Meltzer; Brian Murphy; my sister, Sarah Sorek; and Jonathan Safran Foer. Thanks to my former colleagues at the Jerusalem bureau of the Associated Press for their encouragement and tolerance above and beyond the call of duty in allowing me time off to write, and to bureau chief Steve Gutkin, news editor Joe Federman, and bureau chief Dan Perry, who also contributed incisive comments.

Thanks to Herb and Carol Ginsburg for their generosity in allowing me to write in the legendary Ashtray in Jerusalem for several critical months, to Paul Brykczynski for finding maps of

Aleppo at the University of Toronto, and to Amir Zohar in Israel and Ellis Levine in New York for their legal advice.

Thanks to the staffs at the Central Zionist Archive, Israel's State Archive, and the archive of Hebrew University at Mt. Scopus; to Michael Glatzer at the Ben-Zvi Institute, who always did his best; and to James Snyder, Adolfo Roitman, Galit Bennet, and Dena Scher of the Israel Museum, where this story started.

I owe many, many things to my parents, Imogene and Raphael Zev Friedman, including my interest in writing and history. This book would not have been written without them. Thanks to my children, Aviv, Michael, and Tamar, who have spent most of their lives with the Aleppo Codex and who remind me, beginning before dawn each morning, what is really important. And lastly, and most significantly, thank you to my wife, Naama, without whose support, advice, and unfailing patience none of this would have been possible.

NOTES ON SOURCES

Introduction

The quote from Maimonides, *Guide of the Perplexed,* is from "Introduction to the First Part" in the English translation by Shlomo Pines (Chicago: University of Chicago Press, 1963).

Chapter 1: Flushing Meadow

Descriptions of the UN vote are based on footage from *Day of Decision,* a 1957 documentary preserved by the Spielberg Jewish Film Archive. Further details of the vote are from *Mandate of Destiny: The 1947 United Nations Decision to Partition Palestine* (New York: Jacob Blaustein Institute for the Advancement of Human Rights, 2008), and Benny Morris, *1948* (New Haven: Yale University Press, 2008).

Descriptions of Aleppo on the night of the vote come from interviews with Rafi Sutton at his home in Israel in 2009 and 2010. The description of the sexton's daily rounds comes from interviews with his daughter Batya Ron (formerly Bahiyeh Baghdadi) at her home in Israel in 2009 and 2010.

Quotes from Arab representatives are from Morris, *1948; Mandate of Destiny;* and Norman Stillman, *The Jews of Arab Lands in Modern Times* (Philadelphia: Jewish Publication Society, 2003).

The Zionist delegate to the UN quoted here is David Horowitz, a future governor of the Bank of Israel. The quotes are from his book *A State in the Making* (New York: Knopf, 1953), excerpted in *Momentous Century: Personal and Eyewitness Accounts of the Rise of the Jewish*

Homeland and State, 1875–1978, edited by Levi Soshuk and Azriel Eisenberg (New York: Cornwall Books, 1984).

Descriptions of Jerusalem on the night of the vote and the quote from Golda Meir are from Morris, *1948*, and Larry Collins and Dominique Lapierre, *O Jerusalem* (New York: Simon and Schuster, 1972).

Chapter 2: Aleppo

Descriptions of the Baghdadi family's daily schedule are from interviews with Batya Ron (Bahiyeh Baghdadi) and her sister Carmela Dweck (née Baghdadi) in Israel in 2009 and 2010.

Murad Faham's description of that day comes from the transcript of an oral testimony he recorded at Hebrew University in 1976, provided to me by his grandson Jack Dweck.

Rafi Sutton's account is from interviews in 2009 and 2010, as well as from an extensive oral testimony he recorded at Hebrew University in the late 1980s.

The Aleppo Jews named Lenin, Stalin, and Karl are mentioned in Amnon Shamosh's Hebrew collection *Gluyot Meolam Haemet* (Tel Aviv: Massada, 2010), in the chapter titled "Lenin and Stalin Come to Visit."

The boy who had his beret knocked off is Isaac Tawil, interviewed in Israel in 2009. The boy who remembered sprinting home from school is Yosef Entebbe, interviewed in Israel in 2010.

The text of the ad published by the Jewish youth club in Damascus, and the numbers of Jews killed in the postwar riots, are from Stillman, *The Jews of Arab Lands*.

Chapter 3: The Fire

Descriptions of the riot in Aleppo come from interviews with Rabbi Isaac Tawil in Israel, 2009; Rafi Sutton in Israel, 2009 and 2010; Batya Ron (Bahiyeh Baghdadi) in Israel, 2009 and 2010; Carmela Dweck (née Baghdadi) in Israel, 2010; Yosef Entebbe (the boy who escaped into the alley as rioters entered his home) in Israel, 2009; Professor Yom-Tov Assis in Israel, 2009; Maurice Silvera in New York, 2010; and Leon Tawil in New York, 2010.

The January 2, 1948, edition of *Haaretz,* with the article on the

Crown by Professor Umberto Cassuto, is on microfilm at the national library in Jerusalem. Translations into English are mine.

Chapter 4: The Swift Scribe of Tiberias

The inscription beginning "This is the full codex" is from the colophon of the Crown of Aleppo as copied by Umberto (Moshe David) Cassuto in 1943, published in Hebrew in "Keter Aram-Tzova—Le'or reshimotav shel M. D. Cassuto," by Yosef Ofer, in *Sefunot* 19 (1988–89). The colophon was later among the pages that disappeared.

The account of Eli the Nazir is from Nehemia Aloni's article in Hebrew in *Leshonenu* 34 (1969–70), "Eli ben Yehuda Hanazir vehiburo 'yesodot halashon ha-ivrit.'"

Material on the Masora is from the *Encyclopedia Judaica* and from interviews with Dr. Raphael Zer of the Hebrew University Bible Project in 2009 and 2010. I am grateful to Dr. Zer for his assistance in preparing this chapter.

Material on the creation of the Crown in Tiberias comes from Mordechai Glatzer, "Melechet hasefer shel Keter Aram-Tzova vehashlachoteha," *Sefunot* 19 (1988–89).

Chapter 5: The Treasure in the Synagogue

The number of schools, homes, and businesses destroyed in the riot is taken from contemporary reports cited in Stillman, *The Jews of Arab Lands.*

The description of prayers at the Señor Moshe synagogue and of the chanting of Psalm 83 is from an interview with Rabbi Isaac Tawil in Israel, 2009.

For an example of the claim that "tens" of people were killed, see Hayim Tawil and Bernard Schneider, *The Crown of Aleppo: The Mystery of the Oldest Hebrew Bible Codex* (New York: Jewish Publication Society, 2010).

The description of the Syrian authorities and the wealthy Armenian doctor looking for the Crown comes from the transcript of a conversation in late 1958 between President Ben-Zvi and Rabbi Moshe Tawil. From the archive of the Ben-Zvi Institute.

The first version of the Crown's rescue, from Rabbi Sadka Harari in Mexico City, and the second, about the Syrian minister, are recounted in Amnon Shamosh's history of the Crown, *Haketer: Sipuro Shel Keter Aram-Tzova* (Jerusalem: Yad Ben-Zvi, 1987).

Murad Faham's account of rescuing the Crown comes from his oral testimony recorded in 1976.

The elderly rabbi I interviewed in the synagogue in 2010 was Yaakov Attiyeh. For yet another version of the Crown's rescue, this one from Samuel Sabbagh, see chapter 22.

The account of Asher Baghdadi's rescuing the Crown comes from interviews with his daughters Batya Ron (Bahiyeh Baghdadi) and Carmela Dweck (née Baghdadi) and from a TV interview given by his son Shahoud (Shaul) Baghdadi in 1989 (broadcast in 1993). This version is corroborated in testimony given by Sarah Haver of Aleppo in Jerusalem in 1948; the community's treasurer, Yaakov Hazan, in São Paulo, Brazil, in 1961; and Rabbi Itzjak Chehebar, during Rafi Sutton's investigation, in Buenos Aires, Argentina, in 1989.

The account of the Crown's transfer to a Christian merchant and of the length of time it remained in his hands comes from Rabbi Moshe Tawil's 1958 conversation with President Ben-Zvi, kept in the archive of the Ben-Zvi Institute. The name of the merchant—Fathi Intaki—and the fact of the Crown's transfer afterward to Ibrahim Effendi Cohen, were first uncovered by Rafi Sutton in his 1989 investigation.

Chapter 6: The Jerusalem Circle

Descriptions of Jerusalem in early 1948 are from Morris, *1948,* and from Collins and Lapierre, *O Jerusalem.*

A transcript of the scholars' meeting about the Crown can be found in Shamosh, *Haketer.* In many cases, the original documents used by Shamosh for his investigation were not returned to the Ben-Zvi Institute's archive and have been lost, and the only existing record of them can be found in his book.

Information on Isaac Shamosh and his trip to Aleppo are from an interview with his brother, Amnon Shamosh, in Israel in 2009.

Quotes from the secretary's letter come from a copy of the letter,

written in Hebrew on the stationery of the Palmyra Hotel and provided to me by Ezra Kassin. The reference to an attempt to covertly
photograph the manuscript comes from Shamosh, *Haketer*.

Quotes from Cassuto's diary, and descriptions of his time in Aleppo
in his own words, are from his article about the Crown published
in *Haaretz*, January 2, 1948, and from Shamosh, *Haketer*. Details of
Cassuto's observations of the Crown are from Ofer, "Keter Aram-
Tzova—Le'or reshimotav shel M. D. Cassuto," and Glatzer, "Melechet hasefer shel Keter Aram-Tzova vehashlachoteha."

The rabbi who guarded Cassuto was Yaakov Attiyeh, whom I interviewed in a synagogue in Bat-Yam, Israel, in 2010.

Details of Cassuto's tragic family history are from interviews
with David Cassuto, his grandson and the son of Nathan and Chana
Cassuto, in Israel, 2010.

Chapter 7: The Sack of Jerusalem

Some scholars have posited in the past that the Crown was taken from
Jerusalem not by the crusaders in 1099 but by the Seljuk Turks several
decades earlier. The most recent scholarship, however, attributes the
Crown's capture to the crusaders. See Haggai Ben-Shammai, "Notes
on the Peregrinations of the Aleppo Codex," in *Aleppo Studies I* (Jerusalem: Yad Ben-Zvi, 2009).

The description of the fall of Jerusalem is drawn in part from Benjamin Z. Kedar, "The Jerusalem Massacre of July 1099 in the Western
Historiography of the Crusades," in *Crusades*, vol. 3 (Farnham, Surrey:
Ashgate, 2004). More on the sack of the city and the messianic rum-
blings that preceded it comes from Joshua Prawer, *History of the Jews in
the Latin Kingdom of Jerusalem* (New York: Oxford University Press,
1988). I am indebted to the Crusades scholar Jonathan Rubin of Hebrew University for his invaluable assistance in preparing this chapter.

Gesta Francorum et aliorum Hierosolimitanorum (The Deeds of
the Franks and the Other Pilgrims to Jerusalem) was written by an
anonymous knight, apparently a Norman or Italian, who participated
in the First Crusade and the assault on Jerusalem. Translated by Rosa-
lind Hill (New York: Oxford University Press, 1967).

Gilo's epic poem is from *The* Historia Vie Hierosolomitanei *of Gilo of Paris and a Second, Anonymous Author,* edited and translated by C. W. Grocock and J. E. Sieberry (Oxford: Clarendon Press, 1997).

The description of the Jews being burned in a synagogue is from the Damascene historian Ibn al-Qalanisi, cited in Kedar, "The Jerusalem Massacre of July 1099."

Material on the redemption of Jewish books from Jerusalem is from S. D. Goitein, "Contemporary Letters on the Capture of Jerusalem by the Crusaders," *Journal of Jewish Studies* 3 (1952), and from S. D. Goitein, *A Mediterranean Society: The Jewish Communities of the Arab World as Portrayed in the Documents of the Cairo Geniza,* vol. 5, *The Individual: Portrait of a Mediterranean Personality of the High Middle Ages as Reflected in the Cairo Geniza* (Berkeley: University of California Press, 1988).

Chapter 8: The Jump

The description of Bahiyeh Baghdadi's escape comes from interviews with her in Israel in 2009 and 2010.

Background on the arrival in Israel of Jews from Arab lands is drawn from Tom Segev, *1949: The First Israelis* (New York: Henry Holt, 1986).

The description of Rafi Sutton's escape is from interviews with him in Israel in 2009 and 2010 and from his oral testimony recorded at Hebrew University in the late 1980s.

Chapter 9: The President

The description of Ben-Zvi's preoccupation with the Crown is from an interview with David Bartov in Israel in 2010.

The *New Yorker* article is by John Hersey, from the magazine's November 24, 1951, issue.

Amos Elon's description of Ben-Zvi's generation is from *The Israelis: Founders and Sons* (New York: Penguin, 1983).

Details of Ben-Zvi's attitude toward the Jews of the East are from Gish Amit's doctoral dissertation, submitted in 2010 to Ben-Gurion University, "The Jewish National and University Library 1945–1955:

The Transfer to Israel of Holocaust Victims' Books, the Collection of Palestinian Libraries during the 1948 War, and the Appropriation of Books of Jewish Emigrants from Yemen."

The letter from Chief Rabbi Ben-Zion Ouziel, and the letters from Ben-Zvi and his secretary, are from the Ben-Zvi Institute archive. Translations are mine.

Chapter 10: The Merchant's Mission

Information on Ibrahim Effendi Cohen is from an interview with his great-nephew Moshe Cohen in Israel, 2010.

Information on the condition of Aleppo's Jews at this time, and the fact that one-third were destitute, is from a letter sent by an Israeli immigration agent in Turkey on December 5, 1958. From the Zionist Archive, Jerusalem.

The quote on the Jews' living "in constant fear" is from a confidential report dispatched to the American Jewish Committee by Don Peretz in July 1957, cited in Stillman, *The Jews of Arab Lands.*

The account of Faham's torture is drawn from the transcript of his 1976 oral testimony and from an interview with his son Avraham Pe'er in Israel, 2010.

This account from Faham of his crucial conversation with the rabbis on the eve of his departure is drawn from his 1958 testimony in court. Tawil's account is from the rabbi's own 1958 testimony.

Sarina Faham gave her account of packing the Crown in a washing machine in a TV interview with Rafi Sutton taped in 1989 in Brooklyn, New York, and broadcast on Israel's Channel 1 TV in 1993.

Chapter 11: Maimonides

Details of Maimonides's life and quotes from his letters are drawn from the fascinating and comprehensive *Maimonides: The Life and World of One of Civilization's Greatest Minds,* by Professor Joel Kraemer of the University of Chicago (New York: Doubleday, 2008).

Details of the Crown's journey from Cairo to Aleppo are drawn from Menahem Ben-Sasson, "The 'Libraries' of the Maimonides

Family between Cairo and Aleppo," in *Aleppo Studies I* (Jerusalem: Yad Ben-Zvi, 2009).

I gained much insight into the thought of Maimonides, and especially into the content of the *Guide of the Perplexed,* in conversations with my father, the Maimonides scholar R. Z. Friedman of University College, University of Toronto.

The quote on the Crown from the *Mishneh Torah* can be found in the laws governing the writing of Torah scrolls, section eight, chapter four.

Chapter 12: Alexandretta

Details of Israel's immigration efforts, including information on bribes paid by Israelis and the quote from Shlomo Zalman Shragai, are from Segev, *1949: The First Israelis.*

The letter to Silo on "saving our brothers rotting in the exile of Ishmael" was written by the Israeli immigration agents H. Shadmi and Y. Pa'el in Turkey on December 5, 1958, and comes from the Zionist Archive in Jerusalem. The letter referring to "wild incitement" was written by the same agents to Aliya Department headquarters in Jerusalem on the same date. The lists of Aleppo Jews, the Faham telegram, and the letter from the rabbi—Itzjak Chehebar of Buenos Aires—are also from the Zionist Archive. I am grateful to Professor Yosef Ofer for putting his own extensive research at the archive at my disposal.

Background on Shlomo Zalman Shragai, including his concern at this time for the Jews of Cochin, comes from his extensive files at the Zionist Archive in Jerusalem.

Information on Yitzhak Pessel comes from an interview with his son Avner Fassal in Israel, 2010.

Chapter 13: The Brown Suitcase

The description of that night at Shragai's house is from an interview with his son Eliyahu Shragai in Israel, 2010.

Shragai's letter to Faham, and Faham's letter to Shragai, are preserved in the Crown file at the Israel State Archive, as well as in the file kept by the Jerusalem Rabbinic Court. The translations are mine.

Chapter 14: The Trial

Yitzhak Zaafrani's account comes from his testimony to the Jerusalem Rabbinic Court on May 4, 1958, and from an interview with him in 2010. Faham's account of his interaction with Rabbi Dayan comes from his own testimony in court in 1958 and from his oral testimony recorded in 1976.

The letter from Meir Laniado describing Faham as a "crooked messenger" was sent to Meir Benayahu, Ben-Zvi's secretary, on September 9, 1960, and is kept in the Ben-Zvi Institute archive.

Chapter 15: A Religious Man

Faham's testimony and cross-examination are from the transcripts preserved by the Jerusalem Rabbinic Court.

Ben-Zvi's handwritten notes documenting the reports of the government lawyer, Shlomo Toussia-Cohen, are from the Crown file at the state archive in Jerusalem.

Chapter 16: Our Last Drop of Blood

The letters presented to the court by Shragai are in the file kept at the Jerusalem Rabbinic Court and in the Crown file at the state archive in Jerusalem.

The angry letter from Meir Laniado accusing the state of trying to cut a deal with Isaac Shalom is the same letter cited in chapter 14, sent to Meir Benayahu, Ben-Zvi's secretary, on September 9, 1960, and kept in the Ben-Zvi Institute archive.

Faham's account of how the trial ended is from his 1976 oral testimony.

The Aleppo rabbis testified together in court on March 1, 1960. Tawil, who had arrived in 1958, had previously given similar testimony on December 4, 1958.

The note from Rachel Yanait Ben-Zvi to the government clerk, a Mr. Ziegel, is in the Crown file at the state archive in Jerusalem.

The original trusteeship document, signed by President Ben-Zvi, is in the file at the Jerusalem Rabbinic Court.

Chapter 17: The Book

Translations from the Bible are from the *JPS Hebrew-English Tanakh* (Philadelphia: Jewish Publication Society, 1999).

The letter from three Aleppo rabbis, and Rabbi Dayan's letter mentioning "missing pages," are from the Ben-Zvi Institute archive.

The first detailed reference to what is missing is from the state's first proposed trusteeship agreement, dated only "3.1958—Adar 5718." Provided to me by Ezra Kassin.

Chapter 18: The Keepers of the Crown

The Yemeni book affair is described in detail in Gish Amit's 2010 Ben-Gurion University doctoral dissertation, "The Jewish National and University Library 1945–1955." I am grateful to Amit for generously putting his work at my disposal.

The description of Ben-Zvi's visit to Aden is from Segev, *1949: The First Israelis.*

The number of Jews killed in the 1947 Aden riot is from Stillman, *The Jews of Arab Lands.*

The transcript of the November 1, 1962, meeting of the Crown trustees is from the Crown file at the state archive in Jerusalem, as is the letter from Mordechai Rigbi to Ben-Zvi and the response from Ben-Zvi's secretary.

Ben-Zvi's decision that photographs of the Crown would be published only in his articles is from a letter he wrote on March 8, 1959. From the archive of the Hebrew University Bible Project.

Ben-Zvi's scribbled calculations can be found in the Crown file at the state archive in Jerusalem. The later and more accurate calculation of how many pages were missing was conducted by Professor Yosef Ofer.

The letters to and from the president's office regarding the missing pages are from the archive of the Ben-Zvi Institute.

The diplomat in South America was Alexander Dotan. A copy of his November 7, 1961, letter to Ben-Zvi with Hazan's testimony is included in Shamosh, *Haketer.* Ben-Zvi's note of this testimony and assertion that it was an "utter error" is in the archive of the Ben-Zvi Institute.

Asher Baghdadi's children assert that he was never questioned about the Crown after arriving in Israel. Although a document in the Ben-Zvi Institute archive shows the president was aware that the sexton had been in Israel since 1952, there are no documents suggesting he was ever contacted or interviewed.

Chapter 19: The Officer and the Scroll

Rafi Sutton's account of the Temple Scroll incident comes from interviews with him in 2009 and 2010 and from an unpublished, handwritten memoir he made available to me. Additional information on Sutton's time as an intelligence officer comes from an interview with his then deputy, Samuel Nachmias, in Israel in 2010.

Yigael Yadin's account of these events comes from his English-language book *The Temple Scroll*, vol. 1 (Jerusalem: Israel Exploration Society, 1983), as well as from his Hebrew book *Megilat Hamikdash* (Tel Aviv: Steimatzky, 1985). Yadin's sense that the discovery of the Dead Sea Scrolls was symbolically timed is from his book *The Message of the Scrolls* (New York: Crossroad, 1992).

Chapter 20: Exodus

The scholars' notes from July 11, 1963, and March 11, 1971, describing the conditions in which the Crown was kept, are from the archive of the Hebrew University Bible Project.

The opinion of the head of the Israel Museum's conservation labs, Dudu Schenhav, was expressed at a meeting of the Crown trustees on May 27, 1971, the transcript of which is in the archive of the Ben-Zvi Institute.

The 1970 opinion of the outside conservators, Leah Ofer of the Israel Museum and Esther Alkalai of the national library, is mentioned in a December 6, 1970, document written by M. Peled, acting director of the Ben-Zvi Institute, and labeled "Internal Memorandum." From the archive of the Hebrew University Bible Project.

The late president's widow made her comments to a meeting of the institute's directorate on August 12, 1974. The transcript is in the archive of the Ben-Zvi Institute.

Moshe Cohen recounted the story of his escape from Syria in an interview in Israel in 2010. Additional background on Israel's covert efforts to extract Syrian Jews at this time is from an interview in 2010 with Yitzhak Shushan, an Aleppo-born former spy who helped run the operation on behalf of the Israeli government.

Chapter 21: Aspergillus

Details of the Crown's restoration are from two interviews with Michael Maggen in his office in 2009.

The expert's mistaken assertion in 1970 that "no biotic agent" had damaged the Crown is in a December 17, 1970, letter from Dr. H. Friedman of the Israel Fiber Institute. From the archive of the Hebrew University Bible Project.

The findings of Maggen, Polacheck, and their colleagues were published in *Nature* 335, no. 6187 (September 15, 1988). A scientific article on the same subject was published the following year: see I. Polacheck, I. F. Salkin, D. Schenhav, L. Ofer, M. Maggen, and J. H. Haines, "Damage to an Ancient Parchment Document by *Aspergillus*," *Myco-pathologia* 106 (1989).

The *Jerusalem Post* article that mentioned "parts of the once complete manuscript lost in a fire" is from the paper's March 26, 2010, edition.

Chapter 22: Brooklyn

Leon Tawil recounted his story in an interview in Brooklyn in 2010. Isadore and Renee Shamah spoke to me in Manhattan in 2010.

The arrival of the page from the book of Chronicles was published in Hebrew by Malachi Beit-Arie of Israel's national library in "Daf nosaf le-Keter Aram-Tzova," *Tarbitz* 51 (1981–82).

The description of Michael Glatzer's trip to New York on behalf of the Ben-Zvi Institute is from an interview with him in Israel in 2010.

The researcher in Israel was Yosef Ofer, who published his analysis of the fragment in *Pe'amim* 41 (1989).

Rachel Magen spoke to me in Israel in 2009.

The letters and maps linked to the attempt to divine the location of the missing pages using a psychic are from the archive of the Ben-Zvi Institute. The letter requesting help from the Israeli military was sent by the institute's director, Nehemia Lev-Zion, to his friend Amnon Shamosh in Kibbutz Ma'ayan Baruch on September 12, 1985. Shamosh confirmed the details to me in an interview in 2010.

Chapter 23: The Fog Grows

Amnon Shamosh spoke to me in Israel in 2009 and 2010.

The quote from Toussia-Cohen warning that Shamosh must be steered away from the controversy concerning the Crown's ownership comes from a transcript of a meeting of the Crown trustees on November 19, 1985, kept in the Ben-Zvi Institute archive.

Menahem Ben-Sasson, president of Hebrew University, and Zvi Zameret, head of the Education Ministry's Pedagogical Council, spoke to me in Israel in 2010.

Hayim Tawil and Bernard Schneider's *Crown of Aleppo: The Mystery of the Oldest Hebrew Bible Codex* was published by the Jewish Publication Society in 2010. Tawil spoke to me by phone from New York in 2011. The donor who supported the book, Murad Faham's grandson Jack Dweck, spoke to me in Israel in 2009.

Chapter 24: The Agent's Investigation

Details of Rafi Sutton's Crown investigation are from interviews with Sutton in 2009 and 2010 and from the resulting program aired on Israel's Channel 1 TV in 1993, *Hatoanim Laketer* (The Claimants to the Crown). The program was produced by Miki Laron and directed by Ido Bahat.

The treasurer Yaakov Hazan's testimony that he saw the Crown nearly whole after the riot is mentioned in chapter 18.

Chapter 25: The Collector

Background on the market in Hebrew manuscripts comes from interviews with William Gross in Israel in 2009 and the Jerusalem-based book dealer Angelo Piatelli in Israel in 2009 and 2010.

Chapter 26: The Magicians

This interview with Shlomo Moussaieff took place in Israel on November 16, 2009.

Chapter 27: A Deal at the Hilton

This interview with Moussaieff took place in London on December 2, 2009.

Tammy Moussaieff spoke to me in Israel on January 5, 2010.

The catalogs of the Hilton book shows were made available to me by Angelo Piatelli.

Amnon Shamosh's assertion that he had been called about an attempted sale of Crown pages by Haim Schneebalg came in an interview in Israel in 2009.

Chapter 28: Room 915

The account of Haim Schneebalg's life and last days is drawn from articles by Zvi Singer in the weekend supplement *7 Yamim* of the daily *Yediot Ahronot* on September 1, 1989, several weeks after Schneebalg's death; by Amos Nevo in the same publication on May 14, 1993; and by Ben Caspit of the daily *Maariv* on November 30, 1990.

Chapter 29: Money

Zer spoke to me in Israel in 2008, 2009, and 2010.

This third interview with Moussaieff took place in Israel on January 5, 2010.

Chapter 30: The Missing Pieces

The interview with Edmond Cohen appeared in the ultra-Orthodox paper *Hamodia* on October 21, 1994.

Moshe Cohen, Edmond's son, spoke to me in Israel in 2010.

The quotes from Rafi Sutton's Crown investigation are from a copy of the investigation report provided to me by Sutton.

The passages from Amnon Shamosh's *Michel Ezra Safra and Sons* are from the Hebrew edition. The translation is mine.

Chapter 31: Silo

Ben-Zvi made the assertion that he had received the Crown just one day after Shragai did at the first meeting of the Crown trustees in 1962 (this appears in the transcript of the meeting in the Crown file at the state archive). Many years later, on July 21, 1987, Shragai was interviewed by Michael Glatzer of the Ben-Zvi Institute about his role in the Crown story. He told Glatzer that he had decided to give the manuscript to Ben-Zvi immediately after receiving it but that "Ben-Zvi was not in Jerusalem that day." He continued: "The next day I called Ben-Zvi and he asked me to come and bring the Crown with me." Glatzer's notes of the meeting are in the archive of the Ben-Zvi Institute.

A copy of Shragai's July 28, 1964, letter about a "worldwide public scandal" was provided to me by Ezra Kassin. I later found the original in the archive of Eliyahu Elath, president of Hebrew University at the time, to whom the letter was addressed. (This archive is kept at the university's Mount Scopus campus.) The full text reads:

There are complications in the matter of the Crown of the Torah. The man who brought the book of the Torah, and who is in the United States, can no longer control himself despite all my calming letters and despite my oral conversations with him.

I am very afraid that the matter will be made known and turn into a worldwide public scandal.

If there is no way to arrange the matter, I will have no choice but to insist that the Crown of the Torah be closed and the keys kept by you, that no one be able to use the Crown of the Torah, and that all research work be halted.

This proposal is the result of desperation and of my view of the severity of the situation and of what could happen if we do not find a way to solve the problem in keeping with the law and the conditions of the trusteeship agreement. I am very sorry that I must write this letter, but I do not consider myself free to exempt myself from it.

Faham's testimony regarding the "robbery of immigrants" in Alexandretta is in the Crown file at the state archive in Jerusalem.

Leon Naftali spoke to me in Israel in 2010.

The letter from the immigration agent regarding a complaint about missing luggage was sent to the Aliya Department in Jerusalem on November 29, 1962. From the Jewish Agency archive.

The "David Sasson" note is preserved in one of Ben-Zvi's notebooks now kept in the state archive in Jerusalem. I am grateful to Professor Yosef Ofer, who found this note in the 1980s, for telling me where it could be found among the dozens of files and hundreds of notebooks included among Ben-Zvi's documents.

Silo's son spoke to me in the United States in 2010. Faham's son Avraham Pe'er spoke to me in Israel in 2010.

Professor Yosef Ofer spoke to me in Israel in 2009.

Chapter 32: The Institute

Benjamin Richler of the national library put his knowledge at my disposal on several occasions in 2010.

The termination of Benayahu's employment at the Ben-Zvi Institute in October 1970 is mentioned in an April 9, 1971, letter from the acting director M. Peled to Dudu Schenhav of the Israel Museum.

Dr. Zvi Zameret spoke to me in Israel in 2010.

Professor Joseph Hacker spoke to me in Israel in 2011.

PHOTO CREDITS

THE ALEPPO CODEX

A Note from the Author

Questions for Discussion

A Note from the Author

by Matti Friedman

Although it fell, in retrospect, at the midpoint between the launch of the Kindle and the Kindle 2, I don't think I had more than a vague notion of what a Kindle was on the day in the summer of 2008 when I first descended into a dark room at Israel's national museum in Jerusalem and, standing in front of a dimly lit display case, encountered its exact opposite.

I spent much of the next four years writing the story of the object I found in the museum, a manuscript known as the Aleppo Codex—a millennium-old bundle of animal skins that is the oldest and most accurate copy of the whole Hebrew Bible. In these years I was not cut off entirely from the march of technology. I acquired an iPod. I learned to send e-mail from my cell phone. But I never purchased a Kindle or any of its cousins, nor did I fully understand what they augured.

The Aleppo Codex is a book, one of the most important on earth. I wrote a book about this book. What a book was seemed clear to me, yet when my deadline passed and I finally looked up to find myself staring into the dead electronic eye of the Kindle Fire, I saw that the meaning of the word *book* had been altered and that I had just spent these years of revolution engrossed in a mirror image of the present.

To prepare the codex, tanners scrubbed, stretched, and cut animal hides into folios that were stitched together by craftsmen. Someone scored a grid of lines onto the pages with a sharp instrument, and a scribe, Shlomo Ben-Buya'a, from the town of Tiberias on the Sea of Galilee, used iron gall ink to write the Bible's more than three hundred thousand Hebrew words one by one. Its completion around AD 930 after years of work represented the final condensation of the Hebrew Bible from stories we might imagine recited around Judean campfires to a codified text in black ink on parchment—a book. The codex crowned centuries of scholarship and was meant to be the perfect version of the twenty-four books that made up the Bible, a kind of physical incarnation of the heavenly text in a single manuscript. For Jews, every letter and vowel sound in the Hebrew text is crucial; according to one tradition, the entire Torah is one long version of God's name, which is another way of saying you do not want to get anything wrong. The codex sanctified, even fetishized, the act of reading: above and below the letters were tiny hooks, lines, and circles denoting vowels, punctuation, and the precise notes to which the words were to be chanted in synagogue. It was an object of nearly unimaginable value to the people who revered it.

An electronic book exists in an infinite number of copies; there is no original. The Aleppo Codex, on the other hand, existed only in its original five-hundred-page manuscript. There were no copies at all, and for this reason its physical safety was always paramount. In 1099, it was held in a Jerusalem synagogue when the First Crusade arrived under Duke Godfrey de Bouillon and Raymond of Saint Gilles, Count of Toulouse. The crusaders sacked the city, massacred its inhabitants, and seized property. According to a Muslim historian, they burned a synagogue with Jews inside, but historical records also inform us that the Christians saved hundreds of Jewish books to hold for ransom. The Jews' weakness in this regard was well known, and in some of the correspondences of the time it seems their concern for the stolen books was so great that it rivaled their concern for human captives. The books, each one painstakingly copied, like the codex, by hand, contained priceless and sometimes irreplaceable information. After Jerusalem fell, the Jewish community in Fustat, next to Cairo, raised money and sent 123 dinars with an emissary and instructions to "redeem the Scrolls of the Torah and to [attend to] the ransoming of the people of God, who are in the captivity of the Kingdom of Evil, may God destroy it." The books, in that sentence, came first.

By 1947, the codex had been in a grotto in the great synagogue of Aleppo, Syria, for six hundred years. For the Jews of Aleppo, it had become over time less a scholarly resource than a talisman, the community's mystic power source and a guarantor of its survival: traditions of great age and import made clear that if the book were ever moved, the community would be destroyed. (This, old exiles from that vanished community never tired of telling me, might have sounded fanciful, but it did come to pass.) The physical book had overshadowed the knowledge inside. It became as revered as a cathedral's fragment of saintly hair or bone; even its individual pages, or pieces of pages, came to be seen as valuable. Few had ever seen it, and there were still no copies—requests from scholars abroad to purchase, borrow, or photograph it had been turned down by the Aleppo rabbis who were its keepers.

Then came November 29 of that year, when the United

Nations voted to partition Palestine into two states, one for Arabs and one for Jews. The next day, a mob rioted in Aleppo. The rioters burned Jewish homes and stores. They burned the synagogue. The codex disappeared.

The Aleppo Codex "was devoured by fire in the riots that erupted against the Jews of Aleppo several weeks ago," wrote a heartbroken Bible scholar in the Israeli daily *Haaretz* a few weeks later, in an article best described as an obituary for what he called "this beloved relic of the wisdom of the Middle Ages." The codex had not been destroyed, it later turned out, but this was the meaning of a volume with no copies: the knowledge inside could be lost forever. Here, then, was a book—a single physical book—that meant everything.

Early this year, with my own book squared away, I attended a seminar with a wunderkind Web designer who, as part of a PowerPoint presentation on the twenty-first-century media, showed us a picture of a cloud against a clear blue sky. "The book does not exist," he declared. People nodded. The physical book, he said, was in a theoretical cloud somewhere, and all that existed now were the Kindles and iPads and Nooks and the other "gateways to the cloud." The book had been a step on the evolutionary ladder from those ancient stories recited aloud to information beamed invisibly around the world in an instant, available anywhere and to anyone and present nowhere at all.

My own book, thankfully, would still be a physical object, printed, bound, and placed on shelves. I suppose I'm too old—thirty-four—not to care about that. But it was no longer inconceivable that this would not be the case, that a book would have no pages of its own, no cover, that it would be nothing that could ever be locked in a safe, kept from other people, dismembered, treasured as a lucky charm, coveted, pursued, or stolen as the Aleppo Codex was.

If this great woolly mammoth of a manuscript, in its glorious, inconvenient physicality, in the extreme and occasionally dark impulses it has elicited from men, has a role in this new world of clouds, perhaps it is to remind us, distracted as we are by the metallic gleam of furiously evolving gadgetry, of the essence of what this is all about. The information inside a book remains among our most important possessions: our power source, the guarantor of the survival of our human community. The library is, as Umberto Eco wrote in *The Name of the Rose,* the scene of a "centuries-old murmuring" among pages: "a treasure of secrets emanated by many minds, surviving the death of those who had produced them or been their conveyors." Whether knowledge is encapsulated somehow in disembodied electrons or written on the skins of tenth-century livestock from Galilee, the codex remains in its dark room in Jerusalem to remind us that this has not changed.

Questions for Discussion

1. At the heart of *The Aleppo Codex* is a trial over ownership of the codex —but also over who owns history. On one side is the Jewish community of Aleppo, and on the other the government of the newly created Jewish state, Israel. Did Israel have a legitimate claim to the manuscript? Should anyone or any group own historical treasures? Can they?

2. Who are the likely suspects in the disappearance of the codex pages? What information supports each scenario?

3. What motivations might exist for taking, buying, or keeping the missing pages?

4. *The Aleppo Codex* mentions the Dead Sea Scrolls and the desert fortress at Masada as potent national symbols for Israel. How are objects, places, and symbols used by states to build identity and rally citizens around a shared version of history? What equivalent symbols exist in the United States or in other nations?

5. What did the codex symbolize for the new Jewish state? And what role in general did myths and symbols play in the founding of Israel? How is this related to why Israel's government, and particularly the president, wanted the codex so badly?

6. The codex is the most perfect version of the Hebrew Bible, sometimes referred to as the Old Testament. Why was it so important to have a single, agreed-upon version of the text? And what role has this text had in shaping societies across the world?

7. Why are the Dead Sea Scrolls famous while the Aleppo Codex has remained relatively unknown?

8. While the contours of the Middle East conflict are well known, the world of the Jews of Islam has largely been forgotten. As Friedman notes, in the mid-twentieth century there were approximately one million Jews living in Islamic lands, some of them heirs to communities more than two thousand years old. Today nearly all of them are gone. What can we learn today from the Jews of Arab countries, from their centuries of existence in the lands of Islam, and from their communities' end? Does this alter our understanding of events in the Middle East? If so, in what way?

9. Jewish tradition holds that there is information in the biblical text that is beyond the obvious meaning of the words—and possibly beyond human understanding. Why is it so important to retain a detail like a tiny and seemingly meaningless vowel sign, one that prolongs the syllable *ah* into *aah,* for example?

10. What does it mean that Jews are called the "people of the book," and how does the history of the codex fit into that description?

11. For millennia, religions have sanctified sacred books and the act of writing and reading them. The codex, for example, was written over a period of years by a trained scribe. The Torah, the Five Books of Moses, must be read in a synagogue from a parchment scroll written by hand. How might the age of the e-reader affect those traditions?

Adapted from the Discussion Questions from the Jewish Book Council Book Club, www.jewishbookcouncil.org/bookclub.

SEBASTIAN SCHEINER

MATTI FRIEDMAN'S work as a reporter has taken him from Lebanon to Morocco, Cairo, Moscow, and Washington, D.C., and to conflicts in Israel and the Caucasus. He has been a correspondent for the Associated Press, where he specialized in religion and archaeology in Israel and the Palestinian territories, and for the *Jerusalem Report*. He currently writes for the *Times of Israel*. He grew up in Toronto and lives in Jerusalem.

Milton Keynes UK
Ingram Content Group UK Ltd.
UKHW021627251124
3115UKWH00043B/653

9 781616 202781